COMMUNICATION RULES

Volume 97, Sage Library of Social Research

Sage Library of Social Research

COMMUNICATION RULES
THEORY AND RESEARCH

SUSAN B. SHIMANOFF

foreword by Dell Hymes

Volume 97
SAGE LIBRARY OF
SOCIAL RESEARCH

SAGE Publications   Beverly Hills   London

For information address:

SAGE Publications, Inc.
275 South Beverly Drive
Beverly Hills, California 90212

SAGE Publications Ltd
28 Banner Street
London EC1Y 8QE, England

Printed in the United States of America

Library of Congress Cataloging in Publication Data

Shimanoff, Susan B.
    Communication rules.

    (Sage library of social research; v. 97)
    Includes bibliography and index.
    1. Communication—Philosophy. 2. Social norms.
3. Human behavior. I. Title.
P91.S45   001.5'01   79-25077
ISBN 0-8039-1392-3
ISBN 0-8039-1393-1 pbk.

P91
S45

SECOND PRINTING, 1982

Dialogue 02 on p. 53 is taken from Harold Garfinkel, *Studies in Ethnomethodology,* © 1967, pp. 42-43. Reprinted by permission of Prentice-Hall, Inc., Englewood Cliffs, New Jersey.

Dialogue 05 on p. 96 is taken from Gail Jefferson, "Sequential Aspects of Storytelling in Conversation," in *Studies in the Organization of Conversational Interaction,* edited by Jim Schenkein, pp. 228-229. New York: Academic Press, 1979.

Dialogues on pp. 166-169 are reprinted with permission from: 'The Logic of Nonstandard English' by William Labov, in *Georgetown University Round Table on Languages and Linguistics 1969.* James E. Alatis, ed., pp. 1-39. Copyright © by Georgetown University.

Dialogue 19 on p. 176 is reprinted with permission from Leonard C. Hawes, "Toward a Hermeneutic Phenomenology of Communication," *Communication Quarterly* 25(1977): 30-41.

CONTENTS

LIST OF TABLES AND FIGURES

Tables   **Page**

Figures

DEDICATED TO

Perry S. Shimanoff, my husband
Walter R. Fisher, my mentor
Jerrell D. Bussey and Shirley M. Bussey, my parents

for their encouragement and support

FOREWORD

A foreword should indicate reasons for reading the book it introduces. The main reason, of course, shoud be what the book has to say, but Dr. Shimanoff sets forth her subject so well as to make any additional description redundant. Let me try, therefore, to indicate the interest of the book by adding to its context. I shall try to place the book against the background of some general trends in fields concerned with communication and explore its implications for linguistics and ethnography. These last are fields with which I am especially familiar, but they are relevant beyond that fact. A communication theory must account for language, and the term "rule" has an established place in linguistic research and fields influenced by linguistics; moreover, the use of rule in linguistics conforms essentially to the use defined by Dr. Shimanoff. The case of linguistics may strengthen the case for rules research yet require mutual questioning and clarification. In Dr. Shimanoff's analysis, rules are necessarily concerned with behavior, and rule-governed, or rule-guided, behavior is central to ethnography. Indeed, rules research, as formulated here, is partly a kind of ethnography. Development of the link with comparative ethnography should contribute both to the content of rules research and to refinement of its theoretical models.

I

Human communication theory can hardly help considering itself a perspective on all of human life. Its institutional roots may be particular and diverse: schools of communication, departments of speech and rhetoric, centers of primate studies, parts of social psychology, psychiatry, linguistics, anthropology, sociology. Yet the notion of "communication" implies a claim of universal relevance.

What can be the future of such a theory and such a claim? The rise of the graduate school and university in the last century witnessed a dispersion of knowledge of human life among disciplines, each with some claim to a perspective. Economists may sometimes suspect that the rationality of choice among alternate means to certain ends is a general paradigm for human action. Sociologists must often consider that the origins, maintenance, and transformation of social order is basic to all human experience—societal or personal. Anthropologists know no community without cultural behavior, and avant-garde folklorists none without some sphere in which interaction takes forms shaped by traditional aesthetic values. Theology, according to Tillich, knows no person or people without ultimate concerns, without "god-terms." Amidst so many jostling disciplines, a semblance of harmony seems due to the fact that each, after all, has a certain favored preserve of data and a certain methodology. Whatever may be the ultimate interests of humanity, in unity and free sharing of knowledge, the interests of scholars seeking a place in the academic sun seem to require some claim of uniqueness and monopoly. And as the world becomes more and more one, methodology seems more and more the key.

That conclusion is suggested by the circumstances of anthropology and folklore, two disciplines whose initial niche was protected most by separate subject matter. Although literally the unqualified "study of man," anthropology accepted a division of labor specializing in peoples and cultures separate from its own civilization. Folklore and folklife somewhat similarly specialized in what was preserved or passing away from earlier stages and at the peripheries of that civilization. With the end of explicit colonial relations in most of the world, the usual subjects of anthropological study have become increasingly resistant to research by foreigners except on their own terms. Anthropologists, indeed, may remind them of an unmodern past they wish to put behind them; economists, political scientists, and sociologists may be more welcome. As American anthropology attempts to domesticate itself and find a role in study of the United States, questions of method come to the fore. There is clearly no question of a monopoly on news simply through dint of having been to an exotic place. A role for anthropology has to be argued using the virtues of ethnography as a method of work in competition with others. It is not too much to say that classical anthropology will go the way of classical studies, becoming the counterpart for other vanished cultures of scholarship about Greece and Rome, if it does not succeed in establishing the scientific and social claims of ethnography as a method, distinct from experiment and survey on the one hand, and journalism on the other. Folklorists are divided between those who want to remain devoted to what is past, or passing, and those who see in the aesthetic dimension of small-group interaction—and tradition*alizing* as a dynamic process—universal claims on a part of the future. For the latter group, new methodology has become a focal concern.

This book is an attempt to provide a methodological center for human communication theory in terms of the notion of rule. Such an attempt must be seen as a challenge to major methodological trends already in place, one quantitative, one qualitative.

Much that bears the name "communications research" is cast in a quantitative mode—survey results, content analysis, and the like. That mode goes back to the impetus that led to the institutionalization of the social sciences. When the Social Science Research Council was founded a little more than fifty years ago (Sibley, 1974), one might have seen the dominant trend in the disciplines devoted to systematic study of human life to be quantitative research, research seeking to adapt a methodology associated with the natural sciences. Partly the trend was emulation of sciences more prestigious and successful, but partly it was dedication to the possibility of improving the human prospect through exact knowledge. The growth of departments and divisions of social science in universities, the requirements of industries and government agencies, the availability of certain kinds of data, and, to be sure, the continuing discovery of worthwhile applications, have made such work a permanent part of modern society and intellectual life. When we wish to assess the effects of segregation, or of college education, or to bring the processes of ongoing linguistic change within the sphere of the known, we find ourselves relying on quantitative work.

Since the Second World War, however, there has been a surge and revitalization of qualitative research. The study of one aspect of communication, language, has been at the heart of that revitalization. As a departmental discipline, indeed, linguistics is a creature of the second half of the century. Its success in finding a niche has been based on its discovery of a methodological principle that has enabled it to make the structure of language a general subject of study. Most people have had opinions about language, and many disciplines have dealt with it, but its internal workings, its nature as a system of covariation between form and meaning, did not give rise to a departmental discipline until within the memory of some still alive. Alongside specialization in certain languages and language families (French, Romance languages, Indo-European, Chinese), and in their particular systems of sounds, words, and sentences, there came to exist specialization in sound systems (phonology) in general, the make-up of words (morphology) in general, the make-up of sentences (syntax) in general. And it was generalization not based on illusion, not based, that is, on mistakenly taking the characteristics of familiar languages as the nature of language as such. On the one hand, anthropological linguists such as Franz Goas had worked to purge theoretical conceptions of language of such ethnocentrism. On the other hand, a general methodology was developed that answered to the units and relations of any language. The heart of the method was the question, not of quantity, more or less, but of quality, "same or different." Amidst the infinite heterogeneity of actual utterances, certain relations were constant. Behind the variability of speech lay an invariant system that could be demonstrated and described.

The general principles have evolved and changed in the development of modern linguistics, but their history has throughout had the character of being at once qualitative and rigorous. That has been the source of the attraction to others seeking an alternative to quantitative methodology as a model for the human sciences. The impact was felt first in phonology, the analysis of sounds, because phonology was the great novelty of the new linguistics. Speech sounds had been descriptively measured in the laboratory, identified in the field, and transcribed with more or less adequacy, but only in the 1920s and 1930s did they become the basis of a general science. The key was recognizing that the foundation of a general science of phonology was not measurement, but the intersubjective agreement of speakers of a language. Speakers were not usually aware of their system of sounds as such but were necessarily aware of the qualitative, "same or different," distinctions on which it was based. From these distinctions, the linguist could infer a structure of relations.

A limited example must serve. Perhaps every speech community pronounces some words with a puff of breath after a consonant at the beginning of a word—let us say, a consonant such as "p." In some languages, such as Hindi, the presence or absence of such a puff of breath (called "aspiration" by linguists) indicates the difference between one word and another. In English it does not. A "pig" with little breath and a "pig" with a lot are the same, so far as using the word "pig" is concerned. (A "pig" with a lot of breath, of course, may indicate that the speaker is trying to be especially clear, or amplify an attitude.) Conversely, there are many languages in which the vowel sound of "pig" is not distinct from the vowel sound of "peg," as far as the word one is using is concerned. (The Indian languages of Oregon and Washington are mostly of this type.) In English, on the other hand, "The Three Little Pegs" is not the name of a traditional story, and "Take him down a pig" is not one way of saying a conventional expression.

The principle of covariation between form and meaning employed here is general. Languages differ in the forms that count as differences of meaning. In English, the aspirated and unaspirated "p" count as one unit, from the standpoint of the dictionary, but in Hindi as two. In many Indian languages of Oregon and Washington the vowels of "pig" and "peg" count as one unit, from the standpoint of the dictionary, but in standard English as two. The valid specifics are arrived at by a method of contrast within a frame that is general. That is, the two kinds of "p" are said to contrast in Hindi, but not in English (from the standpoint of the dictionary—from the standpoint of expressive devices, a separate though interdependent system, there is a complementary contrast in English, the aspiration expressing emphasis, either of form [clarity] or meaning [attitude]). The contrast is relative to a specific frame—which sounds contrast with each other may vary with position in word or sentence. The units that contrast are themselves complex, intersections of several dimensions of contrast. Thus an unaspirated and an aspirated "p" are alike in being stops (stoppage of the outgoing breath), voiceless (no vibra-

of the vocal chords), and labial (made with the lips). An English "p" contrasts with an English "f" in that the latter is not a stop (some air escapes), an English "b" in that the latter is not voiceless (the vocal chords vibrate), and an English "t" in that the latter is not made with the lips; and "fig," "big," and (tig- [lic aced]) contrast in English as words, having separate places in the dictionary.

From relations such as these, a model can be derived that one can attempt to apply beyond language. One can seek sets of units that contrast with each other, on a finite number of dimensions, within a certain frame. Given units and structures established in such a way, one can develop models of the more complex relations into which they enter.

The story of the influence of such models cannot be told here, but suffice it to say that the influence has played an important part in anthropology in the United States, has affected ethnomethodology as a movement within sociology, and has entered into the rise of "structuralism" and "semiotics" as general intellectual movements. The common focus of these movements is a concern, first, with the existence of codes underlying messages (structures underlying behavior), and then with the general nature and kinds of codes. In a sense, it is under the rubric of "codes and messages" (or, "codes and modes [of realizing them])" that structuralism and semiotics have laid claim to being central to an understanding of human life in terms of communication. Early on, indeed, the notion of "communication" had been advanced by those influenced by linguistics as model or stimulus— in anthropology (Hall and Trager, 1953; Trager and Hall, 1954; Gumperz and Hymes, 1964; Hymes, 1967), in sociology (Dreitzel, 1970), and in folklore (Ben-Amos and Goldstein, 1957: 6; Paredes and Bauman, 1972).

Rules research, then, does not have the advantage that phonology had. It does not enter an intellectual scene wherein it is the first to propose a general methodology for the communicative phenomena with which it deals. If it has advantages, these must lie in other directions. One may be associated with streams of philosophy long indigenous to Anglo-American thought, those of utilitarianism, empiricism, analysis (Shwayder, 1965: 233ff). A second may be a focus on verifiable and vulnerable theories relating to specific behavior. Much of the impulse of structuralism and semiotics seems to go in the direction of texts, cultural or literary, and into debate about terms and allegiances. A third may be the possibility of integration with linguistics directly. Rather than acknowledge linguistics by analogy, rules research may be able to capitalize on the great body of linguistic work of recent years. For this to happen, however, certain issues must be addressed.

II

The term "rule" has become a normal idiom in linguistics in the last generation, due especially to the work of Noam Chomsky. Chomsky's impact, however, has had to do with his conceptions of the aim and form of a theory of grammar. When he wrote (1961) of the need to consider seriously the notion "grammatical rule," he did not deal on the term "rule" itself but on the need for a theory of grammar to have rules of certain kinds, accomplishing certain purposes. Rule was taken for granted as traditional in grammar (and perhaps in logic and mathematics). In seeking a precise formulation of the notion "grammatical rule," Chomsky's focus was on "grammatical." He inspired many to engage in "rules research" of a kind, but his followers did not debate the use of rule in relation to other generalizing terms within its semantic field. Rather, they debated the merits of one rule, or kind of rule, as against another. They did not ask, "Should grammatical trans-formations be called rules?" but whether or not they should have this or that property.

There has been some critical discussion of the linguistic use of rule, but it has become as common a term in linguistics as "sentence" and "word." And if we consider the decision tree for infer-ring rules presented by Shimanoff (Chapter 3), we find that the three steps to writing an hypothesized rule are quite compatible with linguistic inquiry. To be sure, some linguists rely on reflec-tion for examples, but that can perhaps be considered one way to observe behavior (their own).

Let us consider the three steps (contextual, controllable, and criticizable) in turn.

(1) If a phenomenon of language was not "contextual" in Shimanoff's sense, that is, recurrent, it would not be considered

an object of analysis. The very purpose of a grammar is to describe the finite system that underlies the infinite variety of often unique utterances.

(2) If a recurrent phenomenon is not controllable, then its description would be made part of something other than the rules of the particular grammar. Here, to be sure, linguists distinguish levels of absence of control. On the one hand, it is the hope of Chomsky and many others to determine relations over which speakers have no control, because such features are innate, built into the speaker and the language, as it were. Such relations would be assigned to the general theory of language and would not need to be specified for individual languages. On the other hand, some relations are not controllable within a particular language. For example, most languages have nasal stops, such as "m" and "n," and when they do, the nasals are voiced (the vocal chords vibrate to produce an audible buzz). Some languages, however, have nasal stops that are voiceless as regular parts of their phonology. Clearly, then, human beings can either voice or not voice a nasal stop. Within a particular language, however, the voicing may be invariant, automatic. In such a case, linguists usually relegate the automatic feature to a sphere of what is given with the elements on which rules operate. The feature is not itself an object of rules.

The "basicness" of controllability is revealingly shown in a passing comment by Chomsky and Halle (1968: 298) on labio-velar stops (stops made by coordinated closure of the lips and of the vocal cavity by placement of tongue against the back of the mouth) in some West African languages.

> Since clicklike suction is clearly an independently controllable aspect of the speech event, the data just cited establish suction as a separate phonetic feature, regardless of the fact that apparently in no language are there contrasting pairs of utterances that differ solely in this feature.

Controllability and contrast in some languages are expected to go together, but controllability itself admits a feature to the general system.

Such an exception points out the need to consider rules of language by *two* elementary functions, not just one, as has been typically the case. The feature discussed by Chomsky and Halle does not contrast to distinguish words in the languages in question, but its presence or absence serves to distinguish native from nonnative speakers, and to express emphasis in at least one of them (Bini). The presence of the controllable feature, then, goes together with contrasts after all. Utterances with and without it are not the same, but different in respect not to the dictionary, but to style. One or more stylistic uses of the feature presumably occur in all the languages in which the feature is controllable (Hymes, 1974a: 159-160). An intersection and interdependence of rules both for "what" and for "how" appears to be fundamental to communication.

Controllability enters into the place of "variable rules" in rules research. Shimanoff views the variable rules offered by Labov as probabilistic descriptions, and she contrasts them with prescriptive statements. Labov's prediction is an original and important contribution to the precise description of language and linguistic behavior; it illuminates processes of change; but it is of a kind with other conditioned features that are not usually considered objects of rules in linguistics. (The use of rule here is simply an unexamined extension of its use in linguistics, generally for statements of regularity.) Some of the occurrence of features subject to "variable rules," however, have to do with relations between the social identity of speakers, the settings in which they are speaking, and the topics to which they are attending. The frequency of a feature described by a variable rule may shift stylistically, as between more and less formal circumstances, for example. In such a case, one and the same utterance, from the usual grammatical standpoint, may yet recur and not be a repetition, but a different utterance. The words will not have changed only the way in which the words are said. The contrast will have to do, not with identity in the dictionary, but with style (Hymes, 1972, 1974b).

(3) Shimanoff phrases the third step, "Is the behavior criticizable?" She indicates that one method for assessing the criticizability of a behavior is to ask the actor to judge its appropriateness. In recent linguistic discussion, the question would be, "Do speakers (or speaker-hearers) judge it as grammatical?" There has been indeed considerable discussion of the issues and diffi-

culties involved in such judgment. In a more complex view, sentences which are "grammatical" in terms of a model of grammar may nevertheless not be "acceptable," because of awkwardness or difficulty not part of the grammar but part of short-term memory or other aspects of the processing of grammatical relations in encoding and decoding. Sentences which are grammatical may not be appropriate in a given context. Indeed, the latter fact led me to formulate the notion of the "competence" of a member of a speech community consists of commanding two kinds of rules—rules of grammar and rules of the use of grammar (Hymes, 1967, 1972a, 1974a).

Within grammar itself, indeterminacy may be resolved by fit with well established patterns, rather than direct evidence of judgment by speakers. It is in the nature of a system as complex as grammar that not all of it is directly testable in such a way.

In all three respects (contextuality, controllability, and appropriateness), linguistics is a field within the scope of rules research. It is a field with a rich experience in the issues raised by attempting to base theory on what is controllable and what is judged acceptable. Its success warrants the rules approach. Its debates and difficulties ought to be part of the cumulative experience on which rules research, as a basis of communication theory, proceeds.

The integration of linguistic research into the domain of rules research faces one important discrepancy. The notion of rule developed here carries with it the notion of prescription. It is natural to formulate rules in the "if-then" format developed by Shimanoff with such words as "must," "must not," and "should." Yet linguists typically do not understand their work in that way. Here is a statement representing a long-standing tradition.

> Since natural languages are rule governed systems, the next question is, 'What are the rules of sentence construction and interpretation in different languages?' Linguists try to answer this question by constructing grammars for individual languages and by forming hypotheses about the similarities inherent in all such grammars. In constructing these grammars, linguists are not attempting to tell people what rules they ought to follow when they speak; rather they are trying to formulate rules that correctly describe how people do speak. Thus, the linguist's grammar is

descriptive rather than *prescriptive* [Soames and Perlmutter, 1979: 5].

What linguists have in mind, of course, are the rules that may be laid down in schoolbooks and embodied in dictionaries. Linguists see their role as that of scientists, analyzing phenomena rather than enforcing them. They are well aware that none of us has accurate awareness of all that we say, and that a person may deny a feature that he or she nonetheless uses. It is known that those who embark on prescription, through dictionaries and rulebooks, may not themselves readily agree on many features. When the third edition of Webster's Dictionary appeared, it was attacked for admitting more of what was actually true of the language than some wished acknowledged. Within schoolrooms and some other places, a dictionary may be expected to be a definite arbiter of rules.[1] For most linguists, it is a book that does a better or worse job of getting the state of the language straight.

From Shimanoff's evaluation of the pros and cons of different methods of research; of the difference between rule-controlled and rule-guided behavior; and of the danger that self-reflection may reflect inaccurate folklinguistics rather than actuality, one can see that there need be no essential difference between linguistics and rules research in this regard. In neither case does one attempt to tell people what rules they ought to follow. The prescriptive aspect required for rules of language to be rules in the sense of rules research can presumably be located in the behavior of users of a language as they correct, repair, disattend, admire, and otherwise monitor their own and others' speech. Perhaps a generic prescriptive "must" can be assigned to a grammar as a whole: If you wish to use this language, then you must do the many complex things woven into its grammar.

It remains that linguistics have thought of grammar not as prescriptive but as productive, and that significant issues for both linguistics and rules research may be highlighted by the tension between those two terms. The idiom of rules research tends to be one of "must, must not, should." The idiom of generative grammar and most modern linguistics generally is "can." Given the finite system of a grammar, the competent speaker can do an infinite number of things. The contemporary attitude emphasizes the flexible, creative power of a grammar.

This difference may be associated with another. In rules research the stated rules are directly related to behavior. More general concepts and relations among rules are perhaps to be considered under different terms. In linguistics the term "rule" is very much associated with "rules about rules," with rules that change rules; rules directly related to what is acceptable in speech are assessed as evidence for general conclusions about the kinds of rule and relation among rules, to be found in grammar. The creative power of a grammar is bound up with, and explicated by, these deeper relations among rules. There is a close parallel with the emphasis in ethnomethodological sociology (Cicourel, 1970) on the creative nature of the way members of a society deal with experience and each other. The appearance of stability at one level of rules is contingent on the flexible use of deeper, more general rules.

Perhaps only terminology is at stake. From the point of view of rules research, perhaps it is a question of making distinctions with regard to the patterns and abilities of which rules in a precise sense are a part. At the very least, the terminological relations should be clarified. More may be at stake technically and metaphorically. There is a prescriptive element hidden behind the descriptive stance of linguistics. There is a productive aspect to rule-governed and rule-guided behavior. Mutual clarification of each other's technical problems and metaphorical stances may benefit both.

Formal linguistics focuses on grammar as basic to other considerations of language. It hypostasizes data and problems as general to "English." Yet the relation between "competence" in the sense of English grammar and "competence" in the sense of the abilities of actual people is poorly understood (what is rule-governed versus what is rule-guided in Shimanoff's sense). The tendency of linguists, and many psychologists as well, is to distinguish what I have called the "systematic potential" (Hymes, 1974: 95ff) of the general grammatical system—its ideal productivity—and to assign discrepancies with the scope and content of actual conduct not to the language, but to psychological characteristics (such as short-term memory) of human beings and to unexamined interference from social life. The focus on underlying relations in grammar is accompanied by a reliance in many quarters on self-reflection as a source of data and judgments. As the study of language on a linguistic basis extends further into the use of language, the starting point comes increasingly into question. The social bases of language and of the practice of linguists become more apparent. The general starting point of formal grammar appears as a selected artifact of certain choices about functions and phenomena to recognize (Hymes, 1974; Volophinov, 1973). The insistence of rules research on the relation to behavior can join forces with "behavioral" tendencies in linguistics itself to develop a more adequate general basis for rules in language and conduct alike.

Conversely, the experience of formal linguistics in handling complex relations among rule-related elements of communication can be invaluable to rules research. It is Chomsky's hope to identify properties unique to grammar and indications of innate bases for grammar distinctive of the mind. A growing body of opinion sees properties of grammar as part of general properties of mind or social life. Rules research seems committed to the distinctiveness of human beings at the general level of communication, not at the more specific level of grammar, as Dr. Shimanoff's citation of Kenneth Burke on "action," as distinct from "motion," shows. The commitment, one I share, entails, however, a wide variety of specific systems and modalities. Rules about rules are essential. Adequate modeling of their interconnections undoubtedly will entail using a variety of formal devices, including figures and diagrams, such as have been explored in formal linguistics. The if-then format is excellent for bringing out the character of rules, and rules for specific relations in linguistic data may well take the same form. (Indeed, Soames and Perlmutter [1979: 9] state their introductory instance in such a way: "If the direct object of a verb is coreferential with the subject, it becomes a reflexive pronoun.") But the if-then format is a test of status as a rule, not an exclusive form of presentation.

Rules research could restrict itself to aspects of conduct close to explicit norms. Shimanoff, however, accepts tacitly known rules and considers quite particular features of communicative interaction. A major frontier thus appears to be formulating the relations between rules involving politeness and the like in interaction and the specific implementations in gesture, voice, and word. The general modeling of the relations between ends and means in rule-governed or rule-guided conduct will be complex indeed. It seems unavoidable that it will take on some of the concern of the linguist and ethnomethodologist with productivity and the problems of the connection between the implicit potential productivity of a rule-related system and actual conduct. Ultimately, I would predict, rule-related behavior will be analyzed by the general relation between *strategies* (organizations of ends) and *styles* (organizations of means) within *contexts* (organizations of frames).

The integration of rules research and linguistics research is the more to be desired because many examples of rules in Shimanoff's book come from the study of discourse (Labov on ritual insults, Grice on conversational maxims, Sacks, Jefferson and Schegloff on conversation). It would be odd—and it seems increasingly impossible—for the foundations of the analysis of language beyond the sentence to be different from those of the analysis of language within the sentence. In this extension of the scope of linguistics, the experience of rules research may be of value. It is one thing to be skilled in the discovery of pattern and formal statement of relations. It is another to be sensitive to the different kinds of status, social and theoretical, the patterns and relations may have. Linguists and others influenced by linguistics have readily extended the term "rule" without much analysis. Often enough little is at stake. If Cicourel (1970) were to replace the term "rule," his theoretical argument for two kinds of abilities underlying social order could be restated in interpretive procedures ("basic rules") and norms ("normative rules"). It can only benefit linguists and others to be precise with such terms, however, and it may force more complex, "grammar-like," modeling of the relations among components of an analysis of communicative conduct.

III

Rules research and comparative ethnography have also a mutual contribution to make. What has just been said about discourse applies to ethnography. Conversely, comparative ethnography is essential to the validation of a theory of rules.

There is first of all the question of the relation between the analytical vocabulary of the theory and the analytical distinctions made in particular languages. Any language is itself a metalanguage of its culture. It seems certain that a theoretical vocabulary developed in English will not precisely match the ordinary language vocabulary of action in, say, Russian, Japanese, Arabic, or Samoan. Two issues will arise. One is not to impose the theoretical vocabulary in the description of the local case. Perhaps in a certain community, some of the distinctions noted in English do not obtain; native vocabulary or conduct treats them as the same. Perhaps some additional distinctions, not noted in English, obtain; native vocabulary or conduct shows a contrast where none had been anticipated. The second is to relate valid analyses of local cases to the general framework.

The appropriate procedure is described by Pike (1977). The general framework makes possible the recognition of potentially significant distinctions in new cases. Analysis of what is contrastive and rule-governed in the new case will show what distinctions are significant and what are the relations into which they enter. Open observation may bring to light distinctions new to the framework. The general framework itself can be revised in the light of specific analyses. This three-step process is labelled "etic" (1), "emic," "etic" (2) by Pike (1965), generalizing from the linguistic terms "phonetic" and "phonemic." It is obvious enough, yet the stimulus of seeking universal frameworks today sometimes leads scholars to overlook possibilities of distortion if such a procedure is neglected.

A case in point is that of the conversational maxims proposed by the philosopher Grice and adopted by many linguists. As Shimanoff indicates, these maxims can be stated as rules, e.g., "be relevant," "don't say less than is required," and so forth. Let us leave aside the suspicion of ethnocentrism prompted by the close agreement between the maxims and the maxims of traditional Anglo-American schoolbooks. Let us recognize that Grice does not intend the maxims to be descriptions of conduct, but as bases for the interpretation of conduct. Someone may say less than is required in a conversation, but, given the shared maxim, the fact invites interpretation. The actual meaning of what is said is derived from relating what is said to the maxim.

Such reasoning shows both a universal relevance for what Grice has formulated and the deceptiveness of the formulation. Let us grant that in a society such as that of Madagascar, where normal conservation typically says less than is required or avoids relevance, one still can make sense of what goes on using notions such as saying enough and being relevant. Does it then make sense to say that culture of Madgascar contains as maxims, or rules, such injunctions as "don't say less than is required," and "be relevant?" To say that would require us to consider the people of Madagascar as *normally* violating rules they accept as basic. Children acquiring the culture would have to acquire some such understanding as "don't say less than is required," but "do." The people of Madagascar avoid giving information, not to invite interpretation in terms of politeness but to avoid trouble and danger. A direct analysis of their conduct would formulate such rules as "if asked a question, give as little information as possible" and relate such rules to a general rule or maxim, "be as non-committal as possible, so as to avoid responsibility for unfortunate consequences." The relation of Madagascarian ways of speaking (for Grice) is not in terms of a rule, but in terms of a dimension. Grice has identified *dimensions* of universal relevance to ways of speaking. Different cultures have made different choices, as it were, as to the rules of behavior they find advisable in relation to those dimensions.[2]

This example illustrates again the general problem of the relations one considers to hold among the different components of a theory of communicative conduct. It appears to be equally misleading for the term "rule" to be extended to all regularities, and for the rule-like verbal form (e.g., "Be relevant") to be extended to universal dimensions. Rules research, mediating between the analytical work of philosophers and theorists, and the investigations of ethnographers, may give greater validity and precision to both.

IV

It remains to mention a third trend in the study of communication theory, and this is using the notion of communication as a basis for critical assessment of society.[3] Such use has been present in the work of Raymond Williams and Richard Hoggart in England.

It is central to the work of the German theorist Jürgen Habermas. Habermas distinguishes a sphere of communicative interaction from a sphere of work in relations between persons, as against relations between human beings and nature. The latter is ideally a relation of control, the former is not. Indeed, Habermas finds communicative interaction to presuppose the ingredients of an ideal speech situation in which existing societies can be critically analyzed for systematically distorted communication, an ideal that anticipates a future state of society (Habermas, 1970, 1973; McCarthy, 1973, 1978). Habermas holds forth an ideal that fits the situation of Shimanoff's book. The text (and the foreword) prescribe, but the only sanction to which appeal can be made is that of rational persuasion. The standpoint of Habermas' theory can itself be criticized, as perhaps expressing the interest in a future society of intellectuals (Disco, 1979), but his work shows that communication theory can speak not only in the idiom of science but also in the idiom of human aspiration.

—Dell Hymes

University of Pennsylvania

NOTES

1. The complex interaction among publishers, editors, officials, and members of the public with regard to dictionaries as sources of prescription is illustrated by a recent item in the New York *Times*.

Three years ago, the chief state school officer for Texas removed from the list recommended by the State Textbook Committee the following five dictionaries: The high school edition of the American Heritage Dictionary of the English Language; the Doubleday Dictionary; the Random House College Dictionary, revised edition; Webster's New World Dictionary of the American Language, college edition; and Webster's Seventh New Collegiate Dictionary. The reason: Among the more than 180,000 entries in each dictionary were some 60 words that some citizens found objectionable [8 January 1980].

2. I draw here on the work of Elinor Ochs (1976) and criticize in this one respect the admirable study by Brown and Levison (1978: 100, 298, n. 27).

3. The distinction between what is rule-governed and what is rule-guided should prove central in this regard. It allows for analyzing situations in which the interests of one party are imposed on a situation as its definition in terms of rules, although other parties are (perhaps willy-nilly) guided by other rules. (For a striking historical example, see Hanke, 1965, Ch. III.) A questionable use of the Old Testament and the authority of the people were held to give the Spanish crown the New World for the sake of introducing Christianity there. Indians who surrendered their land peaceably might continue to live on it as vassals, but those who did not could be rightfully killed or enslaved. This "Requirement"

was to be announced to Indians before hostilities could legally be launched. Every con-
quistador was expected to carry a copy. Often enough the Indians could not understand it
or indeed were given no opportunity actually to hear it. But in the eyes of the authorities,
matters were handled in accordance with a rule.

References

Ben-Amos, Dan and Kenneth S. Goldstein [eds.] (1975) Folklore: Performance and
    Communication. The Hague: Mouton.
Brown, Penelope and Stephen Levinson (1978) "Universals in language usage: politeness
    phenomena," pp. 56-289 in Esther N. Goody (ed.) Questions and Politeness: Strategies
    in Social Interaction. Cambridge: Cambridge University Press.
Chomsky, Noam (1961) "On the notion 'rule of grammar.'" Proceedings of the Twelfth
    Symposium in Applied Mathematics 12: 6-24. (Reprinted in Jerry A. Fodor and
    Jerrold J. Katz [eds.] Readings in the Philosophy of Language. Englewood Cliffs, NJ:
    Prentice-Hall.)
Cicourel, Aaron V. (1970) "Basic and normative rules in the negotiation of status and
    role," in Dreitzel, pp. 4-45; Sudnow, pp. 229-258.
Connerton, Paul [ed.] (1976) Critical Sociology. Harmondsworth and New York: Pen-
    guin Books.
Disco, Cornelis (1979) "Critical theory as ideology of the new class: Rereading Jürgen
    Habermas." Theory and Society 8(2): 159-214.
Dreitzel, Hans Peter [ed.] (1970) Recent Sociology, No. 2: Patterns of Communicative
    Behavior. New York: Macmillan.
Habermas, Jürgen (1973) Legitimationsprobleme im Spatkapitalismus (Legitimation
    Crisis). Frankfurt am Main: Suhrkamp Verlag.
    (1970) "Toward a theory of communicative competence," pp. 114-148 in Hans
    Peter Dreitzel (ed.) Recent Sociology, No. 2: Patterns of Communicative Behavior.
    New York: Macmillan.
Hanke, Lewis (1965) The Spanish Struggle for Justice in the Conquest of America.
    Boston: Little, Brown.
Hymes, Dell (1974a) "Studying the interaction of language and social life," pp. 29-66 in D.
    Hymes (ed.) Foundations in Sociolinguistics. Philadelphia: University of Pennsyl-
    vania Press.
    (1974b) "Ways of speaking," in R. Bauman and J. Sherzer (eds.) Explorations in
    the Ethnography of Speaking. New York and London: Cambridge University Press.
    (1972a) "Models of the interaction of language and social life," pp. 35-71 in J. J.
    Gumperz and D. Hymes (eds.) Directions in Sociolinguistics. New York: Holt, Rine-
    hart & Winston.
    (1972b) "Introduction," pp. xi-lvii in Courtney Cazden, Vera John-Steiner, Dell
    Hymes (eds.) Functions of language in the classroom. New York: Teachers College
    Press.
    (1967) "Models of the interaction of language and social setting." Journal of Social
    Issues 23(2): 8-28.
Keenan, Elinor Ochs (1976) "The universality of conversational implicature." Language
    in Society 5: 67-80.
McCarthy, T. A. (1973) "A theory of communicative competence." Philosophy of the
    Social Sciences 3: 135-56.
McCarthy, Thomas (1978) The critical theory of Jürgen Habermas. Cambridge, MA:
    MIT Press.

Paredes, Americo and Richard Bauman [eds.] (1972) Toward New Perspectives in Folklore. Austin: University of Texas Press.

Pike, Kenneth L. (1965) Language in Relation to a Unified Theory of the Structure of Human Behavior. The Hague: Mouton.

Schwayder, D. S. (1965) The Stratification of Behavior. A System of Definitions Propounded and Defended. London: Routledge & Kegan Paul.

Sibley, Elbridge (1974) Social Science Research Council: The First Fifty Years. New York: Social Science Research Council.

Soames, Scott and David M. Perlmutter (1979) Syntactic Argumentation and the Structure of English. Berkeley: University of California Press.

Sudnow, David [ed.] (1971) Studies in Interaction. New York: Free Press.

Toulmin, Stephen (1972) Human Understanding: The Collective Use and Evolution of Concepts. Princeton, NJ: Princeton University Press.

Trager, George L. and Edward T. Hall, Jr. (1954) "Culture and communication: a model and an analysis." Explorations 3: 157-249.

Voloshinov, V. N. (1973) Marxism and the philosophy of language. (L. Matejka and I. R. Titunik, trans.). New York and London: Seminar Press. (The actual author is now widely believed to have been M. M. Baxtin).

Wolff, Robert Paul (1968) The Poverty of Liberalism. Boston: Beacon Press.

ACKNOWLEDGMENTS

This study was completed with the help of several persons, and the author would like to extend her gratitude to them. Walter R. Fisher was the initial supporter of this undertaking; and while others doubted the feasibility of the study, he remained the most enthusiastic and steadfast advocate for its completion. One of his most useful recommendations was that I provide examples to illustrate my assertions. He also pointed out weaknesses in my reasoning by arguing for an alternative position. In the process of defending and illustrating my assertions, I found that they were sometimes in need of revision. I am also grateful for his many suggestions on how to express my ideas more clearly and precisely. It is doubtful that the present study would have been completed without the support of Dr. Fisher, but it is clear that his contributions significantly enhanced the final product.

A special thanks is due Kenneth K. Sereno for his encouragement, support, and advice. He was particularly instrumental in helping me refine my ideas about the contribution of a rules perspective to theory construction in communication. Part of Chapter 6 is designed to answer questions he continually asked me: "Where does a rule fit in the construction of a theory? Is it a theorem, proposition, or what?"

Elinor Ochs introduced me to much of the conversational literature from which communication rules may be inferred. In large part my transcribing and conversational analyzing skills were acquired under her direction.

I would also like to thank Thomas S. Frentz, who has had a significant impact on my thinking about communication; Donald P. Cushman and W. Barnett Pearce, who shared some of their own and their students' unpublished papers with me; and Barbara Ryon Howard, who helped prepare the bibliography for typing.

Throughout the entire process of research and writing this study, Janet L. Weathers proved to be a conscientious friend and colleague. I often called upon her for moral and intellectual support, and I was never disappointed. She served as a sounding board for many ideas, evaluating each carefully. At times, I thought her remarks bordered on "heresy," but these statements were particularly useful in refining my thinking.

This study would not have been completed without the assistance of Perry S. Shimanoff. He supported me in every imaginable way. He typed what seemed to be endless drafts of this study, helped cut and paste various versions, and assumed much more than his fair share of household responsibilities, and yet somehow found the time and energy to be a disciplinarian, a counselor, a lover, and much more.

Chapter 1

INTRODUCTION

"I don't know what you mean by 'glory,'" Alice said.

Humpty Dumpty smiled contemptuously. "Of course you don't—till I tell you. I meant 'there's a nice knock-down argument for you!'"

"But 'glory' doesn't mean 'a nice knock-down argument,'" Alice objected.

"When I use a word," Humpty Dumpty said, in a rather scornful tone, "it means just what I choose it to mean—neither more nor less."

"The question is," said Alice, "whether you can make words mean so many different things."

"The question is," said Humpty Dumpty, "which is to be master—that's all."

—Lewis Carroll

This excerpt from *Through the Looking Glass* has been used by scholars to illustrate a variety of communication concepts—from meaning to the Whorfian hypothesis to one-upmanship.[1] It also demonstrates the importance of rules in communicative interactions. Perhaps this is its clearest message: in order for communication to exist, or continue, two or more interacting individuals must share rules for using symbols. Not only must they have rules for individual symbols, but they must also agree on such matters as how to take turns at speaking, how to be polite or how to insult, to greet, and so forth. If every symbol user manipulated symbols at random, the result would be chaos rather than communication.

Rules of social interaction have become a major concern of a number of humanists and social scientists. Although the exploration of social interaction in terms of rules has been traced to the writings of Aristotle and Immanuel Kant, Ludwig Wittgenstein's 1953 *Philosophical Investigations* has been credited with instigating the current interest in rules.[2] The rules perspective has emerged for two fundamental reasons: (1) dissatisfaction with mechanistic/deterministic interpretations of nonrandom regularities in human behavior and (2) adherence to the presuppositions that human beings make and evaluate choices among alternative courses of action and that many of these choices are made on the basis of rules.[3]

Mechanistic/deterministic approaches to human behavior have been associated with the writings of such scholars as Thomas Hobbes, a contemporary of Galileo; David Hume; and, more recently, John B. Watson and B. F. Skinner.[4] A mechanistic/deterministic interpretation of human behavior assumes that humans never act but only react, and that the "language of physics" is used to describe behavior.[5] Behavior from a mechanistic perspective is investigated from a stimulus-response or a stimulus-organism-response model. In either case, stimuli are viewed as impinging upon the actor and determining his/her[6] fate; the person is not viewed as actively participating in the construction of reality. The essential assumption of this perspective is that the behavior of humans is determined by external forces rather than by choice. Underlying the mechanistic approach to the study of human behavior is the idea that people "move" as machines do, and that causation is the only acceptable form for scientific explanations to take.

Rules theorists acknowledge that some behavior is mechanistically determined and appropriately explained by appealing to causal relationships, but they deny that all or even most human behavior is so motivated. Rule theorists consider mechanistic behavior a form of "motion" and controllable behavior as a form of "action."[7]

The action-motion distinction is most clearly expressed by Kenneth Burke.[8] In emphasizing the symbolic and ethical nature of humanity, Burke distinguishes between action and motion. Action, according to Burke, implies the human personality.

> "People" are entities capable of "symbolic action"; to varying degrees they can be addressed, "reasoned with," petitioned, persuaded. "Things" can but move, or be moved. . . . *Action* involves *character*, which involves *choice*; and the form of choice attains its perfection in the distinction between Yes and No (between thou shalt and thou shalt not). Though the concept of sheer "motion" is not ethical, "action" implies the ethical (the human personality).[9]

Romano Harré and Paul Secord also contrast two conceptualizations of human and human behavior, one mechanistic and the other anthropomorphic.[10] The mechanistic model views humans as "helpless spectators carried along the flood tide of physical causes," as objects to which things are done, and as objects which are controlled by external forces. In contrast, the anthropomorphic model views humans as agents directing and monitoring their own behavior, as watchers, as communicators, and as critics. Rule theorists emphasize the anthropomorphic model as indicative of the humanistic rather than animalistic characteristics of humans.

In addition to the motion/action distinction rule, scholars have grounded their work on four observations: (1) much of human behavior is not haphazard; rather, it exhibits regularities; (2) some regularities are governed by mechanistic forces, but for many others, it is possible to deviate from the regularities, and if one can deviate from the regularities, then the regularities cannot be attributed to physical or logical necessity; (3) deviations from certain regularities may be negatively sanctioned; therefore, many of these regularities are not the result of free choice; and (4) many behaviors are controllable, criticizable and recur in similar contexts; in such cases, it is assumed that the regularities are the result of a rule.

Building on the conceptual foundations established by the above assumptions, scholars from various disciplines have investigated communication rules. They include: John J. Gumperz and Dell. H. Hymes in anthropological linguistics;[11] Donald P.

Cushman, Thomas B. Farrell, Thomas S. Frentz, Robert E. Nofsinger, and W. Barnett Pearce in communication;[12] Noam
Chomsky and William Labov in linguistics;[13] J. L. Austin, Joan
Ganz, H. Paul Grice, Romano Harré, John R. Searle, Stephen E.
Toulmin, and Ludwig Wittgenstein in philosophy;[14] Peter Collett, Susan Ervin-Tripp, Paul Secord, and Dan I. Slobin in psychology;[15] and Ervin Goffman, Harold Garfinkel, Gail Jefferson,
Harvey Sacks, and Emanuel A. Schegloff in sociology.[16] The
theoretical treatises and research of these scholars and others
like them have provided important insights into communicative
processes, and they have served as frameworks for additional
studies.

Researchers have used rules to identify how actors perform
certain acts, fulfill specific roles, enact various episodes, and
manage the dynamics of symbolic interaction. Rules analyses
have been applied to communication exchanges as varied as
telephone conversations at a police desk, group therapy sessions,
child-parent interactions, and the Watergate tapes.[17] The practical utility of rules research cannot be underestimated. Research
has demonstrated that those who deviate from rules may be
viewed as "mad or bad," insulting, or less promotable and that
their messages may be thought of as inappropriate or inco-
herent.[18]

Despite the excellence of much of rules research, at present
ambiguity surrounds basic conceptions, methods, and the potential contribution of a rules approach to communication theory.
There is "little consensus about the criteria for evaluating rules
research or the formal requirements of a rules-based theory."[19]
A need exists to establish theoretically sound answers to these
questions: What is a rule? How can rules be inferred from behavior? What are the various ways rules and behavior may be
related? What are the most appropriate methods for rules research? and What are the contributions of a rules approach to
communication theory?

Several scholars have argued that rule as a concept remains
unclear.[20] In Chapter 2 various conceptualizations are presented
and critically evaluated. Based on this critical evaluation, a
definition of rule is offered. The utility of this definition is judged
in terms of the philosophical assumptions of the rules perspec-

tive, internal consistency, the ability to distinguish rules from related concepts, and comparative advantages to previous conceptualizations. In addition, the structure and functions of rules are delineated.

Some communication rules are explicitly stated, but others are only tacitly known. Implicit rules may be inferred from behavior. Chapter 3 identifies the necessary and sufficient evidence to identify implicit rules. Rule-generated behavior is controllable, criticizable, and contextual. This chapter includes a decision-tree that indicates the appropriate procedures for providing this evidence. Finally, it compares rule-generated behavior with other types of behavior regularities.

Rules may be related to behavior in numerous ways. Behavior can comply or deviate from the prescriptions of a rule, and actors may use rules to make behavioral choices with different degrees of rule-knowledge. Chapter 4 proposes a nine-member taxonomy of various relationships between rule and behavior. Since explanations for behavior on the bases of rules require particular types of relationship, this taxonomy is particularly helpful to scholars who wish to construct communication theories from a rules perspective.

Multiple methods have been used to investigated communication rules and rule-related behavior. The comparative advantage of six methods are evaluated in Chapter 5: self-reflection, survey, naturalistic observation, participant observation, quasi-experiment, and experiment. The usefulness of each method is judged in terms of its ability to provide the required evidence that a rule exists or that a particular relationship between a rule and behavior occurred. The probable accuracy and the generalizability of the results for naturalistic communication are also assessed for each method.

Ultimately, the research efforts of rules scholars should lead to theory construction. Chapter 6 illustrates how rules research may be used to construct axiomatic theories of communication. Because there has been some controversy over whether a covering laws, systems, or rules approach would be the most productive for constructing communication theories, all three perspectives are compared. Differences and similarities are illustrated by specific research examples.

The last chapter highlights possible directions for future research. In each of the chapters there are statements that are discussed as rules. These statements are marked by a capitalized R and a number in parentheses. Rule statements are numbered consecutively within each chapter; the numbering sequences begins anew with each chapter. "Rules" that are inaccurate are marked with the asterisk. The asterisk indicates that the statement is not a rule according to the conceptualization offered here. Rules taken from other sources, whether directly or by inference, are documented. If they are direct quotations, they are also enclosed by double quotation marks. The clarity, usefulness, ethics, reasonableness, and so on of rules are not judged. The concern here is with the nature and accuracy of rules, not their quality.

Chapter 2

COMMUNICATION RULES:
NATURE, STRUCTURE, AND FUNCTION

To investigate communicative behavior from a rules perspective, theorists must be able to identify rules. Theorists have not always agreed, however, on what constitutes a rule. In fact, several scholars have argued that rule as a concept remains unclear. Gidon Gottlieb, for instance, has indicated that "the concept of rule is shrouded in confusion and controversy. Yet rules are relied upon and used in a very wide range of fields."[1] In a critical evaluation of a rules approach to interpersonal communication, Art Bouchner has maintained that "my complaint rests not on their [rule scholars'] philosophy of science but on their conceptualization of rules. . . . Given the complexity of the matter, how are we to know a rule when we see one?"[2] Jesse Delia has probably made the most emphatic statement regarding the confusion about the concept of rule: "The terrain covered by notions of 'rules,' then is broad, grossly diffuse, and imprecisely articulated. . . . The 'rules' territory taken as a whole is, in fact, little short of chaotic."[3] Scholars have also argued that the absence of a clear definition has impeded the construction of communication theories from a rules perspective.[4]

The lack of consensus regarding the definition of rule may be attributed at least in part to the fact that definition concerns have not been the primary focus of communication scholars;

thus scholars have offered different definitions without comparing these various conceptualizations to previous definitions
or without fully exploring the implications of their definitions.
In addition to different explicit definitions, diverse phenomena
have been labeled as rules. For example, interpretations and
explanations for behavior, descriptions of empirical regularities,
inferences about cognitive states, and prescriptions for behaviors have all been labeled rules at one time or another, each
implying possible differences in the conceptualization of rule.
This diversity in usage has compounded the confusion.

A clear and sound definition of rule as a concept would provide
several theoretical advantages, including: (1) allowing one to
identify rules and rule-related phenomena for the purpose of
theory construction from a rules perspective, (2) providing a way
to distinguish rules from related constructs like norm, orders,
instruction and so forth, (3) making possible a consistent application of the definition, which would facilitate comparisons and
contrasts across studies.

Although rule scholars have defined rules in a variety of ways,
they have generally agreed that rules are "followable," prescriptive, and contextual.[5] These characteristics are not always explicit
constituents of definition, as we shall see later, but they are part
of theorists' conceptualizations. Further, though there is a
general consensus that "followability," prescriptiveness, and contextuality are characteristics of rules, there is sometimes disagreement about what constitutes these characteristics. The
domain of rules has also received limited attention as a defining
characteristic,[6] but again there is some disagreement about the
nature of this characteristic.

The primary purpose of this chapter is to examine the defining
characteristics of a rule. Points of agreement and disagreement
among rule scholars, as well as alternative perspectives, will
be critically evaluated in order to establish a sound and useful
definition of rule. This conception will be used to contrast rule
with related phenomena, and it will be compared with other
definitions of rule. Finally, the structure and functions of rules
will be identified.

Nature of Rules

Rules are followable, prescriptive, contextual, and they pertain to behavior. Each of these characteristics will be discussed in this section. In each case, areas of agreement will be presented first. This examination will be followed by qualifications, disagreements, and/or alternative conceptualizations regarding the characteristics.

FOLLOWABLE

That rules are followable has been acknowledged by several scholars. Below is a sampling of their descriptions:

> Speakers know and follow the rules, and it is their following of these rules which accounts for the observed regularities of speech.[7]
>
> A rule is something which can be followed.[8]
>
> Rules are followable or specify "see to it"-able procedures.[9]

These sample statements were taken from the writings of language philosophers, John Fisher, Aaron Snyder, and Joan Ganz. Communication scholars have not explicitly identified rules as followable, but one may infer from their discussions about rule-related behavior that they concur with the language philosophers that followability is a feature of rules. Communication scholars associate rules with actions rather than motions, and actions are behaviors that one may choose to perform; hence, a rule must be capable of being followed.[10]

The idea that rules are followable implies that rules may also be broken.[11] Scientific laws differ from rules in that there is no choice whether one can or cannot follow them; they cannot be broken. Both scientific laws and rules relate to behavior, but the relationship between them and behavior is different. Laws *describe* noncontrollable phenomena, including human behavior, whereas rules relate only to human behavior, and only to human behavior that is *prescribed* and can be controlled. Laws describe motion, whereas rules prescribe actions. The notion that rules are breakable has also been expressed by arguing that one must be capable of misapplying a rule or making a mistake in terms of a rule.[12] Rules also differ from scientific láws in terms of changeability.[13] Rules may be changed if actors consider them no longer appropriate, but laws are changed on the basis of empirical evidence.

Although rule scholars agree that rules are followable, it is not always clear what they mean by followability. *Followable*, according to Ganz, means that rules must refer to empirical possibilities, and not contradictory or physically impossible behavior.[14] This description is useful in distinguishing rules from laws. The distinction becomes clearer when one tries to treat a law as if it were a rule as in *$R_{(01)}$.

*$R_{(01)}$: Objects which are dropped should (not) fall to earth.

Objects cannot choose to follow the laws of gravity; rather, they are subject to their control. Below are two statements which typify the contrasting of rules and laws in terms of followability in rules literature:

> People don't see to it that they don't defy the law of gravity any-more than they see to it that the basketball they throw at the backboard obeys laws concerning the angles of incidence and refraction. Scientific laws can only be fulfilled; they are neither followable nor breakable.[15]

> [A] rule appears to be quite unlike a physical law in that it seems possible for him [a person] to violate the former but not the latter. Driving my car, I can break a Pennsylvania speed limit but I can't exceed the speed of light.[16]

Although rules should not prescribe *physically* impossible or contradictory behaviors, it is possible that rules may prescribe behaviors which are *practically* contradictory and/or impossible. For example, American schools have in the past had rules which were not followable for Spanish-speaking children:

$R_{(02)}$: Children must speak English in the classroom.[17]

If one does not know English, one cannot speak English; hence, the rule is not followable. Nonetheless, those generating and enforcing the rule believe it to be followable, and certainly speakers of Spanish are physically able to learn and speak English. Perhaps, then, we can say that rules must be physically followable, though they may not be necessarily followable in practice.

Rules may also contradict one another. Leonard Hawes described a rule dilemma faced by residents in a halfway house for convicted criminals. $R_{(03)}$ through $R_{(05)}$ are taken from his work.[18] Below are the two rules which were competing:

$R_{(03)}$: Convicts must inform the director of any illegal activities.

$R_{(04)}$: Convicts must not "rat" on each other.

If one is aware of an illegality, it is impossible to follow both rules. The conflict is resolved by invoking $R_{(05)}$ which supersedes $R_{(03)}$.

$R_{(05)}$: The director must not do anything that would result in the physical harm of any convict.

Since turning in a fellow convict would probably result in physical harm, rule$_{(03)}$ is not practically followable in light of rules$_{(04)}$ and$_{(05)}$. However, taken independently, rules$_{(03)}$ through$_{(05)}$ are physically followable; hence, they are rules. In summary, then, rules taken independently must be physically followable, and hence also breakable, but they need not be followed or followable in practice to be rules.[19]

Followability is not sufficient to distinguish rules from other constructs which are also followable. One may follow one's intuitions or whims (e.g., having a milk shake at 3:00 p.m.). Or, one may follow the behavior of others (e.g., playing dress up). Additional characteristics are needed in order to define "rule." Prescriptiveness is one of them.

PRESCRIPTIVE

Not only are rules followable, but those who are knowledgeable of a rule also know that they can be held accountable if they break it. Like followability, prescriptiveness is a characteristic of rules, as several scholars have acknowledged.[20] Prescriptiveness is another means of distinguishing rules from scientific laws. Prescriptiveness implies that something should happen and that a deviation from this behavior is subject to evaluation. Laws are not prescribed; thus, they are not evaluative. This difference has been well expressed by W. Barnett Pearce: "It is absurd to praise or blame sodium for combining with chloride to produce salt, but it is far from absurd to critique a person for performing an insult."[21]

Although rules are prescriptive, scholars have not agreed on what to call this quality. Some have described this quality as either normative force[22] or practical necessity[23] rather than prescriptive force. Stephen Toulmin has described normative force in the following manner: "An agent who recognizes that he is deviating from a rule acknowledges . . . a claim on him to correct his behavior."[24] Donald P. Cushman and W. Barnett Pearce have maintained that "practical necessity depends on the type and amount of normative force an actor feels to perform (or not perform) a given activity in a specified way."[25]

Since *prescriptive force, normative force,* and *practical force* are alternative phrases for describing the same phenomena, one may ask: Is there any advantage to be gained by choosing one phrase over the others? There does seem to be a slight difference among the terms. Something may be prescriptive and not normative, in the sense of what is average, or normative and not prescriptive. Or something may be practical and not prescriptive or prescriptive and not practical. Perhaps some examples will make these distinctions clearer.

It may be that most English speakers use *phenomena* as a singular noun. We may describe this tendency of most speakers as normative behavior. However, the dictionary prescribes that the singular form is *phenomenon*. The dictionary rule has prescriptive force, even if it does not represent normative behavior. One of the distinctions between normative behavior and prescriptive rules is that behavior which is consistent with the prescription of rules, but nonnormative, will not be negatively sanctioned. But normative behavior that violates a rule may be negatively evaluated. For example, those who use phenomenon as the singular form will not be negative sanctioned, even though their behavior is nonnormative. On the other hand, editors will undoubtedly insist that writers conform to what is prescribed by the rule regardless what most people do.

Cushman and Pearce apparently chose the phrase *practical necessity* because they see communicators utilizing rules in order to achieve their goals. However, there are rules that are not necessarily practical, at least, in the usual sense of the word. One may be able to accomplish one's goal (e.g., get a request fulfilled) without being polite.[26] Nonetheless, Robin Lakoff has maintained that politeness rules are central to our linguistic behavior,[27] and Susan B. Shimanoff has reported that people generally are polite.[28] One may argue that it is practical to be polite, but if one uses *practical* in the sense of saving face (rather than accomplishing a task), then ultimately following rules is practical, because not following a rule is likely to result in negative sanction. In that case, we are back to the prescriptive force of rules.

Females may utilize manipulative strategies like pouting, sulking, crying, helplessness, and playing the martyr in order to get their way. We can describe their behavior as practical, inasmuch as it may accomplish their goal, but it is questionable that their behavior is the result of following a rule. Females who use manipulative strategies think less of themselves and are rated less positively by others.[29] If their behavior was the result of rules, we would expect them to be evaluated positively, not negatively.

For all of the above reasons, I will use the phrase prescriptive force, rather than normative force or practical force.

In addition to using various labels, scholars have disagreed about the nature of prescriptive force. The strengths and weaknesses of each conceptualization will be considered and an alternative view presented.

Joan Ganz has defined prescriptive force the most narrowly. For Ganz, rules prescribe what behavior is required (correct) or prohibited (incorrect).[30] At one point, Ganz indicated that rules may identify what is permitted,[31] but later, in distinguishing rules from directions, she maintained that rules prescribe what must happen and directions make recommendations. Ganz's two-pronged view of prescriptive force may be contrasted with multifaceted approaches.

Several rule theorists have applied Georg Henrik von Wright's categorization of purposive behavior to rules, and they thus identify four different types of prescriptive force: obligation, prohibition, permission, and indifference.[32] Ganz views rules as having only the first two types of force. Ted Smith drops indifference from his list and adds a fourth sense of normative force, preference, which he has adapted from Gidon Gottlieb's insistence that rules prescribe action which "may, *ought to* or must [italics mine]" be performed.[33] In total, then, we have five potential ways of viewing the prescriptive force of rules: obligation, prohibition, permission, indifference, and preference. The first two have been accepted by all theorists, including the present writer, but the other three require further discussion.

The notation that prescriptive force may be indifferent should be rejected. Von Wright has defined deontic indifference as that which is neither obligatory nor prohibited.[34] He insists that it is important not to confuse indifference with neutrality.[35] However, he does not explain how the two terms are to be differentiated, and neutrality seems like a reasonable connotation of indifference. Jack L. Ray argued that indifference amounts to saying that "there is no norm or convention or rule and so on, governing the doing or not doing of action A."[36] Rules are not neutral. Something cannot be both prescriptive and neutral. The force of rules is related to obtaining favorable evaluations or avoiding unfavorable evaluations; neutrality would result in the absence of evaluation.

Similarly, to say something is permitted is not to prescribe it. Permitted behavior was defined by von Wright as behavior which is not forbidden.[37] The label "permitted" does not imply that the presence or absence of the permitted behavior would result in sanctions. Therefore, it is incongrous to talk of rules prescribing behavior which is merely permitted.

On the other hand, it makes sense to speak of rules prescribing what behavior is preferred. Like obligatory or prohibitive behavior, behavior that is related to preferences is also subject to evaluation. Preferential rules may indicate that one behavior is preferred over another, or they may be meta-rules specifying when one set of rules is preferred over another set. An example of the first type of preferential rule is our apparent preference for agreements over disagreements.[38] Robin Lakoff describes a preferential meta-rule when contrasting rules of conversation and politeness:

> $R_{(06)}$: "When the crunch comes, the rules of politeness will supersede the rules of conversation: better be unclear than rude."[39]

Therefore, unlike Ganz, I hold that the prescriptive force of rules may relate to preferences as well as obligations and prohibitions, but unlike those who have adopted von Wright's classifications of purposive behavior, I believe rules do not prescribe permitted or indifferent behavior.

There is some similarity between the divisions of prescriptive force discussed above and three classifications of rules utilized by William Labov: categorical rules, optional rules, and variable rules.[40] Categorical rules are rules that apply in all cases and refer to correct (obligatory) and/or incorrect (prohibited) behavior. Variable rules indicate the probability of a behavior occurring under certain circumstances. Optional rules state what may occur (permitted behavior).

To posit an optional rule seems to be as much a contradiction as to describe indifference as a prescriptive force. Rules cannot be both prescriptive and optional. Variable rules are not really rules at all; they are scientific hypotheses that predict the probability of a regularity occurring, or they are descriptive statements indicating the probability that a rule will apply in a specific case.[41]

*Rule$_{(07)}$ is one of the variable rules identified by Labov.[42] A verbal equivalent of the rule is provided below the rule.

$$*R_{(07)}: \quad \text{``Z} \left\langle \emptyset \right\rangle / \left\langle \begin{matrix} +Pro \\ +Cons \end{matrix} \right\rangle \quad \#\# \text{---} \#\# \left\langle \begin{matrix} +Vb \\ +Fut \\ -NP \end{matrix} \right\rangle \text{''}$$

In Black English Vernacular (BEV), the copula is deleted more often if the preceding noun phrase is a pronoun or a noun ending in a consonant and the following grammatical environment is (from the least favorable to the most) a predicated noun phrase; adjectives and locatives; verbs and the auxiliary "gonna" before the verb.

This rule may be refined by indicating the probability that the copula will be deleted given the presence or absence of variable constraints like pronouns, consonants, or verbs.[43] Variable rules are written as descriptions rather than prescriptions. They are, however, descriptions of behavior which are probably the result of preferential rules. They describe what behavior seems to be preferred given certain conditions.

Descriptions of empirical regularities may or may not be the result of rules. (How one determines if they are will be discussed in the next chapter.) If they are, such statements may be labeled "rule-descriptions,"[44] but these descriptions are not themselves rules since they are not prescriptive.

Followability and prescriptiveness are important definitional characteristics, but they are not sufficient for defining *rule*. Orders and commands are also followable and prescriptive, but they differ from rules in terms of scope conditions. Orders and commands are issued for a specific situation; rules apply in all similar situations; rules are contextual.

CONTEXTUAL

Several scholars have pointed out that rules are contextual; that is, rules apply in all similar situations, but they may not be applicable under different conditions.[45] The contextual portion of a rule may include references to the physical and linguistic environments, the episode being enacted, the actors, the medium of communication, and purposes.[46] These circumstantial boundaries of rules may be referred to as the scope conditions of a rule. Although a rule is a rule before, during, and after an event,[47] scope conditions indicate when a rule is operable. For example, a rule of poker is a rule even when one is not playing poker, but it is only operable when one is actually playing the game. Similarly, rules for greeting, no matter where one is in the progression of a conversation, are only operable at the beginning of an exchange when actors are acknowledging the presence of another who has been absent for some time. A rule should include references to when it is operable. (The physical manifestations of the scope conditions of a rule will be discussed in the section on structure in this chapter.)

Although scholars have agreed that rules are contextual, they have not agreed upon how generalizable the rule must be. Aaron Snyder has indicated that rules "must be, in principle at least, applicable to more than one case."[48] W. Barnett Pearce has seemingly argued for greater generalizability, maintaining that rules should produce statistical regularities since "regularity attests to the presence and function of rules which account for structure, differentiating it from creative behavior."[49] Pearce was primarily concerned with rule-related behavior rather than rules themselves, but one may infer from his statement that he believes the scope conditions of rules must be general enough to apply in multiple communicative interactions.

Thomas S. Frentz and Thomas B. Farrell seem to draw the conditional boundaries more narrowly, for they write, "The rules which constrain communicative choice in any episode do not generalize beyond the overall encounter-type in which they occur."[50] What they mean by "encounter-type" is not completely clear, but it does seem to be rather narrowly defined. "Meeting the boss" was identified as one encounter. One might assume that meeting someone else would constitute a new encounter-type according to their scheme. Malcohn Kushner has taken probably the most restrictive position with regard to communicative rules. He argues that communicative rules are unique to each situation and that communication theory from a rules perspective can only be constructed out of meta-rules which allow the researcher to discover the rules of a specific interaction.[51]

If one views rules as unique to single situations, several problems arise. It would be impossible to separate rules from commands and orders, which are situation-specific, or to distinguish rules from other influential factors in controllable behavior (e.g., imitation, whim, or creativity). According to Kushner's system, every act could have a corresponding rule. It is this perspective that David Kaufer has criticized as the dictionary approach to rules.[52] Kaufer argues that a researcher who takes this perspective is likely "to concoct a rule formulation for every instance of purposeful behavior he observes," and be unable to stop finding rules. If everything is a rule, then the construct has little meaning; and if every act must be explained by a separate rule, then one's theory is not parsimonious and we gain little from the rule; one might as well just list the acts. In addition, if one took a one-act, one-rule approach, rules would not be linked to behavioral regularities, and the argument that rules produce regularities is one of the reasons given for approaching communication from a rules perspective.

A separate rule should not be written for every act; rather, a rule should cover types of acts (e.g., questions, turn taking, promises, politeness). Gerry Philipsen discussed this principle in research on the ethnography of speaking. What he has to say about ethnographers is equally true for rule theorists. The finite set of "premises" in rules theory could be "rules."

Indeed they [ethnographers] do not produce a rule for every occasion, a fitting remark for every social exigence, rather they aim to produce a finite set of premises by which a potentially infinite number of speech acts can be judged by native persons as appropriate or inappropriate in a particular situation.[53]

Rules must apply in more than one situation to be rules; and the more generalizable the rule, the more parsimonious it is. How many cases a rule must apply to in order to be a useful rule may depend on one's purpose. More general rules may be used to predict and explain types of behavior across multiple situations. They are more parsimonious, but probably less precise. More specific rules may facilitate more precise predictions and explanations in more limited situations. For example, that an initial encounter should begin with a greeting sequence is a general rule that applies in multiple situations. But if one wanted to predict whether the greeting would be formal or informal, one may need to refer to a more specific rule with more restrictive scope conditions. Or, if one wanted to predict whether one would say "Hi, how are you?" or "Hey, what's happenin'?" one might need to refer to a rule of even more specific scope conditions. (That is, if it can be demonstrated that one or the other choices is preferred given certain conditions, that a rule rather than free choice influenced the usage.)

Two constructs which were introduced by Donald P. Cushman and Gordon C. Whiting seem applicable to this discussion about scope conditions: rule range and rule specificity.[54] Rule range refers to the number of cases to which the rule applies. Rule specificity refers to how specific the behavioral prescription is. There appears to be an inverse relationship between range and specificity. As range increases, specificity decreases, and as specificity increases, range decreases.[55]

The range and specificity of a rule are also related to predictability. If a hypothesized rule applies in very few cases (low-rule range), then it will be more difficult to find situations to test whether the hypothesized rule is in fact a rule. If, on the other hand, the rule applies in many cases (high-rule range), there will be numerous settings in which the viability of the rule may be tested. One drawback of high-rule range, however, is that the prediction will be of a general type of behavior (e.g., a greeting) rather than a more specific act (e.g., "What's happenin'?"), because the specificity of the high-range rule will be low.

Two conclusions may be drawn at this point: (1) rules are contextual—they apply in all like situations (there must be a minimum of two); and (2) researchers may investigate rules that differ in range and specificity, with varying payoffs in terms of predictability.

Although rules are contextual and scope conditions are thus part of the structure of rules, some researchers have confused scope conditions with rules. Robert E. Nofsinger did this when he explicated the demand ticket. He referred to his rules as the primary presuppositions (conditions) that constitute the demand ticket.[56] Presuppositions and rules are related, but they are different. John R. Searle described the interconnectedness between conditions and rules: "If we get such a set of conditions we can extract from them a set a rules."[57] Perhaps the interconnectedness yet difference between conditions and rules can be clarified by comparing Nofsinger's rule (presupposition), $*R_{(08)}$, to what would be the rules according to the conceptualization presented in this chapter, $R_{(09)}$ and $R_{(10)}$. $*R_{(08)}$ describes the presuppositions of the person before speaking. Those presuppositions are parts of $R_{(09)}$ and $R_{(10)}$, but note that these two rules also prescribe behavior, whereas $*R_{(08)}$ only describes "wishes."

$*R_{(08)}$: "A wishes to have the floor to say Z to B, and wishes (or is willing) to be obligated to say Z to B."[58]

$R_{(09)}$: If A wishes to gain the attention of B but also wishes B to return the floor to A in order to say Z, then A should utter a demand ticket.

$R_{(10)}$: If one utters a demand ticket and it is answered, then one must make a statement (Z in $*R_{(08)}$) that makes the reason for the demand ticket evident.

Rules *prescribe* behavior under certain conditions; they do not merely *describe* desires, motives, and/or intentions, which may comprise part of the conditions for enacting the rule.

Followability, prescriptiveness, and contextuality are all definitional characteristics of rules. Taken together, they are generally thought of as sufficient grounds for defining a rule, but the present author believes that there is one other defining characteristic of a rule, that being the domain of rules.

DOMAIN OF RULES

Here we are concerned with to what rules refer. Ganz maintains that the domain of rules is "activities rather than people."[59] She uses this criterion to distinguish rules from orders and commands, which are directed toward people. Her examples of the rules of driving on public roads, the rules of chess, the rules of football seem to support her assertion that rules apply equally to all persons engaged in a specific activity. However, her distinction ignores many communication rules that focus on people and their relationships at least as much as they do on activities. $R_{(11)}$ is an example of this type of rule.

> $R_{(11)}$: Superordinates and strangers should be addressed by title and last names, subordinates and intimates should be addressed by first names.[60]

Communication rules may prescribe differential behaviors for superordinates/subordinates, strangers/friends, family members/non-family members, and so forth. Rules apply to people as well as activities, but in either case, rules specify appropriate behavior.

The proper domain of rules is behavior. Behavior may be prescribed and evaluated. Rules may be utilized in making mental evaluations, inferences, judgments, and interpretations of behavior, but rules themselves do not prescribe what one must (must not) or should (should not) think. It is not possible for others to monitor thoughts, except by observing behavior, and it would be impossible to enforce rules (impose sanctions) about cognitions. Therefore, it is vacuous to speak of rules prescribing cognitions.

Unfortunately, in trying to explain communicative behavior, theorists have often advanced interpretative "rules." Such "rules" are explanations of how one might interpret behavior, but they cannot be taken as rules since one cannot effectively prescribe cognitions. Perhaps an example will clarify the point. Nofsinger offered a "shared existential value" rule, *$R_{(12)}$, as the interpretive "rule" for B in the dialogue below.

Dialogue$_{(01)}$

A: Are notebooks allowed during the final exam?

B: Are porcupines allowed in balloon factories?[61]

$R_{(12)}$: "If A asks a question, QS_1, and B responds with a question, QS_2, which is unrelated to A's question or to A's authority for asking it, and which is unrelated to B's ability or obligation to answer, and if it is not plausible for A to regard S_1 and S_2 as mutually exclusive alternate events, then B is heard as asserting that the answer to QS_2, ES_2, is known to both A and B (i.e., is an AB-event), and also as asserting that the existential value of ES_1 is the same as the existential value of ES_2; and from this value is inferred B's answer to A, ES_1."[62]

Nofsinger's "rule" is actually an explanation of how B may be understood as a negative answer to A. *$R_{(12)}$ does not prescribe behavior; it is not a rule. It does not indicate what must, must not, or should happen; rather, it predicts how an utterance will be understood. Further, this prediction can be made by using rules that do prescribe behavior, like $R_{(13)}$; and what is more, $R_{(13)}$ is more parsimonious. Nofsinger wrote six interpretive "rules," all of which can be predicted on the basis of $R_{(13)}$, which also comes from Nofsinger's work.

$R_{(13)}$: "Do not say that which is pointless or spurious."[63]

Nofsinger's interpretive rules should be viewed as six possible ways to use $R_{(13)}$ to interpret indirect answers. Nofsinger maintains that on the basis of $R_{(13)}$ participants tend to interpret an utterance as if it makes sense rather than viewing it as deviant, pointless, or irrelevant.[64] Although this tendency may be a result of inferring that others are following $R_{(13)}$, these inferences are not themselves rules.

This distinction may be clearer if we assume for a moment that *$R_{(12)}$ has prescriptive force. If *$R_{(12)}$ requires that one count B as a negative answer to A, then a violation of this rule should result in some sort of sanction. Let us suppose that the dialogue ends with utterance B and then speaker A simply walks away. Speaker A could walk away thinking his/her question was answered positively, negatively, or s/he could be confused about the answer. No matter what meaning has been attached to utterance B, speaker A's cognitions would not be sanctioned, because there is no way to know if s/he is in violation of $*R_{(12)}$. Further, his/her behavior would not be sanctioned because departing at the close of a dialogue is within the boundaries of acceptable behavior.

But let us take this hypothetical situation one step further. Suppose speaker A brought notebooks to the exam after engaging in dialogue$_{(01)}$. We might expect that A's behavior may be sanctioned (e.g., s/he might be given a failing grade for violating examination rules). One might be tempted to claim that under these circumstances, the lack of following the interpretive "rule" resulted in a sanction. However, it is important to note that it is A's behavior and not A's cognition which is sanctioned. A may have understood B's utterance as a negative answer and still elected to bring in the notebooks. The conclusion that must be made is that, although rules may be utilized to interpret behavior, there are not interpretive rules.

Because we expect actors to abide by the rules, we utilize rules in interpreting the behavior of others. In fact, they are necessary to make sense out of what would otherwise be random noise.[65] But to argue that rules may be used to interpret behavior is quite different from maintaining that there are rules that prescribe those cognitions. Perhaps another example will help to further clarify this point.

Here I shall borrow an example, one originally used for another purpose, from the work of Raymond Gumb: "For example, suppose one were to say to a young minister just out of divinity school 'Congratulations on your graduation from the 'cemetery' instead of '. . . seminary.'"[66]

The above faux pas might result in a strange look, a laugh, a loss of face. However, if we assume that the salutation was offered seriously, we know that the speaker meant to congratulate the young minister for graduating from divinity school, not from the place of the dead. We know this because of the context and rules for word usage. Rules, then, allow us to interpret the behavior, but they do not prescribe interpretations. It would, of course, be possible to assign only the usual dictionary meaning to the word "cemetery." If the speaker is negatively sanctioned, the sanction would be for his/her word usage (behavior) not his/her cognitions. And again, if we assume that his/her cognitions were about divinity school when s/he incorrectly uttered "cemetery," it is the behavior, not the cognition, that is in error and subject to evaluation.

Unfortunately, the interpretation-rule confusion is further complicated by two behavioral rules, $R_{(14)}$ and $R_{(15)}$, which are related to meaning.

$R_{(14)}$: If one wishes to interact symbolically, then one is required to use terms in accordance with preexisting definitions (e.g., those provided by dictionaries, organizations, or groups), or in accordance with agreements made by the communicators.

$R_{(15)}$: If one is engaged in a casual conversation, then one should not question the meaning of every utterance; one's behavior should be in accordance with presumed, preexisting definitions.

Humpty-Dumpty's behavior with regard to glory (see ch. 1) was in violation of $R_{(14)}$. One is not free to use terms at random. Note, however, that while related to meaning, $R_{(14)}$ prescribes behavior, not cognitions. Garfinkel presents some interesting evidence with regard to $R_{(15)}$ in dialogue$_{(02)}$.

Dialogue$_{(02)}$

(S) Hi, Ray. How is your girlfriend feeling?

(E) What do you mean, "How is she feeling?" Do you mean physical or mental?

(S) I mean how is she feeling? What's the matter with you? (He looked peeved.)

(E) Nothing. Just explain a little clearer what do you mean?

(S) Skip it. How are your Med School applications coming?

(E) What do you mean, "How are they?"

(S) You know what I mean.

(E) I really don't.

(S) What's the matter with you? Are you sick?[67]

It is quite possible that it is not clear what "How is your girl-friend feeling?" and "How are your Med School applications coming?" mean; that one's mental images are incomplete. However, it is not the cognitions which are sanctioned, but the behavior of the communicator.

Rules prescribe behavior. Activities (e.g., driving a car or playing chess), personal variables (e.g., status, age, race, or sex), social variables (e.g., formal/informal or party/professional), and the like may influence the relevance of rules in a particular situation, but all rules refer to behavior. Rules may be used to interpret behavior, and communicators are expected to utilize standardized usage; but rules prescribe behavior, not cognitions.

The four defining characteristics of rules have been discussed. Rules are followable, prescriptive, contextual, and they pertain to behavior. Before offering a definition of rule based on these characteristics, however, it must be determined whether a definition should include both explicit and implicit rules, since some scholars argue that rules cannot be implicit.

IMPLICIT RULES

Perhaps the place to begin is with definitions of explicit and implicit rules. Explicit rules are inscriptions or utterances that prescribe behavior. Implicit rules are unstated prescriptions for behavior. Explicit rules have a physical reality of their own; implicit rules must be inferred from behavior. Chapter 3 will identify more precisely how one may infer specific rules from behavior, but here we shall be concerned with providing minimal evidence for the existence of implicit rules.

Ganz's argument that the existence of implicit rules is improbable is predicated on the premise that one cannot follow that which one is unaware of (i.e., one cannot follow implicit rules); hence, behavioral regularities cannot be the result of implicit rules.[68] Ganz's position is tautological, because she defines following a rule as consciously seeing to it that one's behavior complies with that rule. As will be argued in Chapter 4, behavior may be related to rules in a number of ways, in addition to consciously following a rule. Ganz admits that one may fulfill a rule, which is explicitly stated elsewhere, accidentally, without knowing the rule, or that one's behavior may be in "unconscious" accordance with a rule, which one can articulate if asked to do so. But Ganz does not acknowledge the possibility that one's behavior may be influenced by a rule which is not explicitly known by that person or by a rule which s/he cannot articulate.

Is there any evidence that communicators utilize implicit rules in constructing their behavior? A number of language philosophers answer yes, and they provide impressive evidence to support their point: (1) communicators have an intuitive sense of what is appropriate or inappropriate; by intuitive, it is meant that they make judgments about appropriateness without the benefit of explicit rules; (2) communicators correct and evaluate their own behavior and the behavior of others on the basis of their intuitions about appropriateness; and (3) communicators are able to produce behaviors they have never seen or heard before, but which are consistent with their notions of appropriateness, and they repeat these behaviors under similar circumstances; hence, they must be using rules to construct these behaviors.[69]

In addition, it is argued that many of the behavioral regularities observed cannot be accounted for if one argues that implicit rules do not exist. Although a limited number of behaviors (e.g., knee jerks, eye blinks, and other reflex motions) may be law-related, most communicative behavior is controllable and can be willfully performed. Some of the controllable behavior may be attributed to free choice (e.g., running at 5:00 a.m.). Free-choice behavior may be performed or not performed without evaluation, but much of human behavior is evaluated. Parents, teachers, preachers, politicians, peers, and others often tell us what we should or should not do, and we often serve as critics of our own behavior. We may utilize explicit rules (e.g., one must stop at a stop sign) to evaluate our behavior. But there are still patterns of behavioral regularities which cannot be explained by laws or explicit rules, but can be explained in terms of implicit rules.

Robert Nofsinger's explication of the demand-ticket provides a useful demonstration of the existence of implicit rules. I will begin by presenting two dialogues from the many analyzed by Nofsinger.

Dialogue(03)

A: Yuh know something? (X)

B: What?   (Y)

A: It's time for lunch.   (Z)

Dialogue(04)

A: Jim, guess what.

B: What?

A: (Silence)

B: What?!

A: (Silence)

B: Nofsinger, is this one of your communication games?![70]

Dialogue(03) is consistent with the general pattern for a demand ticket: A utters X, which results in B uttering Y, which returns the floor to A in order to utter Z.[71] If this pattern was law-governed, then there could be no violations, and no alterations in the pattern. Dialogue(04) indicates that the pattern can be broken. If the pattern were the result of consistent but free-choice behavior, then deviations from the pattern could occur, but they would not be negatively sanctioned. Again, dialogue(04) indicates that deviations are negatively sanctioned, and B's frustration, plus the other examples like dialogue(03) provided by Nofsinger, indicates that A's behavior and B's response are related to implicit rules. Neither speaker refers to the rules, and it is highly unlikely that either communicator had ever seen or heard the rule before Nofsinger's formulization. Nonetheless, it is clear that speaker B perceives speaker A's behavior as inappropriate in dialogue(04). It seems apparent that speaker B is evaluating speaker A's performance on the basis of an implicit rule.

Chapter 3 will specify how researchers may infer implicit rules from behavior. But at this point, suffice it to say, there is adequate evidence that implicit rules do exist, and that any definition of rules should be broad enough to incorporate both implicit and explicit rules. Given the discussion about the characteristics of rules and implicit rules, a definition for rule may be proposed.

SUMMARY: A DEFINITION OF RULE

Rules are followable, prescriptive, contextual, and they pertain to human behavior. Rules may be explicitly stated, or they may be known tacitly. Any sound and useful definition of rule must take these characteristics into account, must be applicable to both explicit and implicit rules, and must be consistent with the basic presuppositions of rule scholars. The following is a definition that meets that criteria: *A rule is a followable prescription that indicates what behavior is obligated, preferred, or prohibited in certain contexts.* This definition has several strengths. First, it is consistent with the presuppositions of the rules perspective on human behavior. It stresses that humans may choose to follow prescriptions, and it implies that following rules should result in behavioral regularities. Second, the definition includes all of the relevant characteristics of rules, and it specifies what kind of prescription is appropriate to rules (i.e., obligatory, prohibitive, or preferred). Third, this definition encompasses both explicit and implicit rules. The strength of this definition will be further tested against its ability to distinguish rule from related constructs and in terms of its relative merit to previous definitions.

Potential Synonyms

By utilizing *Roget's Thesaurus* and the *American College Dictionary*, Joan Safron Ganz identified over seventy synonyms for "rule." A review of the twenty-two definitions of rule in the *Oxford English Dictionary* yielded an additional nineteen potential synonyms. An examination of communication literature revealed eleven synonyms not covered by the other sources.[72] The sheer number of potential synonyms increases the possibility of confusion regarding the conceptualization of rule.

A comparison of these terms with rule may serve to lessen this confusion and to clarify the concept of rule itself. Other scholars have called for such a comparison. "A comprehensive and coherent account of the rules perspective would necessitate . . . a discussion of the relation of the concept rule to other concepts such as norm, value, maxim, standard, guideline, convention, regulation, instruction, agreement, and contract."[73]

In distinguishing rules from related constructs, one important comparison to be made is that between rules and behavior. In contrasting rules and behavior, Ganz defines rules as linguistic entities.[74] Linguistic entity as a distinguishing characteristic has both advantages and disadvantages. This conceptualization allows the separation of raising one's hand to ask a question (a behavior) from the rule that prescribes that behavior. However, there are linguistic entities which are also behaviors such as promises, greetings, questions, compliments, and other speech acts. Hence linguistic entity cannot be used to distinguish rules from behavior.

Further, Ganz's requirement that a rule be a linguistic entity leads her to the curious claim that a person may adopt a rule that does not exist. That is, Ganz maintained that one's behavior may conform to an imaginary rule, to some assumption about what is appropriate behavior, but if that "rule" has never been written or uttered, there is no rule.[75] This position seems untenable inasmuch as unstated rules are followable, prescriptive, and contextual like stated ones, and they influence behavior in much the same way.[76] Contextual prescriptions for behaviors, whether they are articulated or not, are rules. Behavior is any physical activity of an organism.[77] Some behaviors are prescribed by rules.

Although rules need not be articulated to be rules, they must be capable of being, at least theoretically, expressed as linguistic entities. Therefore, in this chapter, rules will be compared with other linguistic entities which are either prescriptions or descriptions of behavior. Comparisons of behavior that is the result of a rule with other types of behavior will be taken up in the next chapter. Hence, the following terms for behaviors, which are sometimes used as synonyms for *rules*, will be discussed in Chapter 3: *custom, ritual, normative-behavior, habit, convention, regularity,* and *mechanistic-behavior.*

Table 2.1 represents a selective sample of potential synonyms for *rule*. They were chosen because they are the terms typically compared or contrasted with rule in communication research. Those terms which were also contrasted with rule by Joan Ganz are marked by an asterisk.[78] Agreements and disagreements with Ganz's positions, as well as extensions of her arguments, will be presented in the discussion that follows.

Rule is compared with related constructs on the bases of the defining characteristics of rules. The constructs are listed in a rough approximation to their similarity to rule, with those constructs that share more in common with rule being listed closer

TABLE 2.1   Comparison of Rules and Potential Synonyms

	Qualities	
Terms	Prescriptive	Contextual
*Rule	X	X
Meta-rule	X	X
*Regulation	X	X
*Principle, Value, Maxim	X	/
Criterion	X	/
Agreement	/	/
Norm	/	/
*Standard	/	/
Expectation	/	/
Logic, Plan, Contract, Episode, Self-Concept	/	/
*Command, Order	X	0
Presupposition	0	X
*Scientific Law and Other Theoretical Statements	0	X
Explanation	0	/
*Direction, Instruction, Guideline, Suggestion	0	/

to it. All of the constructs (except regulation) pertain to behavior, so that characteristic does not appear in the table. There are scientific laws that are about inanimate objects and hence not about behavior, and there are criteria for distinguishing one inanimate phenomena from another, but the concern here is with statements which describe or prescribe behavior. Since that which is prescriptive must also be followable, followability was also omitted from the table. The only constructs in Table 2.1 that are not followable are scientific laws and other theoretical statements. An X in the table means that the feature is true for all cases of a given concept; a / indicates it is true for some but not all cases, and an O indicates that the feature is missing. An explanation for the assignment of these symbols is given below.

META-RULE

Meta-rules are rules that prescribe other rules. The term may be used accurately to refer to alternative rules (rules that trigger a set of rules which occur together)[79] or rules for creating, negotiating, changing, and discussing rules. However, the phrase meta-rule has been used to refer to a phenomenon that might better be described as principles or values in that they indicate what is preferred in general rather than prescribing specific behaviors. The following quote from Pearce shows two principles that were called meta-rules: "Consider the hypothesis that interpersonal relationships in Western society are governed by two meta-rules, one which specifies an equitable distribution of values (Brittan, 1973) and the other which legitimates a heirarchical order (H. D. Duncan, 1968)."[80] From the principle that goods should be equitably distributed and that a hierarchical order is legitimate, specific behavioral rules could be developed.[81] (See the section on principles.)

REGULATION

Regulation is often used as a synonym for rule.[82] Ganz offered two criteria by which we may make a distinction: (1) regulations standardize behavior, but rules may also restrict behavior, and (2) regulations specify antecedent conditions (e.g., "the ball is 'live' as soon as the whistle blows"). Both of these distinctions are inadequate. There is no reason to assume that regulations do not restrict as well as standardize. Ganz's antecedent condition example could easily be the rule that "a whistle must blow in order to begin play." The difference between the two statements is more a matter of form than prescription.

Perhaps a difference can be drawn in terms of what is prescribed. Rules prescribe behavior. Regulations may specify requirements for inanimate objects. Consider the differences between $R_{(16)}$, a rule, and $Rg_{(01)}$, a related regulation.

$R_{(16)}$:   If one is typing the official copy of a dissertation, then one must type it on official thesis paper.

$Rg_{(01)}$:   Official thesis paper must be 8½ by 11 inches; 1½ inch margins must be marked in blue ink, and the official seal of the university must be imprinted on the page.

Although rule and regulation may be used as synonyms, in this study rules refer to prescriptions for behavior and regulations refer to prescriptions for objects.

PRINCIPLE, VALUE, MAXIM

Nofsinger describes conversational principles and maxims as rules: "The cooperative principle and its maxims . . . are clearly regulative rules. . . . Maxims have a strong flavor of 'thou shalt,' or 'thou shalt not.' "[83]

Ganz, on the other hand, makes distinctions among principles, maxims, and rules:

> Principles don't specify the procedures for action as rules do, but rather they provide the ideology, justification, motivation and the like for procedures.[84]

> While rules specify what counts as the one correct way to perform an activity, maxims specify either the most strategic, most practical, most accepted or most well thought of and the like, way to perform an activity. . . . Maxims provide the best policy; rules specify the only acceptable procedure.[85]

Ganz's distinction for maxims must be rejected, because rules prescribe preferred behavior (the "best policy") as well as obligatory and prohibited behavior ("the only acceptable procedure"). One might be inclined to distinguish maxims from rules in that maxims may be proverbial statements such as "Haste makes waste." Such statements do not prescribe behavior. However, this may be more of a problem of form than the absence of prescription. The proverb could be rewritten as a rule:

R$_{(17)}$: If one wishes to be accurate and exact, then one should not rush.

Maxims that prescribe behavior are rules. Grice's conversational maxims (e.g., "Do not say what you believe to be false"; or "Do not say that for which you lack adequate evidence") are rules.[86]

Conversational principles may be thought of as communication values. Ganz's distinction between rules and principles appears to be valid. While principles are prescriptive, the prescriptions are general and abstract. Unlike rules, they do not prescribe particular behaviors. Maxims are also more general and abstract than rules. The relationship between principles, maxims, and rules may be viewed as hierarchical with rules as the most specific prescription and principles as the most general.

In addition, rules can be conceived as being generated from maxims and maxims from principles. Below is an example of this relationship. Note that principles and maxims also differ from rules in that they do not always state the context in which they are applicable.

Principle: Be cooperative.

Maxim: Make your comments relevant to ongoing talk.

$R_{(18)}$: If your turn at talk follows the remarks of another, then link your utterance to previous talk by making additional comments on the topic, relate your topic to the previous topic (topic shade), indicate the discussion reminds you of something (touched-off topic), or mark and justify a change of topic (radical topic shift).[87]

CRITERION

Criteria are followable and are usually thought of as prescriptive. However, one synonym for criterion is yardstick, which implies that criterion may be viewed as a nonevaluative standard by which two or more phenomena can be compared. One might argue, for example, that definitions may serve as criteria for determining whether an item belongs in one group or another. If definitions are conceived of as descriptions rather than prescriptions, then definitions would be an example of a nonprescriptive criterion. On the other hand, definitions are often taken as prescriptions. For example, given scientific classifications, it is considered wrong to label a tomato a vegetable. Thus, even definitions may be viewed as standards of correctness. Therefore, it seems appropriate to view all criteria as prescriptive. Rules differ from criteria, however, on the dimension of contextuality. Criteria may apply in all similar cases or in a single case; rules apply in all similar cases.

AGREEMENT

Agreements are statements that express consensus. Agreements are often associated with prescriptive force in that many agreements involve decisions about how persons should or should not behave. However, it is also possible for individuals to agree that "anything goes." Agreeing that a particular behavior is not subject to evaluation was described by Jay Jackson as "vacuous consensus."[88] Agreements may also be statements about reality. For example, two or more persons may agree that the color of a rose is orange, or that the time is 9:00 p.m. Although these statements of agreement may be related to rules about the use of color and time references, the statements themselves are not rules. They are agreed upon descriptions of reality; they are not prescriptions.

Agreements may be contextual and thus apply in all like situations, or they may be limited to single occurrences. For example, a group may agree on a specific solution to a particular case without agreeing upon a rule to handle similar situations.

A rule may also differ from an agreement in that a rule may exist even if there is disagreement about a rule. For example, two players may disagree about a rule for a game and they may consult a rule book to resolve their differences, but the lack of agreement does not deny the existence of a rule.

NORM

Communication scholars often use the terms rule and norm interchangeably.[89] Ganz list norm as a synonym of rule, but she did not compare the terms. Gottlieb has expressed what seems to be the general consensus:

> It makes little difference at this juncture whether we refer to rules, law statements or to norms. . . . There are a number of concepts like rule, norm, law and precept which all license or warrant inferences. These concepts are related and there is no strict English usage for discriminating between them. They are often used interchangeably.[90]

Though most scholars have been content with using norm and rule interchangeably, I would like to make a case for treating them somewhat distinct. A norm may be defined as:

> (a) a statistical standard of comparison constituted by what is in some sense the average or modal value of the variable on which the items in a population are being compared; (b) the average or modal, i.e., most typical behavior, attitude, opinion, or perception found in a social group; (c) a standard shared by the members of a social group to which the members are expected

to conform, and conformity to which is enforced by positive and negative sanctions.[91]

When norm is used like definition (c), then it has the same meaning as rule as it has been defined here. But a rule prescribes behavior, and such a prescription may not always reflect or describe the average behavior. Therefore, rule differs from the first two definitions of norm. Perhaps some examples will make this distinction clearer. The dictionary indicates that criteria should be used for the plural form and criterion for the singular. Nonetheless, many individuals use criteria for both. Using criteria to refer to a singular subject may be a norm, but the rule prescribes different behavior. A deviation from the rule is subject to negative sanctions, but a deviation from the norm is not.

Another example may be drawn from common practice in experimental research. Most communication scholars who employ the experimental method may use college sophomores. However, few scholars argue that for theories about the general populace it is preferable to use college students; in fact, the opposite has been argued. It may be a norm to use college students, but it is doubtful that there is a rule prescribing their use. In fact, a deviation from this norm in the direction of a more diversified population would probably be positively evaluated.

The importance of distinguishing between norm and rule may also be illustrated by the following statement taken from a recent communication study by Donald G. Ellis and B. Aubrey Fisher: "Future studies should consider conflict a *norm* of group interaction and work toward a more explicit understanding of conflict [emphasis added]."[92] One might assume that the term norm is used in this statement to refer to typical rather than preferred behavior, because one does not usually think of conflict as a positive activity. However, it is also possible that conflict may enhance the group output; thus, there may be a rule that prescribes under what conditions conflict is preferred. Therefore, conflict in a group may be a norm, a rule, or both. It is not clear from Ellis and Fisher's statement whether the authors meant to say that conflict is typical of groups or whether it is preferable for groups to engage in conflict. If they intended to indicate that conflict is typical, the term norm is appropriate;

but if they wished to indicate that conflict is prescribed, then the term rule would be appropriate.

Norms represent average behavior; some rules do not. Rules prescribe behavior; some norms do not. Norms that prescribe obligated, prohibited, or preferred behavior are rules. Rules that reflect the behavior of most members in a community are norms; such rules will henceforth be referred to as normative rules.

Normative rules are contextual, as are most norms; but since some norms are not prescribed, they may not always hold, given the same conditions. Further, it is possible to describe what was normative for one event, but the prescriptions of a rule hold in all similar contexts.

STANDARD

A standard may be a criterion, or it may designate average behavior. As such, it compares with a rule in the same way that criterion or norm does. Standards are followable, some are prescriptive, and some are conditional.

EXPECTATION

Expectations are not always prescriptive, and they may be applicable in a single case; but rules must specify the contexts in which they apply, and their prescriptions for behavior are relevant to all similar cases. Rules may generate expectations, but so can other phenomena. For example, the rumor mill may have indicated that someone is a conceited bore, and one may have formulated expectations about how that person will behave. Peter Collett points out that rule violations may also lead to expectations. "If I know that a rule is repeatedly violated and if therefore I expect you to break that rule, then it makes little sense to speak of a rule as a type of expectation."[93] If a person is commonly late, then others will expect him/her to be late. Neither of the above expectations is on the basis of rule; rather, they are the result of general opinion or recurring behavior. They are not prescriptive, and they may apply only until there is contradictory evidence.

LOGIC, PLAN, CONTRACT, EPISODE, SELF-CONCEPT

One may wonder why concepts as diverse as logic and self-concept are classified together. All of the concepts listed above have one feature in common: all five may have been described as clusters of rules. As a result, these terms may be confused with rule. How these terms have been used in rules literature will be identified in this section.

Leonard C. Hawes described the interconnectedness between "rules" and "logic": "By 'logic' I mean simply a set of assumptions and rules for obtaining implications or entailments of those assumptions."[94] Assumptions are not necessarily prescriptive or contextual, but as long as logic involves rules (as they are defined here), then logic will be prescriptive and contextual.

Not all plans are composed of rules, but those that are may be used on more than one occasion. Such a plan is prescriptive and may be treated as a system of rules.[95] Plans which are designed for a single purpose or those which are suggestive rather than prescriptive are not systems of rules.

W. Barnett Pearce has compared rules and contracts: "Contracts are inclusive of rules. A well-developed contract contains several sets of rules (each of which may be quite different from others), some rules which regulate other rules (meta-rules) and 'switching cues' which signal which set of rules is to be salient at a particular time."[96] When contracts are conceived as Pearce has defined them, they share the defining characteristics of rules.

Romano Harré and Paul Secord have defined episode as "any part of human life involving one or more people in which some internal structure can be determined."[97] W. Barnett Pearce views rules as the operational definition of episodes: "A cluster of rules which specify legitimate and expected behaviors and meanings may be considered an operational definition of an episode with the implicit instruction 'to enact episode X, do this.'"[98] Although rules and episodes may be intertwined, episodes involve more than rules. They include such phenomena as the actors and the environment. Some episodes may be prescribed given certain conditions, but others may happen by chance, and still others may occur even though the actors would prefer that they did not.[99]

Donald P. Cushman and Robert R. Craig argue that self-concept is an organized set of rules.[100] "The composite of all the rules an individual has regarding the relationship of objects to him is his self-conception. These rules provide organization which serves to guide human action. . . . It is the stability of this set of rules which makes an individual's actions predictable.[101]

Since self-concept is one's conception of oneself, it would seem more appropriate to view rules as a means of enacting one's conceptualization rather than self-concept itself. Statements describing one's view of oneself are not prescriptions for behavior, but self-concept rules may be prescriptions for behavior that are consistent with one's conceptualization of self. The idea of self-concepts as rules, as presented by Cushman and Craig, was also criticized by Jesse G. Delia. He saw them as more reflective of a general cognitive theory of social behavior than a rules perspective.[102] The relationship of self-concept statements and rules will be taken up again when the structure of rules is discussed.

COMMAND, ORDER

Ganz distinguishes orders and commands from rules on the basis of three criteria. Rules are (1) made (adopted) (2) for activities; and (3) the push lies in "critique" properties of rules and issuers. Orders and commands are (1) given (2) to people; and (3) the push lies in issuers.[103]

Orders may be given, but rules cannot. It is all right to say "I order you to do X," but "I rule you to do X" is not an acceptable English sentence. The same is true for the following pair with the unacceptable statement marked by an asterisk: "Here are your orders" *"Here are your rules."[104] In following rules, it may be irrelevant who issued the rule, but orders and commands usually have force because of who issued them.[105] Earlier it was argued that rules pertain to activities and people; therefore, Ganz's second criterion is not very useful. However, her second criterion was based on another characteristic of rules (i.e., contextuality) that may be useful for distinguishing rules from orders and commands. Rules are contextual; that is, they apply whenever certain conditions hold; commands and orders apply only to the situation that generates them.[106]

Perhaps an example will make this distinction clearer. If I said to a person entering my office, "Please close the door," I have uttered a command or order which applies in that situation. If, on the other hand, I had said, "Whenever you come into my office, please close the door behind you," I would have uttered a rule by specifying the context in which the prescription applied. It is also possible that an order or command may become an implicit rule, if communicators presume it has prescriptive force in all like situations.

PRESUPPOSITION

Presuppositions may constitute the context that makes a rule operable. They are by definition, then, contextual. They are sometimes labeled rules themselves, but they are actually only a part of a rule. Presuppositions are descriptions of preexisting conditions, motives, assumptions, and so on; they are not prescriptions. The relationship of presuppositions and rules was discussed in the section on the contextuality of rules and will be taken up again in the discussion of the structure of a rule.

SCIENTIFIC LAW AND OTHER THEORETICAL STATEMENTS

Like rules, theoretical statements are contextual; both indicate the scope of their applicability. The most apparent difference between theoretical statements (scientific laws, axioms, postulates, propositions, theorems, hypotheses, and facts) and rules is that the former are descriptions of believed truths which are subject to confirmation whereas rules are prescriptions.[107] As descriptions, these theoretical statements are conditional, but they are not followable or prescriptive. Theoretical statements describe relationships that are thought to exist or that are thought will exist, but they do not evaluate these relationships. Rules, on the other hand, are evaluative; they prescribe what should or should not happen, and hence imply what is "good" and what is "bad." Differences between rules and scientific laws were also discussed in the sections on followability and prescriptiveness in this chapter. They will be further contrasted in Chapter 6 when different theoretical approaches to communication are compared. Chapter 6 will also point out how rules may be integrated into theoretical statements.

EXPLANATION

Unfortunately, explanations of behaviors which utilize rules are sometimes confused with rules themselves. Elaine Litton-Hawes, for example, maintains that explanation is one definition of rule: "A rule is an attempt to demonstrate how one behavior (an utterance) follows another and how the members who perform that behavior understand it. Thus, rules seek to account for speech using behaviors from the perspectives of the members who use them."[108]

The present author, however, maintains that rules and explanations are different entities. Explanations are not followable, nor are they prescriptions for behaviors. A full description of how rules may explain behavior is discussed in Chapter 6; however, a brief illustration here should demonstrate that while rules may be used to explain behavior, rules, behaviors, and explanations are nonetheless different.

$R_{(19)}$: If one is addressing a status superior, then one should address them by title plus last name.[109]

Behavior: A secretary addresses his boss by title plus last name.

Explanation: The secretary addressed his boss by title plus last name because this behavior is prescribed by $R_{(19)}$, he has at least tacit knowledge of $R_{(19)}$, he believes that deviation from $R_{(19)}$ might result in a negative sanction, and he wishes to avoid negative sanctions.

Explanations may be given for individual behaviors, or they may claim to be applicable in similar contexts.

DIRECTION, INSTRUCTION, GUIDELINE, SUGGESTION

Directions, instruction, guidelines, and suggestions are followable and breakable. However, they do not prescribe behavior.[110] They may specify procedures, but choosing not to follow directions, instructions, guidelines, or suggestions will not necessarily result in negative sanctions. For example, a teacher may recommend that a student complete the body of a speech before writing the introduction or conclusion. But the student may prepare the three parts in a different order, and still construct a successful speech. Directions, instructions, guidelines, and suggestions may be required under all similar circumstances, or they may be applicable for a single case; rules are applicable in more than one case. However, directions, instructions, guidelines, and suggestions that are required to complete the task correctly or preferably under the same conditions are rules.

SUMMARY

The definition of rule offered in this chapter is consistent with the presuppositions of other rule scholars. It incorporates characteristics of rules that have been acknowledged by several scholars and includes both implicit and explicit rules. In addition, the definition facilitates distinguishing rule from related constructs. For these reasons, it seems to be a sound definition. But, in order to further test its usefulness, it must be compared with previous conceptualizations of rule. These comparisons should clarify the conception of rule offered here by identifying similarities and differences between it and previous definitions. In addition, comparative advantages and disadvantages for each definition will be considered.

Other Definitions of Rule

The most common definition of rule in communication literature comes from Gordon Gottlieb, who was interested in social laws (rules): "Rule is conceptualized as criteria for choice."[111] This definition is consistent with the presuppositions of rule theorists that humans are capable of making and evaluating choices and that many of these choices are made on the bases of rules. The idea of choice implies followability, and "criteria" seems similar to a notion of prescriptiveness. The conditionality of rules is not part of this definition. However, researchers using this definition often add that rules are conditional. The characteristics of a rule (followability, prescriptiveness, and conditionality) seem to be implied in this definition, but they are not clearly present. This definition does not indicate that rules pertain to behavior. Hence, it would be possible to assume that criteria for choosing among cognitions would also be rules according to this definition. But as previously argued in the section on prescriptiveness, it is vacuous to speak of prescribing cognitions. Further, this definition does not specify the limits of prescriptive force (e.g., obligation, preference, prohibition). Those who use this definition have also adopted von Wright's classification of purpose behavior, so it would seem that they must associate criteria with indifferent and permitted behavior. As argued earlier, it is a contradiction to talk about prescriptions for behaviors that are merely permitted or to which persons respond indifferently. The advantages of the definition offered here over Gottlieb's is that the defining characteristics are explicitly stated and, in the case of prescriptiveness, more delineated.

In addition to describing rules as criteria for choice, Donald P. Cushman and Gordon C. Whiting also have defined rules as "sets of common expectations about the appropriate responses to particular symbols in particular contexts."[112] Rules provide expectations inasmuch as we expect people to conform to the prescription of rules. However, generating expectations is only one function of rules, and rules are not the only source for expectations. The definition seems further limited by focusing exclusively on responses. Rules may pertain to initiative behaviors as well as responsive behaviors. The definition does not mention the followability or prescriptiveness of rules. It does, however, indicate that rules are often context bound.

Janice H. Rushing offers another definition of rule: "a governing principle of symbolic behavior, or human action; rules are normative."[113] There are several terms in Rushing's conceptualization that requires further delineation. In Chapter 4 it will be pointed out that governing symbolic behavior is only one way in which rules are related to behavior. Principle is one of the concepts often used as a synonym for rule, but as demonstrated earlier, it is usually more general in scope and less specific in terms of the particular behaviors prescribed. Rusing appears to be using normative in a prescriptive sense. It is not clear from the definition that rules are followable and contextual unless one infers those qualities from the "normative" quality of rules.

One of the most recent descriptions of rule is that by Elaine M. Litton-Hawes.[114] She identifies three central characteristics of discourse rules. A paraphrase of these characteristics is presented below:

(1) Rules are sets of instructions which formally account for or describe the procedures speakers use in conversing.
(2) Rules categorize acts performed with words.
(3) A set of presuppositions that stipulates relations of the users and the conditions under which the rules operate.

The first characteristic seems particularly problematic because key terms refer to different phenomena. "Instructions" are different from "accounts" (explanation), and both are different from "description." Further, rules are neither explanations nor descriptions but prescriptions, and rules may be distinguished from instructions on the basis of prescriptive force. The second characteristic is one function of a rule, rather than a characteristic of a rule. (Litton-Hawes also describes this characteristic as a function.) Rules may be used to categorize (name) acts, but a rule itself does not categorize. Rather, rules indicate how one should perform a specific act, game, ritual, or the like. The second characteristic is also misleading because it implies that rules do not refer to nonverbal behavior. Researchers have identified verbal as well as nonverbal rules. For example, Edward T. Hall indicates that there are a number of rules related to the use of public and private space.[115] Litton-Hawes's definition does specify that rules are conditional, and one may infer followability from her reference to speakers using rules, but her definition does not mention the prescriptive force of rules.

Gerald R. Miller defines rules as "statements which express consensus, shared at varying levels of generality, concerning the structure, procedures and content of communicative relationships."[116] Art Bochner has criticized this definition on the grounds that rules are not always explicitly stated, and therefore statements cannot serve as the only means of verifying rules.[117] Miller's definition does not deal with the qualities of followability, prescriptiveness, or conditionality. Statements such as "We both agree today is Tuesday" or "The group selected Terry president" could be rules, according to Miller's definition. However, these statements differ from rules in that they are descriptions rather than prescriptions; they express relationships which are either true or false, but they do not indicate what must, should, should not, or must not happen. Miller's definition does not seem to very consistent with the basic assumptions about rules held by most rule scholars. However, it is generally true that rules are, at least to some extent, agreed upon; they are concerned with the structure, procedures, and content of communicative relationships; and rules do vary in the generality of their application.

The two definitions that are most similar to the one offered in this book were not written by communication scholars, but by two philosophers, Raymond Gumb and Joan Ganz.

Gumb states that "a rule specifies that a class of behavior is obligatory, permissible or forbidden."[118] Although this definition does not states that rules are followable and contextual, other remarks in his book make it clear that Gumb views these characteristics as qualities of rules.[119] His references to obligatory or forbidden behavior imply a prescriptive quality; but, as pointed out earlier, the position taken here is that rules do not deal with what is merely permissible. Gumb's definition does not consider preferential rules. Since a rule may pertain to a single behavior or a group of behaviors, the phrase "class of" seems unnecessary at best, and perhaps even misleading. Gumb's definition does make it clear that rules pertain to behavior.

Ganz's definition is one page in length,[120] so rather than reprint it entirely here, similarities and differences between it and my definition will be summarized. Ganz explicitly states that rules are followable, prescriptive, and contextual (she uses the term *conditional*). However, she limits prescriptiveness to correctness or incorrectness; she does not allow for preferential rules.

She argues that rules pertain to activities. If behavior is viewed as activity, then her definition is similar to mine in that respect as well. However, she views rules as pertaining to activities rather than people, which would seem to exclude all rules that are based on relationships such as superordinate-subordinate, parent-child, doctor-patient, and priest-parishioner. This is an unnecessary and unfortunate exclusion.

Because Ganz limits rules to linguistic entities, her definition also excludes implicit rules. This restriction is particularly limiting to communication scholars in that many communication rules are not codified. Ganz also argues that to be rules, rules had to be adopted. However, she does not specify what is necessary for a rule to be adopted. [121] Since it is not clear how to identify a rule adoption, this defining characteristic is troublesome. If it is viewed as simply considering one's behavior "critiquable," as Ganz argues at one point, [122] then it is difficult to see how adoption differs from prescription as a defining characteristic.

Ganz maintains that rules lack truth-value and hence are nonconfirmable. This is true because rules are prescriptions rather than descriptions. While Ganz's argument is valid, it is also redundant, and potentially troublesome. It is redundant because the prescriptive quality of rules already establishes rules as "ought" entities rather than "existential" entities. However, her reference to nonconfirmability is potentially troublesome because it may lead one to assume that one cannot confirm the existence of a rule and, hence, that a rule approach to communication cannot be scientific. This is not Ganz's point, but stating that rules are nonconfirmable as part of her definitional requirements makes it easy to misread her. In addition to the above limitations, the very length of Ganz's definition makes it awkward to use. [123]

The definition of rule advanced in this chapter has two advantages over previous conceptualizations: (1) it more clearly identifies the necessary constitutents of a rule, and (2) it avoids unnecessary, contradictory, or otherwise troublesome descriptions. When the characteristics of rules are clearly specified, phenomena which are not rules are less likely to be erroneously identified as rule and rules may be more easily compared and contrasted with related but distinct concepts. Having identified what rules are by delineating their nature, it is now possible to explore both the structure and functions of rules.

Structure of Rules

Most typically, rules are thought to be directives stated in an imperative form. [124] However, several scholars have pointed out that rules may be expressed in many different ways. Below is a sampling of the statements scholars have described as rules, though they are not in the imperative mood.

$R_{(20)}$: "Trespassers will be prosecuted" (sign on private property fence).[125]

$R_{(21)}$: "The dealer at bridge always bids first" (statement in a book on bridge rules).[126]

$R_{(22)}$: "We take off our hats in church" (said to a child entering a church).[127]

$R_{(23)}$: "White moves first" (a rule of chess).[128]

Although these statements are not written as prescriptions, their prescriptive quality is implied by the context. They pertain to behavior, they are followable, and they are contextual. The defining characteristics of a rule, rather than the form, identify rules. However, it will be argued that for scientific purposes there are advantages to adopting one particular form for rules.

STRUCTURAL QUALITIES

Gottlieb's four structural qualities of rules is a good place to begin specifying the properties theoretical rules should have:

(1) an indication of the circumstances in which the rule is applicable;
(2) an indication of that which ought, or may, or must be, or not be, concluded or decided;
(3) an indication of the type of inference contemplated, whether under the rule it is permitted, required or prohibited;
(4) an indication that the statement is indeed designed to function as a rule or inference-warrant.[129]

The first property refers to contextuality of a given rule. Gottlieb referred to this as the *protasis*. The second element, the apodosis, specifies the behavior which is prescribed. The third element, the "character of the rule," indicates whether the behavior specified by the rule is permitted, required, or prohibited. Finally, a rule needs to indicate that it is a rule. In light of the definition of rule offered in this chapter, Gottlieb's specifications require some revisions.

Rules do not indicate what behavior may (be permitted to) happen, but rather they refer to behavior which is preferred, required, or prohibited. The fourth characteristic of rules is circular and adds nothing, because the third element makes it clear that the statement is a rule. Behavior that does not conform to what is prohibited, preferred, or obligated by a rule is in violation of the rule, and subject to negative sanctions. Further, it is not always possible to specify what the sanction will be. A rule need only indicate that behavior is prescribed. Therefore, two revisions are needed in Gottlieb's list of structural qualities: (1) "permitted" in quality number three should be changed to "preferred," and (2) quality number four should be deleted.

THE IF-THEN FORM

The structural qualities of rules can be expressed in an "if-then" format.[130] The if clause states the scope conditions of a rule, and the then clause specifies what behavior is prescribed by the rule and the nature of the prescription (that is, obligation, preference, or prohibition). "If-then" statements can be used to express causal relationships, but they are not limited to such relationships, and the if-then structure of rules should not be taken as expressing a causal relationship.[131] Prescriptive markers in rule statements (e.g., obligated, preferred, prohibited, required, should, must not) indicate that the action prescribed in the then clause is ethically entailed; the then clause of a rule implies what *ought* to happen and not necessarily what *does* or *will* happen.[132] This perspective is consistent with deontic logic and the work of philosopher von Wright, which has informed the work of some communication rule scholars.[133]

Ray points out that a deontic utterance may be prescriptive or descriptive.[134] As a descriptive statement, however, he argues that the if-then format must be preceded by a phrase such as "there is a norm, rule, command, permission, piece of advice, such that . . . ."[135] Descriptive deontic statements have truth value, but prescriptive deontic statements, like rules, do not have truth value. Deontic logic includes statements about behavior which is ethically permitted, obligated, or prohibited. Insofar as prescriptive statements express obligated, preferred, or prohibited relationships they are rules.

Rules, then, should take the general form: "If X, then Y is obligated (preferred or prohibited)." The prescriptive markers in a rule may be expressed in a number of ways. Below is a list of the primary terms and their various alternatives.

Primary Prescriptive Markers	Alternatives
obligated	must, required
preferred	should, should not
prohibited	should not, *cannot

The asterisk in front of "cannot" indicates that it should not be used in rules for scientific purposes.

The terms *can* and *cannot* sometimes appear in informal statements of rules. For example, a railroad conductor may say "You cannot smoke in this car."[136] However, since one is physically able to smoke in the car, the rule would more appropriately be expressed in the form "You must not smoke in this car" or "The rules prohibit smoking in this car." A teacher may say, "You can write either a term paper or take a final examination,"[137] but if s/he is stating a rule, rather than commenting on one's ability, it should take the form "You must write either a term paper or take a final examination." The modal terms of rules (e.g., *must, should, must not*) should be distinguished from the model terms of theoretical statements that may be generated from rules. Theoretical statements may express relationships such as what "will," "will not," "might," or "might not" happen; they do not evaluate these relationships. The modals of rules imply evaluation.

By way of a summary, the structural properties of the if-then format will be illustrated by identifying the parts of a specific rule, $R_{(24)}$.[138]

$$\begin{array}{cc} 1 & 2 \\ \hline \end{array}$$

$R_{(24)}$: If one is summoned and one hears that summons,

$$\begin{array}{ccc} 3 & 4 & 5 \\ \hline \end{array}$$

then one must answer the summons.

A rule should begin with *if* (1) to introduce the if clause which specifies in what context the rule is operable (2); the if clause should be followed by then (3) which introduces the clause that specifies the nature of the prescription, by way of a prescriptive modal (e.g., must, must not, should), (4) and the behavior that is prescribed (5). In this particular rule the indefinite referent "one" was used because the rule applies to any one who is summoned, but for rules that apply to only certain individuals references to those individuals may be substituted for "one."

IMPLICATIONS

It has been demonstrated that rules can be expressed in the if-then rule format, but the utility of this format has yet to be demonstrated. There are four advantages of adopting this format for formal rules: (1) several scholars have advocated this form and if researchers use a consistent form, it would be easier to compare rules across studies; (2) the if-then structure represents the underlying logic of a rule; (3) the form can help one separate rules from nonrules, and (4) the form facilitates the refinement of the scope conditions of a rule and the statement of what behavior is prescribed by focusing on these aspects of a rule. The first advantage is somewhat self-evident, but the last three advantages warrant further discussion.

The if-then format represents the underlying logic of rules. The if clause indicates that rules are contextual by specifying the context which makes the rule operable. The then clause specifies the behavior which is prescribed, and it indicates whether the behavior is obligated, prohibited, or preferred. Because the if-then format reads as a directive given a particular context, it implies that it is followable. The if-then format highlights the defining characteristics of a rule; it is followable, prescriptive, and contextual, and it pertains to behavior.

The if-then format is useful in determining whether purported rules are actually rules. If one takes a purported rule that is not in the if-then format and tries to restate it in that form, one of four outcomes is likely: (a) the rule will be successfully rewritten because the original statement conforms to the defining characteristics of a rule, (b) it cannot be restated because it lacks all the characteristics of a rule, (c) the restatement is questionable because the original researcher did not provide evidence of the prescriptive quality of the statement, or (d) the restatement in the if-then rule format is nonsensical as a rule. Illustrations of these potential occurrences will be provided.

In the beginning of this section on structure, four statements that were not in the if-then format were labeled rules. If they are in fact rules, then one should recognize them as rules in the if-then format.

$R_{(25)}$: If one is not the owner or guest of the owner, then one is prohibited from being on the land marked off by this sign.

$R_{(26)}$: If one is playing bridge and is the dealer, then one must bid first.

$R_{(27)}$: If one is wearing a hat and is entering a church, then one must remove his/her hat.

$R_{(28)}$: If one is playing chess and one's chess pieces are white, then one must move his/her piece first.

Although it is clear that $R_{(20)}$ through $R_{(23)}$ can be successfully rewritten as $R_{(25)}$ through $R_{(28)}$, one might question the advantage of doing so. $R_{(20)}$ through $R_{(23)}$ are as clear as the second set, and they are certainly more parsimonious. For everyday usage, the first may even be preferable to the if-then format. But for scientific purposes, the if-then format is appropriate because it makes explicit what is implied in a less formal statement, and this explication sometimes points out conceptual weakness in the less formal versions. Some examples of attempts to rewrite purported rules that are not rules, or at least questionable as rules, may make this point clearer.

One kind of purported rule that cannot be restated in the if-then rule format proposed here is an interpretation rule. $*R_{(29)}$ and $*R_{(30)}$ are examples of such rules.

$*R_{(29)}$: "If a patient answers a doctor's question with an ellipsis, the patient is heard as implying the same topic as the doctor."[139]

$*R_{(30)}$: "If A asks a question, QS_1, and B responds with a proposition—if S_2 then ES_1—then if it is plausible for A to believe S_2, B is heard as asserting that the antecedent, S_2, is true; and from this is inferred B's answer to A, ES_1."[140]

$*R_{(29)}$ and $*R_{(30)}$ are not rules because they do not prescribe behaviors, and this limitation also prevents them from being expressed in the if-then rule format. The reader will note that $*R_{(30)}$ does have an if and a then clause, but the then does not prescribe behavior; it explains how an utterance might be understood. In $*R_{(29)}$ one does not know if answers with ellipsis are preferred, obligated, or prohibited. Nor is it known whether the doctor should behave as if the patient and the doctor are talking about the same topic if the patient uses an ellipsis, or if it is preferable to ask the patient to be more explicit in his/her responses. A similar analysis of $*R_{(30)}$ can be given. For example, one does not know whether such indirect responses as described in $*R_{(30)}$ are preferred or not. $*R_{(29)}$ and $*R_{(30)}$ are explanations of behaviors, not prescriptions for behavior. When attempting to rewrite them in the if-then rule format, the missing elements, a prescriptive model and a clause prescribing behavior, become immediately apparent.

So-called permitted rules are also easily distinguished from actual rules by using the format recommended because they lack the appropriate modals (e.g., should, must, must not). While $*R_{(31)}$ was labeled a rule, it merely indicates what a doctor may do if a patient answers a question with an ellipsis; it does not indicate that a doctor must or should repeat the same or similar question. Further, the researcher did not provide any evidence of prescriptive force; rather she maintained that the doctor's behavior may be attributable to factors such as habit or not listening.

$*R_{(31)}$: "If a patient answers a question with an ellipsis a doctor may repeat the same or similar question."[141]

Permitted rules are often descriptions of behavioral regularities without regard to whether those regularities are prescribed. Rewriting permissive statements as prescriptive rules will bring to the attention of researchers the necessity for additional evidence to claim that a behavior is obligated or preferred, and not merely that it happens. The nature of that additional evidence will be discussed in the next chapter.

Rewriting purported rules in the if-then rule format sometimes makes it clear that it makes little sense to think of those statements as rules. One area where problems could have been avoided by stating the rules in the form identified above is the research on self-concept rules. Below is an example of what

Donald Cushman and Robert Craig have labeled as self-concept rules:

*R(32): "I am the kind of person who (given certain circumstances) attempts to be logical."[142]

According to the authors, any statement taking the form "I am . . ." or "X . . ." may be a self-concept rule.[143] Later, these rules are referred to as self-concept categories.[144] Below is a list of what those self-concept categories might look like:

*R(33): "Don Cushman is aggressive."

*R(34): "Don Cushman is organized."

*R(35): "Don Cushman is arrogant."

*R(36): "Don Cushman is thoughtful."

*R(37): "Don Cushman is helpful."[145]

*R(32) through *R(36) are descriptions of personality characteristics, but they are not prescriptions for behavior. Further, there is some doubt about whether they could be as illustrated by *R(38) and *R(39).

*R(38): If one is Don Cushman, then one must (should) be aggressive.

*R(39): If one is Don Cushman, then one must (should) be arrogant.

We do not typically think of aggressiveness or arrogance as obligated or preferred behaviors. But, even if one does not conclude that such prescriptions are reasonable, one needs to state the condition for which they apply and specify behaviors which enable one to be aggressive or arrogant in order for such statements to become rules.

Although personality characteristics may be distinguished from rules, it is possible for an individual to have rules that s/he applies to him/herself only. R(40) indicates one type of behavior that might be prescribed for the person who thinks s/he is logical. In essence, it is a rewrite of *R(32) and it represents the kind of rule that might be generated from a self-concept.

R(40): If one considers him/herself logical and if one's utterances have been challenged as logically inconsistent, then one is obligated to either demonstrate how the utterances are consistent or revise one's statement.

The structure of $*R_{(29)}$ through $*R_{(39)}$ helps to distinguish them from rules. However, it is important to recognize that they are not rules, not because of their structure but because they fail to meet one or more of the four criteria of a rule (i.e., followability, prescriptiveness, contextuality, and pertaining to behavior). The if-then structure helps one identify a rule, but it is not a defining characteristic. As noted in the beginning of this section on structure, rules can be expressed in different forms. However, as argued earlier, there are several advantages to be gained for researchers if they adopt the if-then format.

One final advantage of the if-then rule format is that it encourages researchers to refine their statements by specifying the contexts in which the rule applies and by indicating what particular behaviors are prescribed by the rule. This happens because the two major clauses of the format embody the contextual requirements (if clause) and the behavior prescribed (then clause). To illustrate this process, the metamorphosis of two rules based on this format will be presented. $*R_{(41)}$ and $*R_{(42)}$ were initial statements about hypothesized rules. The first statement under them represents the initial rewrite using the if-then format, and this is followed by a second rewrite.[146]

$*R_{(41)}$: The girls in our group gossip in the beginning of the meetings.

If one is a female in the group studying used car salesmen, then one should talk about fashion for the first ten minutes of each group meeting.

If one is a member of the group studying used car salesmen in SPCH 2010, then one should engage in social conversation before beginning work on the task.

$*R_{(42)}$: Those who do well in school are smart.

If one wants to do well in school, one must be smart.

If one wants to maximize the learning potential of classroom instruction, then one should study at least two hours outside of class for every hour one is in class.

In the case of $*R_{(41)}$, when the author of the rule tested the initial rewrite, he found that he had drawn both the scope conditions and the range of acceptable behavior too narrowly, but that further probing provided support for the third version. After rewriting $*R_{(42)}$ in the if-then format, it was clear to its author that one cannot prescribe IQ, and further investigation into what behavior is preferred by the academic community yielded the last version. Notice also that the third version is more concrete than the other two. The if-then rule format encourages greater specificity than less formal alternatives, and because of this specificity, it facilitates rule testing.

One temporary drawback of this specificity is that researchers may limit the scope condition to include only those contexts in which they tested the rule when in fact the rule has a much wider application.[147] For example, the final version of $*R_{(41)}$ may apply to more groups than the one specified. The problem, however, can be eliminated by incorporating the results of additional research, and the initial restriction of the scope conditions informs researchers as to the context in which the rule was tested. Hence, the if clause should be viewed as one context in which the rule is operable and not necessarily the only context, unless so specified.

SUMMARY

Rules should indicate in what context they hold. These contextual features should be expressed in an if statement. Rules should also specify what behavior the rule prescribes and the nature of the prescription, that is, whether it is obligated, preferred, or prohibited. Rules should take the form "If X, then Y is obligated (preferred, prohibited)." Four advantages to adopting this form have been discussed: (1) it is easier to make comparisons across different investigations, (2) it represents the logic of a rule, (3) it helps to identify actual as opposed to purported rules, and (4) it facilitates the refinement and testing of rules.

Functions of Rules

Rules may function to regulate, interpret, evaluate, justify, correct, predict, and explain behavior. Each of these functions will be explored in turn.

REGULATING BEHAVIOR

Since prescription is a defining characteristic of rules, it is not surprising that most of the functional descriptions for rules have focused on the regulating quality of rules. Below is a sampling of these descriptions:

> The method by which human beings manage their affairs and create society, is by the invention and promulgation of rules, in the following of which social behavior is generated.[148]

> What do rules attain? Order and regularity in the communication process.[149]

> Speakers know and follow the rules, and it is their following these rules which accounts for the observed regularities of speech.[150]

Several scholars make a distinction between rules that regulate behavior and those that constitute acts. The distinction between constitutive and regulative rules has been attributed to Immanuel Kant and is most often associated with the work of the contemporary philosopher John R. Searle. Searle defined each type of rule as follows: "Regulative rules regulate a pre-existing activity, an activity whose existence is logically independent of the rules. Constitutive rules constitute (and also regulate) an activity the existence of which is logically dependent on rules."[151]

This distinction has been described by some scholars as an important one.[152] Max Black and Raymond D. Gump, however, have questioned the value of this distinction.[153] The present author also adheres to the position that it is futile to try to dichotomize rules as either constitutive or regulative. Apparently, even Searle has trouble keeping them separate, because after carefully distinguishing constitutive and regulative rules, he writes that constitutive rules constitute and regulate an activity.[154] Searle's examples also fail him. He argues that etiquette rules are regulative rules. However, they can also be viewed as constituting politeness. Constitutive rules have been viewed by some writers as definitional, interpretative rules.[155] But, it has been argued here that cognitions cannot be monitored, and thus deviations from an interpretive rule cannot be sanctioned, except as cognitions are manifested in behavior; therefore, there is no such thing as an interpretive rule.

Searle maintains that constitutive rules take the form "X counts as Y in context C."[156] Constitutive rules have been viewed as definitions which do not result in an appraisal of the actor's behavior.[157] Consistent with that perspective, Robert Sanders and Larry Martin argue that violations of regulative rules result in censure whereas violations of constitutive rules (statements that specify behavior that must occur in order for a ceremony, ritual, game, or the like to take place) result in incoherence— "the transgressor might be ostracized, might be pitied, might be instructed, *but would not be censured* [emphasis added]."[158] The major distinction between the two rules seems to be the consequence of violation. This distinction, however, is questionable. First, the assumption that ostracism, pity, and instruction (particularly if it is condescending) are not forms of censure must be rejected. Second, violation of regulative (procedural) rules might also result in ostracism, pity, and instruction. Finally, if one desires to enact a ceremony, ritual, game, episode, speech act, or the like and his or her behavior fails to constitute a ceremony, ritual, game, or the like in a given community, then from that person's point of view, his/her behavior has been evaluated negatively. Rules are prescriptions for behavior, and a violation of any rule is subject to negative sanctions.

Viewing constitutive rules as nonevaluative definitions fails to meet the definitional requirements of a rule. Constitutive rules are also viewed as rules for performing specific speech acts. From this perspective it is possible to rewrite Searle's basic form ("X counts as Y in context C") so that it meets the definitional requirements of a rule: "If one wishes to perform act X in society A, then one must (should, must not) do Y." Cast in this format, the rule is both prescriptive and contextual. In addition, it regulates what behavior ought to occur. Therefore, it seems more appropriate to view all rules, rather than just certain types, as regulating behavior.

INTERPRETING BEHAVIOR

An interpretive "rule" indicates the meaning for a particular act or class of acts. It has been argued that these so-called rules

are not rules, because one cannot prescribe cognitions. However, rules may be utilized to interpret behavior by assuming
that an actor follows a particular rule in producing an utterance.
This is precisely what H. Paul Grice does when he describes conversational implicatures.[159] The interpretative utility of rules
has been further highlighted in Nofsinger's explications of
indirect answers.[160] Communicators assume certain rules are
operable; and so assuming, they assign meaning to behavior.

EVALUATING BEHAVIOR

Because rules are prescriptive, they may be utilized to evaluate
behavior. Psycholinguists take the evaluation of behavior as the
most stringent evidence that a rule exists.[161] In addition to evaluating behavior, rules are used to evaluate actors. Berger et al.
report that communicators who violate self-disclosure rules are
viewed as less attractive and less mentally healthy than those
who follow the rules.[162]

JUSTIFYING BEHAVIOR

When asked why one is doing something, one may answer
"Because I am supposed to." Because rules specify what behavior
is preferred, obligated, or prohibited, one can justify one's behavior by indicating that one's behavior is in accordance with
the rules. For example, if one asked a man why he opens doors
for women, he may answer, "I'm supposed to. It is polite." If
pushed, he may even state the rule. If, for example, one then
asked, "Well, if it is polite, why don't women open the doors?
Are women rude?" he may reply, "No, women are not impolite;
it is just that men should open the door for women." The following two statements on the justifiability of rules typify the
position of rule theorists. "It is in the preparation of excuses and
justification that rules and rule-surrogates enter the process
(rehearsal of an episode)."[163] "The most notable feature of such
rules (rules of behavior) is that if one accepts them, they provide
reasons for or against behaving in a certain way."[164]

CORRECTING BEHAVIOR

Closely related to using rules to criticize behavior is the utilization of rules to correct behavior. Rules may be made explicit

in corrective processes, as in "No, you did it wrong. The rule is . . ."[165] Slobin reports that the corrective behavior children (i.e., corrections of their speech and others') is taken as an indicator that they have acquired the rules of a language.[166] Scholars who have investigated corrective (repair) behavior have argued that these repairs reflect the rules that the communicators presume are salient.[167]

PREDICTING BEHAVIOR

Rules may be used to predict behavior. If one has knowledge of a situation and the rules that are appropriate to it, and believes that another actor shares that knowledge and desires to perform in accordance with the rules, then one may predict that the actor will perform the behaviors prescribed by the rule. For example, if a question is addressed to a native speaker in the United States, one could predict that that person would respond to that question immediately following its being asked. This prediction would be based on rules for answering questions. Rules may be used by actors and researchers alike to predict behavior. How rules may be used to predict behavior will be discussed further in Chapter 6.

EXPLAINING BEHAVIOR

Ultimately, rule scholars hope that they can explain behavioral patterns and the other five functions of rules (prescription, interpretation, evaluation, justification, and correction) by appealing to rules and their prescriptive force. "The interest in rules and knowledge of rules is based on trying to understand and explain behavior and action."[168] "Communication rules form general and specific patterns of choice which provide the basis for the explanation, prediction and control of comunication behavior."[169]

It is this final function of rules that is of primary concern to communication scholars, and it will be explored in further detail in Chapter 6. (See also the discussion of explanation in this chapter in the section on Potential Synonyms.)

SUMMARY

. Rules may serve several functions, including regulating, interpreting, evaluating, justifying, correcting, predicting, and explaining behavior. One task of the rule scholar is to explicate these functions and their relationship to communicative behavior. For the purpose of theory construction, the predictive and explanatory power of rules are their most important functions.

Conclusion

A number of scholars have puzzled over a definition of *rule*, and they have argued that the ambiguity of this term has impeded the development of communication theory from a rules perspective. Although there has been general agreement on the defining characteristics of rules, these characteristics are not always stated explicitly in definitions and there has been disagreement about what constitutes these characteristics. Perhaps it is for this reason that phenomena which are related to rules in some way but which fail to meet the defining characteristics have been mistakenly labeled rules. The presentation of the nature, structure, and function of rules in this chapter has several advantages over previous conceptualizations in communication literature: (1) it makes the characteristics of rules explicit; (2) it avoids unnecessary, contradictory, or otherwise troublesome characteristics; (3) it presents characteristics that are internally consistent; (4) it distinguishes rules from related phenomena (e.g., norms); and, (5) it distinguishes rules from parts of a rule (e.g., presuppositions or scope conditions), results of a rule (e.g., descriptions of empirical regularities), functions of rules (e.g., interpretations and explanations) and sources of rules (e.g., self-concepts). Using the criteria presented, scholars may accurately identify a rule by identifying a followable prescription that indicates what behavior is obligated, prohibited, or preferred in certain contexts. For scientific purposes, rules should take the form "If X, then Y is preferred (obligated, or prohibited)." Four advantages to using this form have been presented, and seven functions of rules have been identified.

Chapter 3

IDENTIFYING RULES FROM BEHAVIOR

Using the defining characteristics outlined in Chapter 2, one can determine whether or not a linguistic entity is a rule.[1] However, many communication rules have not been explicitly stated. To identify implicit rules, researchers must observe the behavior of communicators.[2] The purpose of this chapter is to specify what evidence is necessary and sufficient to infer rules from behavior.

The distinguishing features of rule-generated behavior emanate from the defining characteristics of a rule. This relationship is illustrated below:

A rule is:	Rule-generated behavior is:
(1) followable	(1) controllable
(2) prescriptive	(2) criticizable
(3) contextual	(3) contextual

A description of what counts as evidence that a given behavior is controllable, criticizable, and contextual will be presented. This description will be followed by a decision-tree that illustrates the steps involved in constructing this evidence. Finally, rule-generated behavior will be compared with other types of behavioral regularities on the basis of these three criteria.

Controllable

Rule-generated behavior is controllable.[3] By controllable, it is meant that one can physically perform or not perform that behavior. It does not mean that behavior is always performed willfully. One may conform to a rule in such a habitual manner that s/he acts "without thinking," as if the behavior was a reflex reaction. For example, given the question "How are you?" a speaker may automatically answer "Fine" without really thinking about the question, his/her actual condition, or the answer. This behavior can be attributed to complying with rules regarding greetings, questions and answers, and the specific exchange. Although this behavior appears to be reflexive, it is in fact controllable. When brought to the attention of actors and asked to change their behavior, actors are physically capable of making any utterance following "How are you?" or even of remaining silent.

The notion that rule-related behavior must be controllable can also be expressed in terms of the construct "volition." Actors must be able to choose, at least theoretically, whether or not to perform a behavior prescribed by a rule. If it is not within the actor's physical ability, or presumed ability, to choose whether or not to perform the behavior, it would be meaningless to hold the actor responsible for his/her behavior.[4]

The controllability of rule-generated behavior is one of the characteristics that distinguishes it from the mechanistic (reflexive) behavior, which is not controllable. Further, it is closely related to the criticizability of rule-generated behavior. We neither praise nor blame actors for blinking when they get dust in their eyes, but we do hold them accountable for their use of obscenities, even if they "speak without thinking," because we know that it is not possible to control the former but that the latter is controllable.

The primary test for whether a behavior is controllable is the physical ability to deviate from that behavior. Controllability is a necessary feature of rule-generated behavior, but this is not sufficient evidence to infer a rule. One can skip on the sidewalk, but observing someone skipping would not be sufficient evidence to argue that one must or should skip on the sidewalk. In addition to being controllable, rule-generated behavior is criticizable.

Criticizable

To say that rule-generated behavior is criticizable is to indicate that it is open to evaluation. It may not always get appraised, since there are factors that inhibit sanctions, but actors must view evaluations of rule-generated behavior as legitimate in given contexts. Critiques of rule-generated behavior may be positive or negative.

POSITIVE AND NEGATIVE EVALUATIONS

Adherence and deviations from rules are not universally praised or blamed. In some cases, actors "enhance their reputations by observing rules but lose nothing by failing to do so," whereas in other situations, actors "derive no special distinction by adhering to rules, but stand in danger of foregoing something by violating them."[5] Peter Collett's position is that rules that are empowered by the threat of negative sanctions for deviation are central to the maintenance of the social system, easy to perform, and expected, but that those that are empowered by the promise of reward for compliance are peripheral, arduous to perform, and not really expected.

These distinctions are embodied in differences between obligatory and prohibitive rules, on the one hand, and preferential rules, on the other hand. Compliance with rules that prescribe what one must (obligatory) or must not do (prohibitive) will probably go unrewarded, but a deviation from such a rule may be subject to negative evaluations. Compliance with preferential rules, however, will probably result in a positive evaluation whereas a deviation may go unnoticed. Perhaps an example of each will help to clarify this point.

$R_{(01)}$: If a question is addressed to a person, then that person must respond to that question.[6] (obligatory)

$R_{(02)}$: If one is walking on a public street, then one must not be nude. (prohibitive)

$R_{(03)}$: If one is concluding a pleasant telephone conversation, then the called should express his/her appreciation for the phone call. (preferential)

People who answer questions addressed to them or who walk on public streets clothed receive little attention for their compliance with $R_{(01)}$ and $R_{(02)}$, but a violation of either rule is likely to be negatively sanctioned. Persons who fulfill social amenities, like $R_{(03)}$, are likely to be rewarded for their courtesies, but the absence of these behaviors will probably not be negatively sanctioned. There is a limitation, however, on how much they will be ignored, and a person who fails to comply with preferential rules will be viewed less favorably than one who fulfills their prescriptions.

So far, preferential rules have been treated as if they are linear; the more one does the preferred behavior, the greater the reward. But it is also possible for them to be curvilinear. For example, there is a general preference for agreements in conversations.[7] Therefore, the greater the number of agreements, the higher the expected reward. However, there is also a preference for honesty. If an over-abundance of agreements leads to the impression that the agreements are fictitious, then as the number of "yes-man" statements go up, the evaluation of the person will decrease. These relationships can be illustrated by using Jay Jackson's Return Potential Model, which plots the approval or disapproval curve of a behavior in conjunction with its frequency.[8]

The utility of distinguishing obligatory and prohibitive rules from preferential rules can further be demonstrated by providing additional insight into previous research. The research of Charlene Edna O'Brien will serve as an illustration. O'Brien found that "Company members perceived individuals most favorably, especially managers, in the social episodes when they behaved in a rule consistent manner. Company members perceived individuals least favorably in task episodes when they behaved in a rule inconsistent manner."[9] Using this evidence, O'Brien concluded that compliance with the rules in a task setting was a minimal expectation, resulting in little reward for compliance but significant negative sanction for deviation. On the other hand, she argued that compliance with the social rule was optional. However, her evidence does not support the notion that the social rule studied was optional, since those who complied with it received a more favorable evaluation than those who did not. Rather, it seems likely that the company's rules for task situations were obligatory or prohibitive, and its rules in the social setting were preferential.

To demonstrate that a particular behavior is criticizable, that it may be evaluated positively or negatively, one may draw upon three different types of evidence: (1) judgments of appropriateness, (2) negative sanctions for deviation, and (3) repairs of deviations.

JUDGMENTS OF APPROPRIATENESS

If behavior is rule-generated, actors may be able to indicate what behavior is appropriate and what would be considered inappropriate in that context.[10] Statements about appropriateness may range from articulation of the rule to rating the behavior on approval/disapproval scales, to choosing preferred behaviors for alternatives.

Unfortunately, even when a behavior is rule-generated, a researcher may be unable to secure judgments about its appropriateness. Sometimes actors are hesitant to claim that one behavior is correct or preferred and the other is incorrect or not preferred, even though their behavior reflects standards of appropriateness. Edward T. Hall, in his research on spatial rules, reports that communicators are often "unable to formulate specific rules for their informal behavior patterns. In fact, they often deny that there are any rules, and they are made anxious by suggestions that such is the case."[11] Peter Collett, who recommends seeking judgments of appropriateness above all other techniques for determining if the behavior is rule-generated, indicates that there are potential problems with it.[12] For example, he doubts that English subjects, who consistently walk to the right side of the pavement, would be likely to label walking on the left side as wrong or inappropriate.

While adults may be hesitant to make judgments about what is appropriate or inappropriate behavior, children may avoid making comparisons of behavioral choices all together. Consider dialogue$_{(01)}$:

Dialogue$_{(01)}$:

Interviewer: Now Adam, listen to what I say. Tell me which is better
. . . some water or a water.

Adam (two-year-old): Pop go weasel.[13]

Finally, the term *appropriate* may not be the best choice for soliciting judgments about behaviors. Janet L. Weathers has found that asking students and teachers whether a particular communication act was appropriate was not as effective for assessing the prescriptive force as asking them to rate the behavior on positive/negative and comfortable/uncomfortable scales.[14] Researchers might also consider using comparative terms like *best, better, good, bad, worse,* and *worst.*

Even though actors may be unable or unwilling to make formal judgments about the appropriateness of a given behavior, researchers should not automatically conclude that the behavior is not the result of a rule. Actors demonstrate the criticizability of behavior in other ways, including imposing negative sanctions on deviating behavior and actors.

NEGATIVE SANCTIONS

In fact, that one is conforming to an implicit rule may be most apparent when a deviation occurs: "Rules and conventions governing such social interactions become apparent only when members make communicative mistakes at which time embarrassment, humiliation, rage, disappointment, and laughter are a few of the possible responses."[15]

Earlier it was argued that preferential rules were empowered by rewards rather than punishments, but smaller or fewer rewards may be viewed as a type of punishment. If an actor wishes to be popular and his/her noncompliance with preferential rules makes him/her socially less desirable than s/he would like, then this reduction in popularity can be viewed as one type of negative sanction.

Types. Negative sanctions may take many forms in addition to those mentioned above, including: (1) staring at the deviator,[16] (2) explicit reprimands, (3) demands that the noncompliance be corrected, (4) calling the noncompliance to the attention of the actor, (5) "loss of face," and (6) loss of credibility or attraction. Some of these sanctions will be manifested in communicative behavior, but other sanctions, like loss of face or attraction, may require that one ask the participants about their reactions to particular behaviors and actors.

Dialogue$_{(02)}$ is an example of an explicit reprimand for not conforming to rule$_{(04)}$. In dialogue$_{(03)}$, the mother demands an apology for nonconformance with rule$_{(05)}$. In dialogue$_{(04)}$, a noncompliance with rule$_{(06)}$ is called to the actor's attention. If an actor fails to conform to rule$_{(07)}$, other actors may negatively sanction the speaker by ignoring his/her remarks, as illustrated in dialogue$_{(05)}$.

Dialogue$_{(02)}$:

Terry: What is the purpose of the assignment?

Teacher: The assignment has many purposes. First, it is to help you get to know one another. Second . . .

Terry: [Talking to another student.]

Teacher: Terry, when you ask me a question, I expect you to listen to the answer. I consider your talking through my answer to be quite rude.

Terry: I'm sorry; go on.

R$_{(04)}$: If one has asked a question, then one is obligated to listen to the answer.

Dialogue$_{(03)}$:

Child: You old bag.

Mother: Don't talk to me that way. Show some respect. Apologize to your mother.

Child: I'm sorry, but you made me mad.

R$_{(05)}$: If one is a child, then one should not use derogatory references when referring to one's parent.

Dialogue$_{(04)}$:

F$_1$: You didn't give me the newspaper back. . . .

F$_2$: Oh, I'm sorry. [Pause.] I was just. . . .[17]

R$_{(06)}$: If one has borrowed something which belongs to someone else, then the borrower has an obligation to return what was borrowed to the original owner.

Dialogue(05):

Roger and Dan have been talking about the contributions of schizophrenics. Ken's remarks are ignored because he fails to make them
relevant to the ongoing conversation and hence he violates rule(07).
The dialogue between Roger and Dan continues as if Ken's remarks
were never made.

[GTS:IV:1:12]

Dan: Alright, except that again, you're—you're—you're— using an
example of maybe one or two individuals.

Roger: Yes.

Dan: Uh::m and saying well look what these people did. And the
other idea is that most schizophrenics, most psychotics are
not really able to produce very much of any thing.

                                      [
                                  I'm not

Roger: saying don't cure schi—I'm taking it as an individual case.
I'm taking this individual and=

                [

Dan: Mm hm, it's *true*—

Roger: =referring to only this individual.

Dan: 'S true, and I'm sure that his artwork uhm all you have to
do is go over t'Brentwood and see some very interesting
artwork I find it interesting.

                [

Roger: Where at the hospital?

Dan: That's right.

Ken: Yeah and you c'n also go into some of these millionaires' hou-
homes. And they've bot-boughten some of these uh artworks
from different places in the world? You c'n look at 'em and—
I mean I don't know anything about art. I can't—I can't draw
that well. I can draw cars, and junk like this when I want to,
but uh::go into some of these houses and they—it looks like
somebody took a squirtgun with paint in it an' just squirted it.
Justa buncha *lines* goin every which way an' "Oh isn't that
terrific?" "Yeah. What is it." Y'kno(h)w? "Didjer child have a
good time when he was drawing that?" "Whad-diyuh *mean* that
cost me—" Y'know hhh.

Dan: See but the other al—the alternative that you're giving me is to
say well, look, m-m-maybe uh maybe a person has to be sick in
order to be able to see these things.

Roger: No, this man—

    [[

Dan: And I don't think—

Dan: And I don't think that's true.

Roger: I don't think so either. But this man. . . .[18]

$R_{(07)}$: If a speaker is not the first speaker in a conversation, then the speaker must demonstrate the relevancy of his/her remarks to ongoing talk.[19]

Problems with Sanctions as a Measure of Criticizability. Using negative sanctions of deviations as a measure of prescriptive knowledge may, however, be a troublesome indicant for two reasons: (1) rule deviations are not always negatively sanctioned, and (2) criticisms may occur for reasons other than deviations from rule prescriptions.

The intensity and crystallization of a rule may affect whether or not a deviation from that rule may be sanctioned.[20] The intensity of a rule is measured by the degree of its salience in a given situation: the less important a rule, the less likely deviations from that rule will be negatively sanctioned. The crystallization of a rule concerns the degree of agreement regarding a rule; the more communicators disagree on what a rule prescribes or what is applicable when, the more likely deviations from that rule will not be negatively sanctioned.

Deviations from rules may also escape negative sanction if the deviation does not exceed one's tolerance threshold for deviations.[21] Even if repeated deviations are eventually sanctioned negatively, because their accumulative effect exceeds one's tolerance, the possible delay of a sanction presents a methodological problem of timing; that is, how long should researchers observe before they can reasonably conclude that the nonsanctioned deviation from a regularity is not a deviation from a rule? This issue is an important one to consider, but it is not easily answered. Researchers may need to combine deviation data with other tests for determining if given behaviors are rule-generated.

Gerry Philipsen has reported that deviations from a rule by a superordinate were, in one case, handled in three different ways across time.[22] First, there was an attempt to persuade the actor to change his behavior. When persuasion failed, it was assumed that the actor was following a higher-order rule. And finally, when this rationalization was no longer satisfactory, the actor was viewed as a person above the rule (i.e., a saint). Here, the absence of criticism may indicate a reluctance to evaluate one's superordinate, but negative sanctions may not occur for a variety of other factors.

In choosing among contradictory rules, Ted Smith argues that communicators may choose to avoid negative sanctions by: (1) seeking additional information on the hope that they will learn that one of the rules is not applicable, or that one rule is considered more important than the other, and if the more valued rule is followed, sanctions may be avoided, (2) acting ambiguously so it is not clear that any rules are violated, (3) preventing surveillance of action, or (4) seeking to change one of the conflicting rules.[23]

Mark Knapp points out several reasons why noncompliant behavior may not be sanctioned: (1) an actor may be viewed as unaware, naive, handicapped, boxed in, or fooling around, (2) other contiguous norms are not violated, so that one's total behavior is considered balanced, (3) violations may be defused by acknowledging the norm is about to be broken, (4) the violation was done with class or style, and (5) the violation may be of a norm of little importance.[24]

Five other reasons may be offered to explain why noncompliance may not be negatively sanctioned: (1) negative evaluation of one's behavior and/or one's self threatens face, and since evaluations violate rules of politeness, negative sanctions may not occur, (2) the violation may go undetected; that is, communicators may selectively perceive that the behavior did comply with a rule, (3) the violation may be overlooked because the violator is of higher status, (4) communicators may choose to adopt the violation as a new rule, or (5) the violation may be viewed as a purposeful violation for the purpose of emphasis or humor.

Purposeful violations of rules for emphasis has been discussed by Paul Grice as the characteristic that gives rise to conversational implicatures.[25] In dialogue$_{(06)}$, rule$_{(08)}$, and rule$_{(09)}$ are violated; but in their violation, the speaker is able to make a more forceful statement than s/he might otherwise have been able to make. It is quite possible that these violations will not be interpreted as real violations, and, hence, not negatively sanctioned.

•

Dialogue(06):

A: Is Jones a good student?

B: His handwriting is good.[26]

R(08): "Make your contributions as informative as required."[27]

R(09): "Do not say that which is pointless or spurious."[28]

Intentional rule violations may also occur when one wishes to be humorous. Rules are used to generate expectations; deviations from rules violate one's expectations, and deviations from what is expected is one source of humor.[29] For example, pie-in-the-face routines have delighted audiences for years, and this behavior is a rule violation.

Intentional rule violations for the purpose of emphasis or humor enhance communicative interactions, but purposeful violations may also be used to deceive and manipulate others. If the latter violations go unsanctioned, misunderstandings and the loss of status may occur. What is more, the absence of sanctions makes it difficult to determine whether the behavior is rule-conforming.

John Waite Bowers et al. have argued that by exploiting (violating) the rules for answering questions, actors can send devious messages.[30] For example, in dialogue(07), speaker R's response to V's question is devious. Gildersleeve had already been selected commissioner. It is true that he was not being considered, but the "no" is likely to be taken as indicating that he did not get the job.

Dialogue(07):

V: Is Gildersleeve being considered for water commissioner?

R: No.[31]

Deceptive use of rules is only effective if the violation goes undetected.

Several scholars have maintained that rule violations may be used purposely to manipulate other actors. Janice Hocker Rushing reports that a communicator can disorient another person by violating rules, and if one allows the deviation to go unchecked, the violation can serve as means to gain power over another person.[32] Similarly, Rebecca J. Cline and Bonnie McD. Johnson indicate that actors who violate rules of verbal focus increase the discomfort and defensiveness of other actors.[33] Thomas S. Frentz and Thomas B. Farrell argue that in violating the communication rules of the Oval Office, John Dean changed the role relationships and increased his power.[34] Wayne A. Beach and William Wilmot argue that violation of self-disclosure rules can be used to gain power, and the present author has argued that manipulation (violation) of politeness rules can also be used to increase one's power over another.[35]

When a violation of a rule goes unchecked, the possibility that the violator may gain status is increased. The increase may occur because communicators allow those of higher status to violate rules more often than those of lower status, and the absence of negative sanction may imply that the deviator is of higher status. (This issue is discussed in more detail later under the heading of rule-allowance behavior.) Rule-abiding actors are then caught in a bind, if they are aware of the violation to respond negatively to someone is to violate politeness rules but to allow others to violate rules increases the possibility that the violator will gain power. Like deceptive violation, manipulative violations may also go undetected and thus not be negatively sanctioned.

If a deviation from a behavior is not negatively sanctioned, then researchers will have to demonstrate the criticizability of the behavior by securing judgments of appropriateness or by observing repairs of the deviation in the direction of the hypothesized rule. Before discussing repair data, however, one last caution with regard to using sanctions as a measure of criticizability needs to be given.

One may criticize someone and his/her behavior for reasons other than not complying with the rules. For example, one may dislike someone because of his/her personality, religion, ethnicity, and so on; one may be in a cantankerous mood; one may be argumentative by nature; one may sanction someone else's and his/her behavior in an effort to establish himself/herself as the higher-status person, and so forth. To establish that the criticism is related to rule-generated behavior, researchers need to combine sanction data with either judgments of appropriateness or repair data, or demonstrate that the behavior and the criticism are similarly contextual. That is, given a particular context, the behavior recurs, and on those occasions when it does not, the deviations are negatively sanctioned.

REPAIR

A repair is an attempt to preempt, eliminate, or fix a communication trouble source.[36] Deviation from a rule may be a source of trouble. Actors may preempt that trouble and related criticism by repairing the deviation.[37] Dialogue$_{(08)}$ provides an example of a repair marked by the phrase "wait a minute," which may be the result of Rule$_{(10)}$. That is, the speaker's original utterance misinforms the hearer with regard to the timing of an event. R$_{(10)}$, however, requires that the speaker give the correct time if s/he knows it.

Dialogue$_{(09)}$:

E: Anyways, when this (.2) happened a week ago—wait a minute, a year ago next week.[38]

R$_{(10)}$: "Do not say what you believe to be false."[39]

Repair data have been used to support hypothesized rules related to clarity, accuracy, politeness, and sequencing. When a communicator repairs a message, one may infer that s/he has violated a rule (actual or imagined) or that s/he is trying to preempt a violation. One nice feature about using repairs as a means of identifying and verifying rules is that repairs are signaled or "flagged" by behavioral cues, such as: unfilled pauses at non-transitionally relevant places, filled pauses, cutoffs, lexical markers, and brackets.[40] Researchers can use these flags to locate repairs and then utilize the repairs to infer rules.

Repairs are not, however, a foolproof method for determining that a behavior is rule-generated. Repairs may also be indicative of psychological trouble (e.g., anxiety or memory lapse), or they may be in respose to the behavior of listeners (e.g., apparent non-attentiveness or interruption). Some researchers have even indicated that sometimes what appears to be a repair is actually a conversational strategy.[41] Repair data may be used as additional evidence of a rule, but they are not sufficient evidence by themselves. At a minimum, repair data must be coupled with judgments of appropriateness, negative sanctions, or contextual data that indicate the behavior recurred under similar conditions and that the repairs corrected deviations so that they conformed to this regularity. Finally, one cannot count on every deviation being repaired. Communicators may let "hearable" errors[42] pass for a number of reasons, including: the error goes undetected, the error falls within the actor's tolerance for deviation, the actor is focusing on content rather than form, or the actor is in too much of a hurry to correct errors consciously.[43] If deviations are not repaired, then the researcher must rely on judgments of appropriateness or negative sanctions to establish the criticizability of a behavior.

Emanuel A. Schegloff et al. have demonstrated that in conversation there is a preference for self-correction over other-correction of trouble sources.[44] Erving Goffman, however, describes a repair process involving multiple actors. He calls these processes "remedial interchanges."[45] A remedial interchange involves a rule deviation that needs to be remedied. The deviation may be remedied in one of three ways: accounts, apologies, and requests to violate the rule before the deviation (e.g., "Can I ask you something personal?").[46] Like repairs in general, remedial interchanges may facilitate the identification of rules. In fact, G. H. Morris has used remedial interchanges to identify the rules of student-teacher interactions.[47] Researchers can maximize the probability of acquiring remedial data if they investigate episodes that are likely to include remedial interchanges, for example, performance reviews or "gripe" sessions. In a remedial interchange, all parties agree that a behavior must be remedied. Therefore, such interchanges are sufficient evidence of the criticizability of the behavior.

The criticizability of a behavior can be demonstrated by providing one of three types of evidence: (1) judgments on appropriateness, (2) negative sanctions of deviations, or (3) repairs of deviations. Given all of the potential problems of securing evidence of the criticizability of a rule, it is possible that a rule exists even though the researcher has been unable to provide this evidence. However, if the researcher strikes out on all three counts, then s/he should take a more conservative position and assume that there is no rule prescribing that behavior. The importance of providing evidence of the criticizability of the behavior to rules research cannot be underestimated. This evidence is not merely necessary to meet definitional requirements; it is essential to the explanatory power of the rules perspective. One of the basic assumptions of the rules perspective is that actors comply with the dictates of rules because rules may be used to critique their behavior and they wish to receive favorable evaluations.

Since behaviors other than those prescribed by rule may be controllable and criticizable (e.g., behavior resulting from orders or commands), these necessary features must be combined with a third one, which is contextual.

Contextual

Rules prescribe what behavior is appropriate in a particular context; hence, behavior that is rule-generated recurs in similar contexts.[48] This stipulation may lead some scholars to argue that the behavior thought to be prescribed by a rule must occur 95 percent of the time if one is to infer a rule.[49] Although researchers need to know that the patterns they observe are not due to chance alone, a requirement of 95 percent regularity seems both arbitrary and inappropriate.

As noted, actors can deviate from rules for a number of reasons, including mistakes, interruptions, conflicting rules, exploitation, humor, and anger. Although each of these factors would reduce the degree of behavioral regularity, none denies the existence of a rule. In arguing that a behavioral pattern is the result of a rule rather than chance, researchers should report the occurrence of behavioral regularities, repaired deviations, negatively sanctioned deviations, and they should offer alternative explanations for deviations, such a conflicting rules, humor, and interruptions.

Obligatory rules should result in the consistent presence of the prescribed behavior, and its absence should be taken as a deviation. Prohibitive rules should result in the consistent absence of the prescribed behavior, and its presence should be taken as a deviation. Prohibitive rules may be more difficult to identify than obligatory rules because they are inferred from the consistent absence of some behavior. To identify prohibitive rules, researchers may have to perform, or have performed, a variety of behaviors which are typically absent in a given case, hoping that one or more of them will be either repaired or negatively sanctioned, in order to determine which behaviors among a multitude of alternatives are prohibited by rules. Preference rules should result in the preferred behavior occurring more often than not occurring, and its nonoccurrence should be viewed as a deviation from the rule.

Following communicators around hoping to catch them in enough similar situations in order to infer rules may be a tedious and inefficient research method. To determine if a behavior recurs in similar contexts, researchers may ask actors to role play situations, or they may create similar situations. Jean Berko has developed a procedure for measuring the extension of linguistic behavior in similar contexts. For example, a child is presented a picture of an unknown creature and is told that it is a wug. The child is then shown a picture with two creatures and asked to complete the sentence "There are two. . . ." If the child answers "wugs," the child's behavior is thought to be rule-related, in that it is generalized to similar situations.[50] Perhaps modifications of these procedures could be used to test other communicative behaviors.

It is possible that the recurrence of a particular behavior may become so routine that it goes unnoticed. Such regularities may lead one to assume that all human beings in all situations behave similarly, overlooking the possibility that the behavior may be prescribed by a rule. One approach for surmounting this problem is to consciously look for changes in behavioral patterns. Dell H. Hymes argues that "a shift in any of the components of speaking may mark the presence of a rule."[51] One scholar who has been particularly successful in using code-switching to identify rules is John J. Gumperz. By using this method, he has explicated rules related to status, social distance, solidarity, classroom behavior, and Afro-American sermons. He has also used this method to resolve a controversy about the meaning of a disputed statement.[52] In addition to searching for shifts in behavioral patterns, researchers may use cross-cultural observations to challenge assumptions about the natural order of communicative behavior.

Since code-switching and cross-cultural data demonstrate the possibility of deviation, they may be used to argue that a behavioral regularity is neither logically nor physically necessary but that it is prescribed by a rule. Inasmuch as a pattern is most easily recognized when there is a deviation from that pattern, such data may also serve to draw attention to a regularity that might otherwise go unnoticed.

If communicators conform to rules, their behavior should be repeated under similar circumstances, but this evidence is not sufficient to conclude that the behavior is rule-conforming. Actors may replicate their behavior under certain circumstances for reasons other than trying to conform to rules. They may do so because they have no control over their actions (e.g., breathing or reflex movements) or replication may happen by accident, by imitating others, or by choosing to do so without perceiving that their behavior may be subject to evaluation. In addition to demonstrating consistent extension of the behavior, researchers need to provide evidence that the behavior is critiquable to infer a rule.

By demonstrating that a behavior is controllable, criticizable, and contextual, a researcher provides all the necessary and sufficient evidence to infer a rule from that behavior. Based on arguments above, it is possible to construct a decision-tree for identifying rules from behavior.

Decision-Tree for Inferring Rules

Figure 3.1 illustrates the steps a researcher should follow in identifying rules from behavior. Beginning with behavioral observations, the researcher should determine if the behavior recurs in similar contexts. If it does not, if it is random or limited to a single case, then the researcher need not proceed as the behavior is not rule-generated. If the behavior is contextual, then it must be determined whether or not it is controllable. It is if deviation from the behavioral pattern observed is physically possible. If deviation is not possible, then the investigation can be stopped, the behavior is not rule-generated. If the behavior is eventually found to be criticizable, then the test of controllability is unneeded because only behavior that is controllable may be cri-

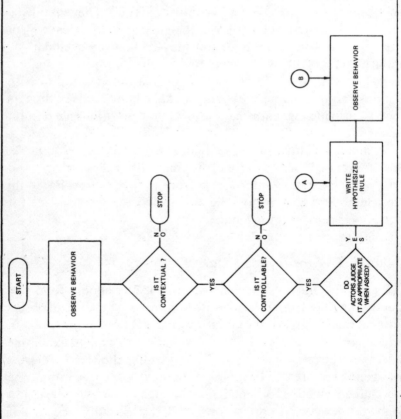

FIGURE 3.1: Decision-Tree for Inferring Rules

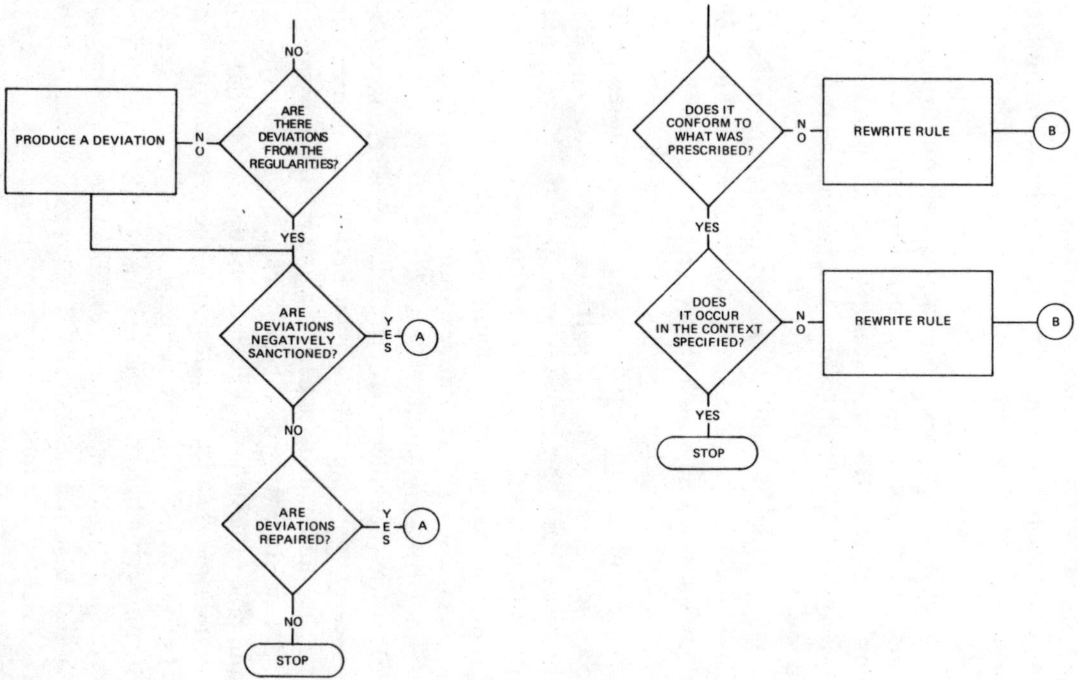

FIGURE 3.1: (Cont.)

107

tiqued. However, since whether behavior is controllable or not is a much easier question to answer and since it is not possible to infer a rule from behavior that is not controllable, the controllability question should be asked before the questions on criticizability. If the behavior is both contextual and controllable, the researcher must then seek to determine if the behavior is criticizable.

Since the criticizability of a rule may be demonstrated in a number of ways, the procedures for providing this evidence are more complex. Researchers may seek three different types of evidence: (1) judgment of appropriateness, (2) negative sanctions for deviation, or (3) repairs of deviations. In combination with contextual data, only one of them is needed. Researchers may set out to find this evidence in any order. The order presented in Figure 3.1 parallels the order in which the types of evidence were discussed above, but any order would be just as good. If any one of these three questions is answered affirmatively, then researchers can proceed with writing the rule. If one or two are answered negatively, researchers can still seek an affirmative answer to the other. Of course, if all three are answered affirmatively, then the evidence that a rule exists is very strong. If all three are answered in the negative, then the researcher should conclude that the behavior is not rule-generated.

If there is sufficient evidence that the behavior is rule-generated, then the researcher should write a hypothetical rule in the if-then rule format recommended in Chapter 2. Since this format requires a specific statement of the context and the behavior prescribed and since the original evidence used to infer that a rule exists may not provide an adequate test of the specific rule hypothesized, the validity of the rule needs to be tested. This can best be done by observing behavior and asking whether it conforms to the behavior prescribed in the rule and whether it occurs consistently and only in the context specified. If the answer to either question is no, the rule should be rewritten and retested. When the answer to both is yes, then the researcher can stop, for s/ he has identified a rule.

It is possible to infer rules from methods other than direct behavioral observations. These methods (e.g., self-reflection and questionnaires) along with various types of behavioral observations will be discussed in Chapter 5. But whatever method used, researchers must be able to demonstrate that the behavior they claim is prescribed by a rule is controllable, criticizable, and contextual.

Other Types of Behavioral Regularities

Rule-generated behavior is sometimes confused with other types of behavioral regularities. Using the defining characteristics of controllable, criticizable, and contextual, rule-generated behavior may be distinguished from these other regularities. Table 3.1 compares these regularities with rules on the bases of the defining features.

CONVENTIONS

Conventions are behavioral regularities that occur because individuals want to conform to the behavior of others.[53] Conventions have been contrasted with rule-related behavior on the grounds that some rules will be followed regardless of how others act.[54] David K. Lewis offered the following examples of rules that are not conventions ($R_{(11)}$ is a direct quotation; $R_{(12)}$ and $R_{(13)}$ are paraphrases of his remarks).[55]

$R_{(11)}$: "Employees are not to smoke within 100 yards of any acetone vat; violation will be considered grounds for immediate dismissal."

$R_{(12)}$: Library books are to be returned within two weeks from the check out date; borrowers who return books late will be fined $1.00 a day.

$R_{(13)}$: Authors must submit papers in standard notation; those papers not in standard notation will not be published.

One will probably choose not to smoke, to return books on time, and to submit papers on standard notation, regardless of what others may do.

Although there are rule-related behaviors that may not be conventions, it is difficult to conceive of a convention that is not rule-related. Not following a convention results in negative evaluation, because conformity is desired. Conventions seem to be predicated on rules—at least on one rule: "One should behave

TABLE 3.1   Rule-Generated Behavior Versus Other Types of Behavior

Behavior	Qualities		
	Controllable	Contextual	Criticizable
Rule-generated	X	X	X
*Convention	X	X	X
*Custom	X	X	/
Ritual	X	X	/
Normative	X	/	/
*Habit	X	/	/
Regularity	/	/	/
Rule-symptomatic	X	X	0
Rule-allowance	X	X	0
Mechanistic	0	X	0

X= true for all cases of a given concept.
/ = true for some but not for all.
0 = (feature is) missing.
*also compared with rule by Joan Ganz.

like everyone else." Conventions, then, are one type of rule-related behavior; they are the result of normative rules.

CUSTOM, RITUAL

Customs and rituals are controllable behaviors that recur in similar contexts. Most of them are also criticizable in that a rule prescribes that the custom or ritual must or should happen. A few, however, may not be prescribed.[56] For example, it may be a custom (ritual) to begin one's Christmas shopping the day after Thanksgiving, but it is not a rule. One may elect to begin during the July sales, or just about any other time, without incurring sanctions. Many customs or rituals are rule-governed, but not all are. Those that are, are also rule-generated behavior.

NORMATIVE BEHAVIOR

Normative behavior is behavior that happens on the average. It is controllable, and it is often contextual, but not always. Something can occur on the average without being criticizable. Examples of this distinction were provided in Chapter 2 when prescriptive force was contrasted with normative force, and when norm was compared with rule. Therefore, for clarification of this issue, readers are encouraged to refer to those earlier sections. One can speak of normative behavior for a single situation, but rule-generated behavior must recurr in similar contexts.

HABITS

Habitual behavior is physically controllable and usually contextual. However, when bad habits become consciously controllable, they often cease to recur; but, because rule-generated behavior is prescribed, it continues to occur even when conscious control is possible. Rule-generated behavior may become habitual, but all habits are not prescribed by rules.[57] For example, I may regularly have breakfast at a particular restaurant whenever desiring steak and eggs; but if I choose to eat elsewhere, there will be no sanctions imposed upon my behavior. Munching while studying, pacing while trying to solve a problem, and verbal mannerisms such as "ok," "you know," "uh," and "er" are also examples of habits. That these regularities are probably not the result of rules may be illustrated by what would be the rules if we assumed these actions were guided by rules; this is the purpose of $*R_{(14)}$ through $*R_{(16)}$.

$*R_{(14)}$: If one is studying, then one must (should) munch.

$*R_{(15)}$: If one is solving a problem, then one must (should) pace.

$*R_{(16)}$: If one is speaking publicly, then one must (should) use "ok," "you know," "uh," and "er" repetitively.

One might argue that for some people, the above statements are, in fact, rules, in that if these persons do not comply with the behavior prescribed, they are not comfortable. Further, they may prefer munching, pacing, or repetitive utterances to other alternatives such as giving up, screaming, or wringing their hands. If this is the case, then $*R_{(14)}$ through $*R_{(16)}$ would be rules for those individuals. If, on the other hand, such persons would prefer not to munch, pace, or rely on certain verbal mannerisms, these behaviors are not prescribed by rules. Perhaps the best way to distinguish behavior that is prescribed by rules from habitual behavior that is not prescribed is that a deviation from those habits will not result in negative sanctions whereas deviations from behavior prescribed by rules are subject to negative evaluation.

REGULARITY

Regularity is a generic term for consistent behavior. It may include rule-generated behavior, habits, mechanistic behavior, and so forth. Some regularities are controllable, contextual, and criticizable, but some are not.

RULE-SYMPTOMATIC BEHAVIOR

Rule-symptomatic behavior is not prescribed by a rule, but is nonetheless the result of a rule. Because it is a by-product of a rule, it is contextual. It is also physically controllable, though it often occurs unconsciously. For instance, regular occurrences of vocal nonfluencies in situations where one may need to make choices may be an example of rule-symptomatic behavior. Percy Tannenbaum et al. have found that individuals often exhibited hesitating behavior (e.g., "uh," "ah," "er") prior to what the researchers believed to be cognitive choice points.[58] However, it is unlikely that this regularity is the result of conforming to a rule. $*R_{(17)}$ indicates what such a rule would have to look like:

$*R_{(17)}$: If one is at a cognitive choice point, then one must (should) hesitate.

What is more likely is that the regularity observed is symptomatic of a rule similar to $R_{(18)}$.[59]

$R_{(18)}$: If one wishes to keep the floor while trying to formulate the next utterance, then one should not allow long pauses to lapse between vocalizations.

$*R_{(17)}$ and $R_{(18)}$ are related to the same regularity, but $*R_{(17)}$ is not a plausible rule, whereas $R_{(18)}$ is. The difference between the two is that noncompliance of $*R_{(17)}$ would not result in a negative evaluation (in fact, the absence of vocal hesitation might result in a more positive evaluation) whereas noncompliance of $R_{(18)}$ (if it is a valid rule) would probably result in a negative sanction (e.g., the loss of the floor). Rule-symptomatic behavior may be distinguished from rule-generated behavior on the basis that its absence would not result in negative evaluations and its presence can be explained by its relationship to a rule.

RULE-ALLOWANCE BEHAVIOR

Rule-allowance behavior is a special type of rule-deviation. It is controllable, and it recurs in certain contexts. Rule-allowance behaviors are regularities that are the result of consistently allowing a person or class of persons to violate a rule. For example, small group research has indicated that leaders are allowed to violate group rules more often than other members.[60] It has also been reported that speakers of high status interrupt speakers of lower status more often than the reverse[61] and that males interrupt females more than females interrupt males.[62] It does not seem reasonable that these regularities could be attributable to *rule$_{(19)}$, *rule$_{(20)}$, or *rule$_{(21)}$.

*R$_{(19)}$: Leaders should (must) violate the rules of the group.

*R$_{(20)}$: High-status speakers should (must) interrupt low-status speakers.

*R$_{(21)}$: Males should (must) interrupt females.

Rather, it seems more plausible that the regularities exist because certain allowances are given to those considered to be of higher status; because violating certain rules, like rule$_{(22)}$, seems to be a way of expressing dominance;[63] and because we expect those of higher status to dominate.

R$_{(22)}$: If one is involved in a conversation, then one should not interrupt another speaker.

Rule-allowance behavior may be distinguished from rule-generated behavior in four ways: (1) a deviation from a rule-allowance regularity would not result in a negative evaluation, (2) although rule-allowance behavior is not negatively sanctioned overtly, communicators should evaluate, when asked to do so, rule-compliant behavior more positively than rule-allowance behavior, (3) the rule-allowance regularities should occur less often than rule-compliant behaviors (e.g., higher-status speakers should exchange turns more often without interruption than with interruption), and (4) those communicators exhibiting this regularity should be of higher status than those not performing the regularity.

Distinguishing between rule-allowance behavior and rule-generated behavior has two advantages: (1) rules will not be written for permitted rule deviations (rule-allowance behavior); and (2) it will not be assumed that one set of rules (those prescribing rule-generated behavior) apply to one group while another set (those assumed to be prescribing the rule-allowance behavior) apply to another group of people. The first advantage was demonstrated when $*R_{(19)}$ through $*R_{(21)}$ were explicated, but the second advantage still needs to be illustrated.

In her research on company rules, in task and social settings, Charlene Edna O'Brien reports that "female managers were always perceived more harshly when they behaved in a rule-inconsistent manner than were males and were perceived more positively than males when they behaved in a rule-consistent manner."[64] This finding leads O'Brien to conclude that the company has different rules for males and females. However, since both males and females were evaluated negatively when they deviated from the rules, a more plausible explanation is that the same rule applied to both males and females but that males were allowed to deviate from the rule more than females. The fact that females received a more positive evaluation for rule compliance might be explained in terms of the setting. Since some persons still see the business world as a man's world, when a woman complies with the rules, perhaps this less expected occurrence receives greater positive attention.

In one sense rule-symptomatic and rule-allowance behavior are criticizable in that their absence is preferred, but this feature is marked as missing in the chart. The reason for this notation is that they have the opposite valance of rule-generated behavior. Rule-generated behavior is subject to negative sanctions for deviations, but behavioral evaluations become more positive as deviations from rule-symptomatic and rule-allowance behavior occur. Since "criticizability" stems from the prescriptive force of rules and since rule-symptomatic and rule-allowance behavior are not prescribed, the 0 notation seems appropriate.

MECHANISTIC BEHAVIOR

Mechanistic behavior recurs in similar contexts, but it is neither controllable nor criticizable. Examples of mechanistic behavior include: knee jerk reactions, blinking, and breathing for life-support. W. Barnett Pearce suggests one method for determining if behavior is mechanistic (law-related).[65] He recommends that one ask whether a given behavior was the result of a logically or empirically necessary relationship between antecedents and consequents. If the answer is yes, the behavior would not be rule-related. In rule-related behavior, it must be demonstrated that an actor could have behaved differently if s/he chose to do so.[66]

Keith Adler proposes an alternative method for distinguishing rule-related behavior from law-related behavior. He recommends comparing the behavior of those who know what is presumed to be a rule with those who do not know it. If the behavior is law-related, there should be no difference in the behavior of either group, but if the behavior is rule-related, then those who know the rule should comply with it more often than those who do not.[67] His assumption is that the prescriptive force of a rule will encourage compliance. If one assumes that those who know and adopt a rule may be separated from those who do not, Adler's position seems reasonable.

Conclusion

Rules may be identified from behavior by providing certain evidence. Rule-generated behavior recurs in similar contexts, and it is controllable. Unlike other controllable regularities, however, rule-generated behavior is also criticizable. A claim that behavior is criticizable may be supported by judgments of appropriateness, negative sanctions for deviations, or repairs of deviations. Rule-generated behavior may be distinguished from conventions, customs, rituals, normative behavior, habits, regularities, rule-symptomatic behavior, rule-allowance behavior, and mechanistic behavior.

The distinctions made here are important because they will allow scholars to infer rules from behavior accurately. Without

the requisite knowledge, researchers may erroneously write rules
for behavioral regularities that are not prescribed. This is most
likely to happen when frequency data are used independently of
evidence that the behavior is criticizable. Using the if-then rule
format suggested in Chapter 2 is also helpful because it will remind researchers that they must provide evidential support for
the prescriptive modal (e.g., must, should, must not) of a rule.

Chapter 4

Procedural / Regular - Guide
- unwritten

Constitutive - Govern

RULES AND BEHAVIOR

· Who determines the rules?

Rules may be related to behavior in many different ways. This chapter will identify types of rule-related behavior and outline the kind of evidence needed to conclude that a particular type of relationship between a rule and behavior exists. The identification of various types of rule-related behavior and the requisite knowledge of each is important because: (1) different labels have been used to describe the same relationship, and such discordant usage makes comparisons across studies difficult if not impossible; and (2) researchers must be able to establish a particular type of relationship between rules and behavior in order to use rules to explain behavior.

Rules Governing and Guiding Behavior

Communication scholars typically refer to rule-*guided* or rule-*governed* behavior without distinguishing between them.[1] When a distinction is made, it is based on the assumption that constitutive and regulative rules are different.[2] Constitutive rules are said to govern; procedural rules are thought to guide behavior. Those who make the distinction between "govern" and "guide" on the basis of constitutive and regulative rules do not offer a reason for the differentiation, and there is no apparent reason to justify it. Furthermore, the distinction is sometimes dropped in a single article. For example, Donald P. Cushman and Gordon C. Whiting asserted, "Constitutive rules govern, the procedural rules guide."[3] But later they wrote that "procedural rules guide and govern."[4] What is more, it has been argued (see Chapter 2) that the distinction between constitutive and regulative rules is untenable. In short, the distinction between rule-guided and rule-governed behavior based on the supposed difference between constitutive and regulative rules is not productive. However, a useful distinction between these two terms can be made on other grounds.

The rules that govern a situation and those that guide behavior may be the same rules, or they may be different. The rules that govern a situation are those that are held to be appropriate for that situation. The rules that guide behavior are those that influence the behavior of a particular actor.[5] If the actor's rules are taken as the rules that govern the situation, then the rules that govern and those that guide behavior are the same rules. On the other hand, if the rules of someone other than the communicator are viewed as those governing the situation, then the rules that govern and those that guide behavior in this case are different rules. An example should make this distinction clear. One may argue that the rules of standard English govern classroom behavior. But these rules, unknown and/or unaccessible to the nonstandard speaker, would not be said to guide his/her behavior. Thus, it is possible to have rules that govern but do not guide behavior.

Is it also possible to have rules that guide but do not govern? The answer may depend on who "determines" the rules. If a speaker elects to guide his/her behavior on the basis of some assumed rule, then for that speaker that is the rule which governs the situation. For example, the black child in an American classroom may have a rule such as $R_{(01)}$.

$R_{(01)}$: If one is interested in the material being presented, then one should become actively involved both vocally and physically.[6]

If the child assumes this rule applies in classroom situations, the child may comply with the rule. For the child, $R_{(01)}$ both governs and guides his/her behavior. For the child's Anglo teacher, however, $R_{(02)}$ may be the governing rule.

$R_{(02)}$: If one is interested in the material being presented, then one should sit very still and remain silent.[7]

Thus, if the researcher takes the point of view of the teacher, then $R_{(02)}$ can be said to be the rule governing the situation whereas $R_{(01)}$ guides the behavior. When talking about rule-governed behavior, researchers need to specify whose rules they are investigating (e.g., the teacher's rules or the child's).

There are situations in which the rules that govern behavior are the same ones which guide behavior. In fact, one would suspect that this is true of most situations. However, because behavior may be rule-governed and/or rule-guided, both terms should be retained. The distinction is particularly useful in explaining research on language attitudes which often involves a comparison between rule-governed behavior (standardized rules) and rule-guided behavior (nonstandard speaking).[8]

Rule-governed and *rule-guided* are the most common adjectives for rule-related behavior, but some rule researchers also use such adjectives as: rule-accordance, rule-applying, rule-bound, rule-conforming, rule-confirming, rule-constituted, rule-fitting, rule-following, rule-fulfilling, rule-generated, rule-regulated, rule-reflective, and rule-satisfying.[9] The diversity of terms suggests that behavior and rules may be related in a number of ways. Because the terms are often used without precision, it is difficult to determine an author's meaning. However, three useful taxonomies of rule-related behavior have been proposed: one by Stephen E. Toulmin, which has been given the most attention in communication literature, and ones by philosopher Joan Safron Ganz and psychologist Peter Collett.[10] The strengths and weaknesses of these three taxonomies are discussed below.

Taxonomies of Rule-Related Behavior

TOULMIN'S TAXONOMY

Toulmin provided a seven-part taxonomy.[11] Toulmin's taxonomy is often described as a list of seven different types of rules.

However, these "rules" are not prescriptions; hence they are
not rules according to the definition used here. They are actually
different labels for rule-related behavior. The taxonomy is predicated on a hierarchy of rule-related descriptions from the least
rational and conscious to the most rational and conscious behavior. What follows is a paraphrased explanation of Toulmin's
taxonomy:

As a rule. This refers to physiological phenomena. A regularity that
occurs "as a rule" has nothing to do with rationality or consciousness (Example: After a passage of a cold front, the cloud layer,
as a rule, breaks up, producing a clear sky.)

Regularity. Regular occurrences of behaviors which one performs
without being cognizant of the reasons are regularities. (Example:
An emotionally disturbed student regularly loses the paper on
which he has jotted down his class assignments.)

Rule-governed behavior. Behavior which is the result of rules that
specify standardized series of distinctive actions is rule-governed
behavior. The rules which apply need not indicate absolute standards of correctness, but may specify latitudes of acceptable
behavior. Rule-governed behavior need not be rational or conscious. (Example: peek-a-boo.)

Rule-conforming behavior. Standard sequences of behavior which
may be judged as "correct" or "incorrect" are rule-conforming
behavior. (Examples: the grammaticality of utterance.)

Rule-applying behavior. Problem-solving behavior which occurs
because one is consciously applying the rules is rule-applying
behavior. (Example: making mayonnaise while consciously observing the rules.)

Rule-following behavior. Problem-solving behavior which occurs
because one is unconsciously following the rules is rule-following
behavior. (Example: making mayonnaise according to the rules
without thinking about them.)

Rule-reflective behavior. Applying rules with conscious critical
attention is rule-reflective behavior. (Example: critical evaluation of various procedures.)

The hierarchy specifies that rule-governed behavior is less
conscious and rational than rule-conforming behavior. This
implies that preferential rules, which allow latitudes, would
result in less rational behavior than obligatory or prohibitive
rules. However, one may reasonably ask if this is true. One could

argue that more conscious, rational consideration is required for choosing among a variety of responses than between simple dichotomies (i.e., right/wrong). Without additional reasoning or evidence, it is impossible to determine if guiding one's behavior via obligatory and prohibitive rules or via preferential rules requires more conscious use of rules. Toulmin's distinction between "rule-conforming" and "rule-governing" seems to be based on the specificity of the behavior rather than on rationality or consciousness. Therefore, there seem to be no grounds for including these categories in a system based on rationality and consciousness.

Toulmin's labeling of subconscious behavior as "rule-following" is also questionable. To use "rule-*following*" to describe a subconscious application of rules would seem to be a contradiction in terms. How can one follow something of which s/he is not consciously aware. Ganz recommended that subconscious compliance with a rule be called rule-accordance behavior.

Two of Toulmin's "rules" do not designate rule-related behavior: "as a rule" and "regularity." "As a rule" behavior is law-related behavior; it is the result of causal, nonchoice phenomena. The term *regularity* is a generic term for all patterned behavior, including regularities that are law-related. Therefore, *regularity* is too general a term to be used as a distinction among rule-related behaviors.

Although some of Toulmin's examples of regularities are probably not prescribed by rules, others may be the result of following rules. For instance, Toulmin's example of an emotionally disturbed student losing his/her assignment with regularity is probably not the result of a rule prescribing that behavior. However, some of Toulmin's other examples of regularities are not any more or less consciously related rules than the examples he labels "rule-following." For example, he cites going to church and saving money as examples of regularities. These regularities could be the result of rules. Such rules might be stated as:

R(03): If one wishes to be a Christian, then one must (should) attend church regularly.

$R_{(04)}$: If one wishes to be a thrifty householder, then one must (should) save money regularly.

Toulmin's distinction between regularities (e.g., attending church) and "rule-following" behavior (e.g., following a recipe by rote) does not appear to be clearly based on rationality and/or consciousness. Both may involve subconscious application of rules for behavior.

Perhaps it is the ambiguity in Toulmin's taxonomy that has resulted in its being used inconsistently. Elaine Litton-Hawes has reversed the attributes of a rule-conforming and rule-governing behavior, and Donald Cushman has reversed the order of rule-applying and rule-following behavior in the hierarchy.[12] These reversals are not surprising when one considers that it is questionable whether rule-conforming behavior is any more rational than rule-governing behavior as they are defined by Toulmin, and that the description of rule-applying behavior suggests more consciousness than rule-following behavior, though Toulmin places them in the opposite order in the hierarchy. What seems to be needed is a taxonomy with clearer divisions and labels.

In summary, then, some of Toulmin's categories overlap others, some are not predicated on a degree of rationality/consciousness, still others are not even the results of rules, and the taxonomy has been used inconsistently. Joan Ganz's taxonomy of rule-related behavior provides some solutions to the problems in Toulmin's list.

GANZ'S TAXONOMY

Joan Ganz's three-part taxonomy of rule-related behavior is paraphrased below.[13]

> *Rule-fulfilling behavior.* Behavior which is consistent with the rules but which is not motivated by the rules is rule-fulfilling behavior. The actor in this case has never heard, seen, or constructed the rules that his/her behavior is fulfilling. (Example: playing by the rules of chess without ever seeing, hearing, or constructing those rules.)
>
> *Rule-accordance behavior.* Behavior which is consistent with the rules and is unconsciously motivated by the rules is rule-accor-

dance behavior. The actor knows the rules and could articulate them, but his/her behavior has become habitual and s/he does not refer to the rules when acting. (Example: an experienced chess player playing according to the rules habitually.)

Rule-following behavior. Behavior which is consistent with the rules because the actor knows the rules and sees to it that his/-her behavior is consistent with the rules is rule-following behavior. The actor makes constant reference to the rules as s/he follows the rules. (Example: someone learning how to play chess who constantly refers to the rules to be sure his/her behavior fulfills the rules.)

Like Toulmin's classification of rule-related behavior, Ganz's taxonomy is hierarchically ordered according to the level of rule-consciousness. Ganz's taxonomy is superior to Toulmin's in several ways: it does not label non-rule behavior as rules; the categories do not overlap; all hierarchical distinctions are predicated on the degree of rule consciousness; and, it includes a rule-behavior relationship not acknowledged by Toulmin's taxonomy. There is no parallel to "rule-fulfilling" behavior in Toulmin's list. His "rule-applying" behavior is similar to Ganz's "rule-following" behavior, and her "rule-accordance" behavior is like his "rule-following" behavior. Ganz has no parallel to Toulmin's "rule-reflective" behavior; she does not discuss behavior which critically evaluates rules. Because communicators do evaluate rules critically, Toulmin's taxonomy provides a useful label, and it should be included in any taxonomy.

Ganz's taxonomy is also useful because each level in the hierarchy requires additional evidence for determining a higher-order association between rules and behavior. To classify behavior according to Ganz's system, one must know the answers to three questions: (1) What are the operative rules in a given situation? (2) Does the actor know the rules? and (3) Does the actor refer to the rules when acting? One must know the answer to the first question to determine if the behavior is related to rules at any of the levels in the taxonomy. Rule-accordance and rule-following behavior require an affirmative answer to the second question, and rule-following requires an affirmative answer to the third question.

One determines what the rules are, according to Ganz, by locating the written inscription or oral utterance that has been adopted as the rule. For a rule to be adopted, the appropriate means must "have been taken by the appropriate people so that an utterance or inscription specifies what counts as correct or incorrect procedure for some activity."[14] Precisely what the appropriate means are and who the appropriate people are is not completely clear, but Ganz's examples imply formal adoption, for example, the adoption of legal rules or the rules of a game. A rule does not exist in Ganz's system unless it has been articulated and adopted. These criteria are met in the rule-accordance and rule-following conditions inasmuch as the actor must be able to articulate the rule s/he has adopted. But in order to label behavior "rule-fulfilling," one must identify the rule independent of the actor.

For Ganz, the dilemma of identifying the rule that is relevant to "rule-fulfilling" behavior is resolved by looking for physical evidence of a rule, that is, an inscription or utterance of the rule by "appropriate people." In addition to the problem of trying to determine who are appropriate people, this solution is also troublesome for communication scholars, because communication rules rarely appear in print. Nor are they often a topic of conversation. But as argued in Chapter 2, there are implicit communication rules. One major weakness of Ganz's taxonomy is that it cannot incorporate relationships between implicit rules and behavior.

Ganz's taxonomy is also inadequate in one other regard. It assumes that all rule-related behavior is also rule-compliant. However, noncompliance with a rule is also rule-related behavior. An adequate taxonomy of rule-related behavior must take into account both rule-compliant and rule-noncompliant behavior. Ganz's and Toulmin's taxonomies both fail to acknowledge noncompliant behavior as rule-related. Peter Collett's taxonomy of rule-related behavior includes both rule-compliant and rule-noncompliant behavior.

	Person does not know the rule	Person knows the rule
Person's behavior does not accord with the rule	A	C
Person's behavior does accord with the rule	B	D

FIGURE 4.1: Collett's Taxonomy of Rule-Related Behavior

COLLETT'S TAXONOMY

Peter Collett identified a four part taxonomy of rule-related behavior. His scheme is depicted in Figure 4.1.[15]

In situation A, the person is ignorant of a rule and his/her behavior does not comply with it. In situation B, the person is unaware of a rule, but his/her behavior is nonetheless consistent with it. Collett argued that in B, the behavior is not guided by the rule but is merely "rule-fitting." This category is similar to Ganz's "rule-fulfilling" category. In situation C, the person knows the rule, but his/her behavior does not comply with it, whereas in D, the actors know a rule and his/her behavior is in accord with it.

In C and D, the actor may or may not make conscious reference to a rule in acting; thus, Collett's taxonomy will not allow one to distinguish between rule-violations and rule-mistakes, or between following a rule consciously and subconsciously. Collett acknowledges that these distinctions may be worth making, but his taxonomy is not helpful in this regard. He does not discuss rule-related behavior that varies in rule consciousness. Further, his taxonomy fails to discuss rule-reflective behavior. Finally, Toulmin's and Ganz's taxonomies provide labels for various types of rule-related behavior, whereas Collett's scheme lacks these useful labels.

By combining the strengths of Toulmin's, Ganz's, and Collett's taxonomies, it is possible to construct a taxonomy of rule-related behavior that takes into account: (1) various levels of rule-consciousness; (2) explicit and implicit rules; (3) rule-compliant and rule-noncompliant behavior; and (4) rule-reflective behavior.

A Proposal for an Alternative Taxonomy

The taxonomy offered here incorporates the strengths of Toulmin's, Ganz's, and Collett's categories, and avoids their faults. It is structured on a continuum of rule-consciousness in acting. Rule-consciousness is the degree to which actors are aware of the rule in acting. It can range from subconscious, tacit knowledge to conscious reflection on the merits of the rule before acting. Rule-consciousness was chosen as the criterion variable to distinguish between levels of rule-related behavior because: (1) this variable affects one's ability to predict and explain rule-related behavior, and (2) establishing different levels of rule-consciousness requires different supporting evidence. In addition to varying levels of rule-consciousness, the taxonomy presented here includes both compliant and non-compliant behavior.

The taxonomy, which is organized from the most conscious rule-compliant behavior to the most conscious rule-noncompliant behavior, may be viewed as a nine-point continuum. Figure 4.2 illustrates this continuum.

Each step in the continuum will be explained in turn by beginning with rule-absent behavior and then moving toward the most conscious rule-compliant behavior; then noncompliant behavior will be discussed from the least conscious to the most conscious. This procedure was chosen because as one moves away from the center of the continuum toward the outer edges, more evidence is needed to establish a particular relationship between rules and behavior. It is important to remember that at each level, except rule-absent, this taxonomy assumes the existence of a rule and then compares that rule to behavior. To identify rules from behavior, one must use the system identified in Chapter 3.

RULE-ABSENT BEHAVIOR

Rule-absent behavior fails to exhibit one or more of the properties of rule-related behavior. Because a rule prescribes what behavior is obligated, preferred, or prohibited under certain conditions, rule-related behavior must be controllable, recur

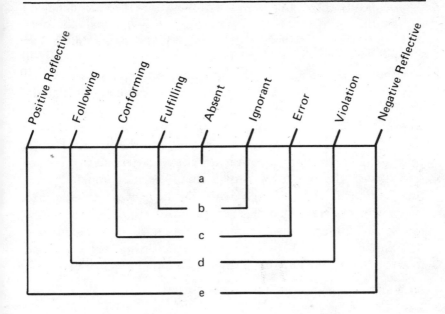

Key

a: noncontrollable, noncriticizable, or noncontextual
b: rule-governed, but no knowledge of the rule
c: tacit knowledge of a rule
d: conscious knowledge of a rule
e: conscious knowledge, plus evaluation of a rule

FIGURE 4.2: Rule-Related Behavior

under similar conditions (contextual), and be subject to evaluation (criticizable). Behavior that fails to meet any one of these
criteria is rule-absent behavior. Toulmin's "as a rule" category
corresponds to "rule-absent" behavior.

RULE-FULFILLING BEHAVIOR

If a person's behavior corresponds to a specific rule, stated,
written, or hypothesized by someone other than the actor, it is
rule-fulfilling behavior. The person's behavior may fulfill the
rule by accident, by imitation, or by design. For example, one
may observe that a particular graduate student addresses all

professors by "Dr." plus last name. We know that this behavior
fulfills the rule which specifies those of lower status should
address those of higher status by title plus last name, but it may
be that this particular student does not know the rule tacitly
or explicitly. S/he may use the last name only because s/he does
not know the first name; s/he may be imitating the behavior
of others; s/he may use the address form to establish distance;
so s/he uses a consistent form or s/he may use the form for some
so s/he uses a consistent form; she may use the form for some
other reason. In observing that a behavioral regularity is consistent with the prescription of a rule, one may conclude that
the behavior fulfills the rule. However, more evidence is needed
if one wants to claim that the rule had some impact on the behavior. Rule-fulfilling behavior corresponds to Ganz's category by
the same name, to what Collett calls "rule-fitting" behavior, and
to what Raymond D. Gumb calls "rule-satisfying" behavior.[16]

RULE-CONFORMING BEHAVIOR

If a person's behavior corresponds to the specifications of a
rule and if that person has tacit knowledge of that rule's prescriptive force but s/he does *not* refer to the rule while conforming
to it, the behavior is rule-conforming. By referring to a rule, I
mean, at a minimum, mentally noting it and consciously making
sure one's behavior is consistent with it. (What kind of evidence
a researcher needs to conclude that the actor took mental note
of the rule in acting will be discussed later in the section on rule-
following behavior.) In rule-conforming behavior, rules influence
behavior on a less conscious level than in rule-following behavior.
One need only have a tacit knowledge of what is appropriate.
The rule-related behavior may have become so habitual that
one acts without thinking. A rule influences behavior at a tacit
level in rule-conforming behavior.

Communicators may demonstrate their tacit knowledge of a
rule in a number of ways: (1) the actor's ability to verbalize the
rule; (2) the actor's ability to distinguish appropriate from inappropriate behavior; (3) extensions; (4) negative sanctions of
deviant behavior and actors; and (5) repairs. The advantages
and disadvantages of each measurement will be evaluated.

Verbalization. Ganz argues that if a communicator knows a rule, s/he must be able to articulate it.[17] Other scholars maintain verbalization is not the only means by which one can determine if someone knows a rule.[18] Max Black points out that even when pushed, actors are not always able to articulate rules they know. For example, chess players know that no two pieces may occupy the same square simultaneously, but few will state that as a rule of chess when asked to give a complete list of rules.[19] Similarly, communicators do not always seem able to state the rules that influence their behavior. For example, communicators may be able to utter grammatical sentences such as "Will Mary have left?" but probably few could articulate the rule$_{(05)}$:

R$_{(05)}$: "Given a sentence whose first element is Q, move the first auxiliary verb in that sentence to the left of the subject NP."[20]

If an actor can articulate a rule for his/her behavior, it is safe to conclude that the behavior is rule-conforming. But if an actor cannot articulate it, one cannot automatically conclude the behavior was not rule-conforming; an actor may be able to indicate his/her knowledge of the rule in another manner.

Appropriate Versus Inappropriate Behavior. If the actor knows the rule, then s/he should be able to distinguish correct and preferred behavior from incorrect or less-preferred behavior.[21] However, communicators may not be sufficiently conscious of alternative behaviors to be able to generate examples by themselves. Therefore, researchers may have to provide examples for the comparisons. However, even when researchers provide examples of what are rule-compliant and rule-noncompliant behaviors, actors may be hesitant to admit one behavior is correct or preferred and the other is incorrect or not preferred. (See Chapter 3 for more details on this phenomena.) If an actor's behavior complies with a rule and the actor can make judgments about appropriateness, then one can conclude that the behavior is rule-conforming. But if the actor cannot make such judgments, the researcher may be able to secure other evidence of the actor's tacit knowledge.

Extension. One indirect method of demonstrating that a speaker knows a rule is to indicate that the speaker extends the behavioral prescriptions of the rule to similar situations.[22] This extension may be manifested in the actor's behavior in recurring interactions with others, or it may be demonstrated in an artificial setting designed to measure one's ability to extend the rule. (See Chapter 3 for a discussion of Berko's method for measuring the extension of linguistic behavior.)

If communicators are conforming to rules, their behavior should be repeated under similar circumstances, but this evidence is not sufficient to conclude that the behavior is rule-conforming. Communicators may replicate their behavior under certain circumstances for reasons other than trying to conform to rules. (See Chapter 3.) Extension evidence strengthens the argument that the behavior is rule-conforming, but it is insufficient; it must be combined with one of the other measures of tacit knowledge.

Negative Sanction. Communicators may demonstrate their tacit knowledge of a rule's prescriptive force by imposing negative sanctions on deviating behavior and actors.[23] To claim that a behavior is rule-conforming, one must demonstrate tacit knowledge of the rule by the actors observed; therefore, the negative sanctions must be for their own deviations, or if for the deviations of others, the deviations must be of behaviors that actors perform consistently in similar contexts. Deviations from rules are not always sanctioned. (See Chapter 3.) Therefore, the absence of negative sanctions does not necessarily mean that the behavior is not rule-conforming; researchers can look for other evidence of tacit knowledge like repairs of deviations.

Repair. One alternative to asking someone directly to evaluate behavior and/or actors associated with that behavior is to infer their attitudes by observing not only the regularities of their own behavior, but also their repair behavior.[24] In rule-conforming behavior, deviations from regularities should be corrected in the direction of rule-compliance. Since all rule deviations are not repaired (see Chapter 3), an unrepaired deviation does not necessarily mean that the behavior is not rule-conforming. One may rely on one of the other types of evidence to argue that the behavior is rule-conforming. If, however, all of the possible indicators of tacit knowledge are absent, then the researcher should label the behavior rule-fulfilling rather than rule-conforming.

Summary. Conforming to rules is a subconscious act. To conform with a rule, one must give some indication that s/he has a sense of what is appropriate behavior and his/her behavior must conform to that sense of appropriateness. The minimum evidence needed to conclude that the behavior is rule-conforming is that: (1) a behavior must be compliant with the prescriptions of a rule and (2) the actor must indicate tacit knowledge of the prescriptive force of the rule by (a) verbalizing the rule, (b) correctly judging behavior as approriate or inappropriate according to it, or (c) demonstrating his/her ability to extend the application of the rule, plus negatively sanction or repair deviations. Confidence that a rule exists increases with the amount of evidence provided, but, if these two criteria are met, the absence of additional evidence should not lead to the conclusion that the behavior is not rule-conforming.

The term *rule-conforming* as it is used here is parallel to Toulmin's "rule-following" and similar to Ganz's "rule-accordance." However, it also includes conforming to both implicit and explicit rules, whereas Ganz's term refers only to rules that the actor can articulate. The narrow focus of Ganz's category was the reason for rejecting her label. Toulmin's term did not seem appropriate, because "following" signifies a higher level of consciousness than is implied by "rule-conforming" behavior. "Rule-following" is a label reserved for the next level in the hierarchy.

RULE-FOLLOWING BEHAVIOR

In following a rule, a communicator's behavior must be consistent with the specifications of a rule, s/he must have conscious knowledge of a rule, and s/he must consciously make sure that his/her behavior complies with it. To conclude that behavior is the result of the following a rule, one must be able to provide all of the evidence needed for rule-conforming behavior, plus additional indicators. Communicators must be able to articulate the rule they followed, and there must be some evidence that they referred to the rule when making a conscious choice. Oral or written references to the rule given as a reason or justification before, during, or after a behavior may be taken as evidence that it was rule-following behavior.

Rule-following behavior differs from rule-conforming behavior in a number of ways. It is a more conscious application of a rule; it requires that an actor know precisely what behavior is correct or preferred according to a rule; tacit knowledge of appropriateness is not sufficient; and, the actor must know that his/her behavior is the result of following a rule.

"Rule-following" behavior, as it is used here, is consistent with Ganz's use of the term, and it is similar to Toulmin's "rule-applying" category.

POSITIVE RULE-REFLECTIVE BEHAVIOR

This type of behavior requires all of the criteria for rule-following behavior, plus one added dimension. In positive rule-reflective behavior, the actor must evaluate the rule itself. S/he must determine whether the rule is a valuable rule. For example, does it encourage ethical, just, or elevated behavior? If one concludes that the rule is valuable and should be followed and s/he complies with it, his/her actions may be labeled positive rule-reflective behavior.

Four ways in which behavior may be positively associated with rules have been examined: rule-fulfilling, rule-conforming, rule-following, and positive rule-reflective behavior. At each successive level, behavior has complied with rules with increasing consciousness. However, one may also consciously or unconsciously not comply with a rule. Therefore, four terms for non-compliant-rule behavior will be offered as the parallels to the compliant labels.

RULE-IGNORANT BEHAVIOR

If a person's behavior fails to fulfill a rule because s/he is unaware of it, the behavior is rule-ignorant behavior. To label an action rule-ignorant behavior, the researcher must demonstrate that it does not comply with a rule and that the actor is unfamiliar with a rule. The actor should be unable to articulate it, s/he should be unable to distinguish correct and preferred behavior from incorrect or not preferred, s/he should not evaluate those who follow it any differently from those who do not follow it, and s/he should not view negative sanctions of his/her behavior as reasonable. Thomas S. Frentz and Thomas B. Farrell present dialogue(01) as an illustration of what happens when rules are not shared or one communicator is ignorant of the other speaker's rules. In this case, speaker A gets interrupted. However, A's criticism of B's interruption and B's acceptance of the criticism as legitimate (indicated by "Sorry") and his/her attempt to justify the deviation from the rule all seem to indicate that B is not ignorant of turn-taking rules, but rather that s/he has failed to comply with them.

Dialogue(01):

A: You see, we could introduce this thing with a quote from McBowis and. . . .

B: McBowis! Are you crazy? I refuse to be associated with that turkey!

A: Hey! Why don't you let me finish?

B: Sorry. Go ahead. It's just that you have to draw the line somewhere.[25]

Communicators who accept negative sanctions of their behavior without indicating that they were previously unaware of the rule (e.g., they do not say something like "Oh, I didn't know that was the rule") should not be viewed as being ignorant of the rule or not sharing the rule. Rather, if their behavior does not comply with the rule and if they view negative criticisms as legitimate, as in dialogue(01), then their behavior should be viewed as rule-error or rule-violation behavior.

RULE-ERROR BEHAVIOR

An inadvertent or unconscious failure to comply with a rule when one has either implicit or partial knowledge of a rule or a deviation from rules without conscious reference to rules is rule-error behavior. Under these conditions, one's behavior may not comply with a rule for two reasons: (1) inadequate knowledge or (2) inadvertent noncompliance due to forgetfulness, inattention, or the like. If a communicator's action is rule-error behavior, it will be inconsistent with a rule, the communicator will acknowledge his/her error if it is pointed out to him/her, and s/he should be able to demonstrate rule-knowledge similar to that of the person whose behavior is rule-conforming.

RULE-VIOLATION BEHAVIOR

To violate a rule, a communicator's behavior must be inconsistent with a rule, an actor must know the rule, and s/he must consciously make sure his/her behavior does not comply with it. Rule-violation behavior is as conscious as rule-following behavior, and it requires the same kind of evidence, except the behavior is noncompliant rather than compliant. Rule-violations may occur for a number of reasons. For example, one may be purposively rude when one wants to be disrespectful or incite conflict; one may be purposively unclear when clarity may cause conflict; one may lie when honesty may be incriminating.

NEGATIVE RULE-REFLECTIVE BEHAVIOR

Negative rule-reflective behavior requires the same activities and consciousness as positive rule-reflective behavior. The only difference is that an actor concludes that a rule is not valuable and s/he chooses to reject and violate it.

Implications of the System of Rule-Related Terms

In the beginning of this chapter, rule-guided and rule-governed behavior were contrasted; now that a hierarchy of rule-related behavior has been presented, these terms can be further explored with regard to the hierarchy. Rule-guided behavior may be rule-reflective (positive and negative), rule-following, rule-conforming, and rule-violation behavior. Rule-fulfilling and rule-ignorant behavior cannot be rule-guided behavior because the actor does not know the rule, and rule-error behavior is not rule-guided because the actor does not consider the rule in acting. These distinctions are important because if one wishes to explain behavior in terms of rules the behavior must be some form of rule-guided behavior. (See Chapter 6 for more details on the explanatory power of rules.)

With the exception of rule-absent behavior, every other term in the hierarchy may be analyzed from a rule-governed perspective. To identify the rules that govern a situation, one may utilize the communicator's perception, ask for a majority vote (e.g., official rules of a group), or appeal to an authority (e.g., prescriptive grammarians, Emily Post). If the rules of someone other than the communicator are viewed as the source for determining which rules govern the situation and the rules which guided the communicator's behavior differ from the governing rules, then one should compare these two sets of rules to determine the source of difference. It would be useful to know whether an actor deviated from the governing rules because s/he was ignorant of them (e.g., s/he assumed different rules were operative); s/he forgot or confused them (e.g., s/he knows different rules are operative, but s/he continues to use the rule s/he knows best—for example, speakers learning a new language or dialect); s/he chose to violate the rules (e.g., s/he was angry and did not want to comply with the rules); or s/he did not value the rules and chose to guide his/her behavior by different rules (e.g., the feminist who rejects traditional sex-role rules).

Eleven rule-related terms have been discussed: the nine part hierarchy and *rule-governed* and *rule-guided.* This system of rule-related terms provides several advantages for research and theory construction from a rules perspective:

(1) Rule-related behavior is distinguished from rule-absent behavior.

(2) Distinguishing between rule-guided and rule-governed behavior allows for a comparison between the two.

(3) The taxonomy recognizes that both compliant and noncompliant behavior may be rule-related behavior, and it gives the researcher labels for discussing both types of relationships.

(4) Various gradients of rule-related behavior are labeled according to the degree of rule consciousness. These labels may be important for several reasons. Because each label corresponds to certain kinds of evidence, researchers may indicate the kinds of relationships their evidence provides. For example, if all one has is a rule and some behavior but no test of the actor's knowl-

edge or conscious use of the rule, then a researcher can claim only that the behavior does or does not fulfill the rule. In order to claim a stronger relationship between the rule and the behavior, a researcher needs additional evidence. The labels may also be useful in trying to explain evaluations of behavior. For example, one might expect that rule-violation would be more negatively sanctioned than rule-ignorance.

Chapter 5

METHODOLOGICAL APPROACHES

Communication research from a rules perspective is designed to identify communicative rules, to specify relationships between rules and behavior, and to provide explanation, prediction, and possibly the control of behavior. Such research has utilized various methodologies, including self-reflection, survey, naturalistic observation, participant observation, quasi-experimentation, and experimentation. This chapter evaluates the comparative strengths and weaknesses of each of these methods in identifying rules and specifying relationships between rules and behavior. The role of rules research in providing explanation, prediction, and control of behavior will be discussed in Chapter 6 under the heading of the criteria of scientific knowledge.

In examining how rules—prescriptions that indicate what behavior is obligated, preferred, or prohibited under certain conditions—may be identified through self-reflection, survey, naturalistic observation, participant observation, quasi-experiments, and experiments, the comparative advantages and disadvantages of each method will be considered. Examples of relevant research from each method will be presented. In some instances, research will be cited in which no formal rule is identified. In these cases, the type of rules that might be inferred from the research will be presented.

Self-reflection

One of the most common methods for inferring rules from behavior involves self-reflection. In self-reflection research scholars rely on the personal experience of native speakers. In many cases, this means that researchers draw upon their own experiences and/or the experiences of their associates. Researchers use their experience to construct communicative interactions on paper, and they infer the rules from these hypothetical dialogues. The method has been associated with speech act theory because researchers using it have focused on rules for performing particular acts, but the method need not be limited to such rules.[1]

ALTERNATIVE LABELS

The method has been known by alternative names: (1) intuition,[2] (2) linguistic case study,[3] and (3) ordinary language methodology.[4] These labels were avoided because they connote images that are not implied by "self-reflection." Intuition is often thought of as a mystical, possibly irrational process. Self-reflection research is neither mystical nor irrational; scholars may systematically consider perceptions of previous experiences; they may consciously draw upon their recollections of past behavioral interactions, or they may contemplate behavioral exchanges in hypothetical encounters. They are not engaged in fictional composition. Their aim is to formulate illustrative anecdotes of real-life experiences.

The phrase *linguistic case study* is too vague. It could refer to the linguistic behavior of a single individual, group, organization, or so on. Joseph N. Cappella defined *linguistic case study* as the use of a small class of linguistic examples to determine the principles of the set. This definition seems unacceptable for the purpose of this chapter because a "small class of data" could be collected by a number of methods.

The phrase *ordinary language methodology* seems equally imprecise. It could refer to any method investigating ordinary rather than mathematical language. "Self-reflection," on the other hand, more clearly identifies the source of the data.

RESEARCH EXAMPLES

Several scholars have utilized the self-reflection method for identifying rules. For example, John R. Searle has used it to explicate the rules for promising; H. Paul Grice has outlined the rules (maxims) of conversational implicature; Robert E. Nofsinger has laid out rules for a demand ticket; and Thomas S. Frentz and Thomas B. Farrell have presented the rules for a delay game.[5] Below are some sample rules drawn from the research examples cited above. In addition, sample dialogues have been provided to help illustrate the rule.

Dialogue$_{(01)}$:

H: I asked you to do the windows.

S: I promise to do them tomorrow.

$R_{(01)}$: "A promise is to be uttered only if the hearer (H) would prefer the speaker's (S) doing some future act (A) to his not doing A, and S believes H would prefer S's doing A to his not doing A."[6]

Dialogue$_{(02)}$:

A: Is Jones a good student?

B: His handwriting is good.[7]

$R_{(02)}$: "Do not say what you believe to be false."[8]

Dialogue$_{(03)}$:

A: Guess what?

B: What?

A: Mary had her baby. (Z)

*$R_{(03)}$: "A wishes to have the floor to say Z to B, and wishes (or is willing) to be obligated to say Z to B."[9]

Dialogue$_{(04)}$:

A: Could I have a drink of water?

B: Mark, it's bedtime.

A: But I'm thirsty.

B: Really?

A: Yes.

B: Just a second, I'll get it.[10]

R$_{(04)}$: "Given question/request for basic need fulfillment, it is not only polite, but obligatory as institutionally defined responsibility that parents fulfill such requests for their children."[11]

Dialogue$_{(05)}$:

A: Going to be working at the office?

B: The kids are sick.[12]

*R$_{(05)}$: "If A asks a question, QS$_1$, and B responds with a proposition —if S$_2$ then ES$_1$—then if it is plausible for A to believe S$_2$, B is heard as asserting that the antecedent, S$_2$, is true; and from this is inferred B's answer to A, ES$_1$."[13]

Rules like *R$_{(03)}$ and *R$_{(05)}$ came under attack in Chapter 2 for not being rules; *R$_{(03)}$ is a presupposition to a rule, and *R$_{(05)}$ is an interpretation of behavior. Neither one of them prescribes behavior. This problem, however, is not inherent in the self-reflection method; rather, it is contingent upon the conceptualization and structure of the rules. Behavioral rules can be written for dialogues$_{(03)}$ and $_{(05)}$. Although the other three rules are not written in the if-then format, they could be rewritten according to that form.

ADVANTAGES

There are several advantages to the self-reflection method. Most of these advantages stem from the ease of data "collection." As daily participants in conversations, native speakers (especially trained ones) have a wealth of knowledge about how conversation operates. It is from this knowledge that researchers construct rules.

Access to Communicative Behavior. The self-reflection method is particularly useful in the construction of rules for less frequent communicative behavior. For example, in analyzing rules for indirect answers, Nofsinger demonstrated the utility of his "rules" in explaining communicative interactions that are probably part of every communicator's experience, but may not be easily observed every day. Dialogue$_{(06)}$ through dialogue$_{(08)}$ are three of his examples of indirect answers to questions.[14]

Dialogue(06):

A: Going to be working at the office?

B: Is the Pope Catholic?

Dialogue(07):

A: Going to work at the office?

B: Do I dress up like this to mow the lawn?

Dialogue(08):

A: Are notebooks allowed during the final exam?

B: Are porcupines allowed in balloon factories?

Even if one assumes that a behavior occurs daily, for example, "promises," these behaviors may constitute one-thousandth of one's total utterances. Following a person all day, taping all of his/her remarks, transcribing them all, or even listening to them all to analyze the one or two promises may not be the most efficient means of studying specific speech acts. In contrast, native speakers have years of experience with these behaviors in interactions with numerous persons (not one person for one day in our example above), and they can probably judge what is acceptable or unacceptable behavior. In addition, the researchers' conclusions are always subject to the scrutiny of others, who compare them with their own experiences.

Rule Refinements. By constructing dialogue examples from one's desk, one can try out several dialogue variations in order to provide greater rule refinement or to specify the scope of the rule. Nofsinger, for example, provides four variations for answering questions indirectly: plausible antecedent, implausible antecedent, shared existential value, and contrasting existential value.[15] Even if Nofsinger had been able to follow enough native speakers around with tape recorders long enough to gain enough examples to claim questions can be answered indirectly, one must wonder how many years it would have taken to collect enough examples of the four variations to conclude they were each possible. The self-reflection method is a time-efficient method. It is based on years of experience, but the researcher begins with this experience when s/he attempts to identify the rules. S he does not decide to identify the rules and then spend years collecting data to find them.

Explication. Another advantage of the self-reflection method is that it simplifies the explication of rules. In naturalistic dialogue, a single turn at talk may involve the use of several rules (e.g., politeness, answer, status, and turn-taking). Hence, parceling out what behavior is the result of which rule may be troublesome, and examples may not demonstrate the principles a researcher wishes to illustrate as clearly as s/he would like. Further, manifestations of a rule in naturalistic dialogue may occur across turns at talk; hence, illustrating a point from such data may be a long process. Consider, for example, dialogue(05) in Chapter 3. In the conversation, Roger and Dan have been talking about the possible contributions of schizophrenics. The remarks of a third speaker, Ken, about abstract art, are ignored because he fails to show the relevancy of his remarks to the previous ongoing talk. The dialogue which fills a page was presented to help document a rule regarding conversational relevancy. If one was to construct a self-reflective example to support this rule, one could shorten the example by deleting behavior which was not directly related to the rule. When one creates one's own dialogues, they can be cleaned up and simplified in order to focus the reader's attention on the "relevant" variables.

DISADVANTAGES

Although the self-reflection methodology has made valuable contributions to the study of human communication, it is not without its faults. In fact, it has probably received the greatest criticism of all the methods. The criticism focused on five major issues: (1) the accuracy of the rules, (2) the type of the behavior prescribed by the rules, (3) the oversimplification of communicative processes, (4) the low parsimoniousness, and (5) the predictability of the rules.

Accuracy. Because the self-reflective method relies on personal perceptions, memory, reflection, and the creation of hypothetical dialogues rather than on actual behavior it has been argued that rules generated in this manner may reflect inaccurate folk-linguistics (common beliefs about language) rather than actual behavior.[16] For example, there is a folklinguistic belief that women talk more than men, but most research demonstrates that in mixed groups men speak longer.[17] If researchers had offered rules based on the above folklinguistic belief, inter- subjective agreement might have been high due to cultural con- ditioning, but the rule, nonetheless, would have been inaccurate because it would have been predicated on a presumed regularity that has not been demonstrated empirically.

In addition to creating rules based on folklinguistics, self- reflection might result in confusing rule-symptomatic and/or rule-allowance regularities with rule-compliant behavior; thus, researchers might erroneously construct rules for these regu- larities. Researchers need to demonstrate that not only will the proposed rule account for the regularity that is believed to exist but that this regularity also occurs because it is obligated, pre- ferred, or prohibited; in other words, s/he must demonstrate prescriptive force.

In self-reflective research, the evidence for rules often consists of a limited number of examples. In explicating the "demand ticket," Nofsinger presented twelve examples, and he utilized eight examples when he outlined the rules for indirect answers. He could have generated more examples, but without knowing how many examples out of what total number are accounted for by his rules, one has no way of knowing how typical or atypical his examples are. Rules supported by a handful of examples are always open to question by counter examples. When the con- clusions of researchers have been questioned, some have re- sponded, "Well, this conclusion is correct according to my dialect."[18] Such responses make it impossible to prove con- clusions false, or to test rules; hence the "rules" are of little scien- tific value. William Labov has argued that relying on one's intuition alone contributes little to theory construction.

> We return to the painfully obvious conclusion—obvious at least to those outside linguistics—that linguists cannot continue to produce theory and data at the same time. . . . It is now evident that the search for homogeneity in intuitive judgments is a failure. . . . In many ways, intuition is less regular and more difficult to interpret than speech. If we are to make good use of speakers' statements about language, we must interpret them in light of unconscious, unreflecting productions. Without such control, one is left with very dubious data indeed—with no clear relation to the communicative process we recognize as language itself.[19]

Even when scholars agree upon rules, it is still possible to question their judgment for speakers in general. Not only are the sample dialogues few in number, they also are often drawn solely from the limited population of academicians. One may ask legitimately whether the speech and rules of academicians should be the primary data for theories about human communication in general. In addition, the judgments of academicians are not always accurate. Christina Abdul-Ghani has reported that actual stress patterns in conversation differed from both linguistic theory about stress and intuitive judgments of linguists who marked, on a written copy of a conversation, where they thought stress had occurred in the original interaction.[20] Presumed rules generated by the self-reflection method should be tested against data from naturalistic interactions.

Uncommon, Obvious, or Trivial Rules. Rules which are generated via self-reflection have also been criticized on the grounds that they prescribe uncommon, obvious, or logically necessary behavior. Earlier it was pointed out that one of the advantages of the personal reference method is that it may allow one to write rules for behavior that may not occur very often. Some may view this as a disadvantage in that while these rules may explain unusual behavior, they will not be very useful for prediction and control. Donald P. Cushman argues that this kind of research is precise but antiseptic in that the scope conditions are so restricting that the rules only apply in limited cases.[21]

The criticism that the self-reflection method can produce only obvious and trivial rules is easily challenged. If the rules are so obvious, then native speakers in general would be able to cite the rules for promising, the demand ticket, answering indirectly, and so forth without reading the work of self-reflection scholars. It seems doubtful that they could. The printing, reprinting, and referencing of this research indicates that, at least among many scholars, the conclusions of Searle, Grice, and Nofsinger are not considered obvious or trivial.

Although the self-reflection method does not necessarily produce only obvious rules, it is possible that because this method relies on personal awareness it may not yield rules which are "known" only at a subconscious level. There may even be some resistance to acknowledging rules. This problem has been expressed well by Ronald D. Laing: "I have never come across anyone (including myself) who does not draw a line as to: *what may be put into words,* and, *what words what may be put into.* If my view is right, we at this moment may not know we have *rules against knowing about certain rules.*"[22]

One may expect rule scholars to be more open to the possibility that a behavior is the result of a rule, but there may be rules of which even they are unaware. Therefore, the self-reflection method may overlook rules which may be identified through other methods.

The self-reflection research of Robert Nofsinger has been accused of describing behavior which is logically necessary, rather than practically necessary or prescribed. Further, it has been initimated that this is characteristic of speech act research in general.[23] If something is logically necessary, rather than prescribed, then its status as a rule is questionable. Nofsinger's "rules" are thought to be logically necessary for four reasons: (1) he does not specify the degree of rule crystallization (i.e., how much agreement there is on the rule); (2) he does not specify the intensity of the rule (i.e., how powerful the prescriptive force is); (3) he uses the phrase "some invariant structure or *logic* underlies the process of conversation";[24] and (4) it is presumed Nofsinger is working with closed system.[25] Each of these reasons will be evaluated.

Indicating the crystallization and intensity of a rule provides more information about a rule than not specifying those qualities, but the absence of this information does not automatically mean that the behavior is logically necessary rather than prescribed.

It is quite possible that Nofsinger was using the term *logic* to refer to a set of rules. This interpretation would be consistent with his constant reference to rules. Actors may come to view the behavior by a rule as "logical" in the sense of being expected, but this is because the rule prescribes that behavior. For example, American English speakers consider it logical that a response to a question should follow it immediately, even if that response is "I can't answer that right now." But the Indians of the Warm Spring Reservation do not consider that logical behavior; logical behavior would be to respond after one had time to think about a question. This means questions may not be answered for hours, days, or even a week.[26] It is doubtful that Nofsinger was using logic in a mathematical sense, like "if A = B, and C = B, then A = C." He does not discuss the rules for a demand ticket as if they were logically necessary, but he does demonstrate their prescriptive force by illustrating what happens whey they are violated.

To argue that Nofsinger is operating in a closed system is to ignore the rules he identifies. His rules take into account at least two systems, that is, two interacting individuals. The behavior of these individuals is prescribed by rules, and if one or both of them follows or violates the rules, it will effect the behavior of the other. Nofsinger's rules for the demand ticket are obligatory rules rather than preferential rules, and this character of these rules may have contributed to the confusion. Behavior according to these rules is either correct or incorrect. Perhaps it was this dichotomy that led to the assumption that Nofsinger's rules operate in a closed system, but, in fact, they can be changed and they take into account more than one system.

Nofsinger fails to use open-systems terminology, and he is not very specific about the scope conditions of the rules. He may be accused of assuming greater generality than is warranted (if one provides counter examples, though the critics of his demand ticket rules did not), but he cannot be accused legitimately of working within a closed system perspective or of describing logically rather than prescriptively necessary behavior. Nofsinger's work, as well as the research of other self-reflection researchers, is aimed at explicating rules, that is, prescriptions for behavior and not logically necessary behavior.

Oversimplification. The self-reflection method has also been criticized on the grounds that it oversimplifies the communicative process. Researchers using this method often analyze their hypothetical dialogues independent of environmental constraints, which may influence the applicability of rules. Further, there is a tendency to assume a one utterance, one act, one rule, or set of rules (e.g., all the rules for making a promise) ratio.[27] As pointed out earlier, this assumption facilitates the illustration of a possible behavioral manifestation of a rule, but this simplification may also obscure the complexity of human communication. Perhaps a brief analysis of lines 3 and 4 in dialogue$_{(09)}$ will illustrate this problem.

Dialogue$_{(09)}$:
[This transcript is taken from the closing of a dialogue.]
(1) Jean: Okay.
(2) Mel: Okeydoke.
(3) Jean: Thank you/ / Mel. [Earlier in the conversation last names were used.]
(4) Mel: Thank you/ / Jean.
(5) Jean: Bye/ / Bye.
(6) Mel: Bye.[28]

The utterances in lines 3 and 4 are relatively simple remarks when compared with many conversational turns; nonetheless, these statements may be attributed to adherence to a number of different rules. $R_{(06)}$ through $R_{(10)}$ may be just some of the possible operant rules (the corresponding behavior is identified in parentheses).[29]

$R_{(06)}$: If one is concluding a conversation in which an exchange took place, then one should close the conversation expressing his/her appreciation. (Behavior: "Thank you.")

$R_{(07)}$: If one wishes to reduce social distance, then one should substitute a first name for title plus last name. (Behavior: "Mel.")

$R_{(08)}$: If one member of a conversation has indicated a desire to reduce social distance (Behavior: "Mel"), then it is preferable to reciprocate with a similar expression. (Behavior: "Jean.")

$R_{(09)}$: If one is actively participating in a conversation, then s/he should take his/her turn at the first available opportunity (Behavior: Overlaps [indicate by the double slash marks] of "Mel" at a transitionally relevant place [a space where a turn could end, i.e., "Thank you" could be considered a complete unit]).

$R_{(10)}$: If one party ignores a gesture to reduce social distance (Behavior: Overlap of "Mel"), then the other party should presume that the first party does not want to reduce social distance and s/he should not wait for a reciprocal gesture to reduce social distance but should honor rule$_{(09)}$. (Behavior: Overlap of "Jean.")

There are undoubtedly other rules, but surely the point has been made. Various rules can be inferred from what appears to be a rather simple, straightforward dialogue. Self-reflection research often ignores these complexities in order to explicate one rule for one act. This problem is not, however, inherent in the self-reflection method. In order to make any conversational data manageable, researchers consistently choose to analyze certain aspects of the data to the exclusion of other aspects. It may be that this is just more common or recognizable in self-reflection research where scholars make a concerted effort to simplify their examples.

Dialogue$_{(09)}$, however, illustrates another problem with self-reflection methodology. Typically, examples in self-reflection research stand in isolation; that is, without the benefit of linguistic and nonlinguistic environments. In isolation, it would be impossible to infer rule$_{(07)}$ from "Mel." It is essential that one know that Mel was previously addressed by his title plus last name. The isolation of self-reflection dialogues may make it difficult if not impossible for researchers to construct rules which are based on what has previously happened or what is expected to happen. Again, naturalistic dialogues may reveal regularities that are not present in the relatively short and restricted personal-reference dialogues.

Low Parsimoniousness and Predictability. David Kaufer criticizes the intuitive (his label) approach on three grounds: (1) no independent grounding, (2) low parsimoniousness, and (3) weak predictability.[30] The first criticism has already been discussed by pointing out that rules generated from this method are grounded in the experience of native speakers and subject to the intersubjective agreement of researchers. The last two criticisms need to be further explicated. Kaufer maintains that rules generated intuitively will be easy to find, but that it will be difficult to stop finding them.[31] He then demonstrates that the intuitive method is likely to result in a dictionary of rules, one for each behavior, which would describe rules in an ad hoc fashion but which would not predict future behavior on the basis of rules. He chooses to illustrate his point with one of Robert Nofsinger's rules for answering questions indirectly.

Nofsinger offered an implausible antecedent rule ($*R_{(11)}$) in order to explain why in dialogue$_{(10)}$ B's utterance is understood as a "no" answer to A's question.

Dialogue$_{(10)}$:

A: Going to be working at the office?

B: When hell freezes over I'll go work at the office.[32]

$*R_{(11)}$: "If A asks a question, QS_1, then B responds with a proposition—if S_2 then ES_1—then if it is not plausible for A to believe S_2, B is heard as asserting that S_2 is necessary for ES_1; and from this is inferred B's answer to A, not ES_1."[33]

Kaufer argues that while Nofsinger's rule adequately describes the inferential pattern used in the dialogue, the rule lacks predictive value. He then offers an example to illustrate the failure of $*R_{(11)}$ to predict the meaning of the mother's utterance in dialogue$_{(11)}$.

Dialogue$_{(11)}$:

Friend: Will Tommy ever go camping?

Mother: When Tommy is able to walk, he will go camping.[34]

Kaufer points out that $*R_{(11)}$ is based on an existential *impossibility* but that in dialogue$_{(11)}$ the inferences may be predicated on the *improbable*. Kaufer characterizes Nofsinger's rules as statements which describe ad hoc cases. He further maintains that such ad hoc statements could only result in a dictionary of rules, perhaps one rule for each behavior. To be of theoretical importance, rules must be predictive.[35]

Kaufer's examples and arguments are convincing; Nofsinger's rules seem to lack parsimoniousness and predictability. But is this an inherent failing of the personal-reference method, or can this failing be attributed to another factor? In Chapter 2 it was argued that Nofsinger's rules are not rules at all, but rather that they are explanations. They explain how a particular utterance can be understood as an answer to a particular question. As explanations for particular utterances, they have limited generalizability, and hence, low parsimoniousness and predictability. However, Nofsinger does present one behavioral rule, $R_{(12)}$, which is relevant to all of his interpretive "rules" and is pertinent to Kaufer's example, $R_{(12)}$, which was constructed via the self-reflection method and is both parsimoniousness and predictive.

$R_{(12)}$: "Do not say that which is pointless or spurious."[36]

In interpreting indirect answers, communicators assume that the speaker of an indirect answer is following $R_{(12)}$. Further, based on $R_{(12)}$, one can write a rule for answering questions indirectly which will predict all of Nofsinger's examples and Kaufer's counterexamples. Hence, it is possible to construct a parsimonious and predictive rule via the self-reflection method. $Rule_{(13)}$ might be such a rule:

$R_{(13)}$: If one wishes to answer a question indirectly, then one should utter a statement or question for which the existential value is known to the original questioner.

Unlike Nofsinger's interpretive rules, $R_{(12)}$ and $R_{(13)}$ prescribe behavior. $R_{(12)}$ and $R_{(13)}$ do not predict specific behaviors (e.g., "When hell freezes over, . . . ") but they do predict a certain type of answer, that is, one which is not pointless or spurious and one whose existential value is known. Nofsinger's explanation (interpretive "rules") for indirect answers can all be inferred from these behavioral rules. Nofsinger's explanations identify possible existential values (plausibility, implausibility, shared, and contrasted), and Kaufer adds another (improbability). It is possible that other researchers may refine our understanding of the various existential values from which a speaker may choose. These refinements will add to our knowledge, but they will not reduce the parsimoniousness or predictability of $R_{(12)}$ and $R_{(13)}$. Hence, while it may be true that Nofsinger's explanations (interpretive "rules") suffer from low parsimoniousness and weak predictability, it is not true that the self-reflection method inherently results in rules which are not parsimonious or predictive. How parsimonious and how predictive a rule is depends not on its method of construction but on its scope condition, its range and specificity.

QUALITY

The quality of personal reference research may be judged according to two criteria: (1) degree of intersubjectivity and

(2) the richness of the analysis. The validity of rules identified by the personal reference method has been predicated primarily upon whether or not other researchers agree with the conclusions drawn. Researchers should ask whether all and only promises, demand tickets, indirect answers, and so on can be performed by following the rules. If the answer is yes, there is greater confidence in the accuracy of a rule, but it should still be tested against naturalistic data. If the answer is no, a rule should be rewritten to accommodate the conflicting evidence. Further, confidence in the accuracy and generalizability of a rule would be increased if it was confirmed not only by researchers but also by communicators in general.

David Smith introduced the concept of "richness" as a means of evaluating research.[37] The term is somewhat elusive, but it may be thought of as providing two types of satisfaction: (1) a sense that the explanation is plausible, that there is no alternative explanation which would be superior, and that there is no disconfirming evidence and (2) a new sense of understanding and appreciation for the complexity of human communication. Self-reflection research which achieves intersubjective agreement and richness is valuable research.

SUMMARY

Researchers who use the self-reflection method to construct rules infer rules from their perceptions of what are appropriate and inappropriate communicative interactions. Its advantages stem from the ease of data collection, and they include: (1) the ability to construct rules for possible but perhaps less common communicative behavior, (2) the ability to try out rules on variations of hypothetical dialogues in order to refine the rule and its scope conditions, and (3) the ability to simplify examples in order to focus on certain aspects of communicative behavior. Disadvantages of the self-reflection method stem from the source of the data collection. The accuracy of the rules and the value (i.e., uncommon or trivial) of the behavior prescribed by the rule have been questioned. The criticism that the self-reflection method describes logically necessary rather than prescribed behavior was refuted. Other criticisms of the method (e.g., oversimplification, low parsimoniousness, and weak predictability) were shown not to be inherent in this method. The utility of rules generated by the personal reference method may be assessed by intersubjective agreement and the richness of the analysis.

Survey

Survey research consists of asking communicators what they believe are communication rules. Typically, this would involve questionnaires, but the data might also be acquired by interviewing native speakers. Rules research does not typically consist of only survey research; rather, data gathered from questionnaires or interviews is usually integrated with data collected by other means. However, it is possible to use the survey method by itself.

RESEARCH EXAMPLE

Carole Edelsky used the survey method in order to explicate the rules for talking like a lady.[38] Edelsky asked native speakers to indicate whether specific behaviors were more likely to be performed by men in general, women in general, or both men and women with equal likelihood. The behaviors Edelsky had her subjects respond to had been identified by Robin Lakoff as sex-linked or sex-neutral behavior.[39] The judgments of the respondents in Edelsky's study corresponded to Lakoff's assessments.

Edelsky does not state any formal rules, but she makes references to communicative competence rules, sociolinguistic and single versus complex rules. She reports that expressions like "adorable," "oh dear," and "my goodness" were categorically associated with females and that "I'll be damned" was categorically associated with males. These regularities might prompt one to write rules like $R_{(14)}$ through $R_{(17)}$.

$R_{(14)}$: If one is a male, then one must not say "adorable," "oh dear," or "my goodness."

$R_{(15)}$: If one is a female, then one must (should) say "adorable," "oh dear," or "my goodness."

$R_{(16)}$: If one is a female, then one must not say "I'll be damned."

$R_{(17)}$: If one is a male, then one must (should) say "I'll be damned."

Edelsky's research, however, does not permit one to determine if the perception of regularities she reports are perceived by her subjects to be the result of prohibitive rules like $R_{(14)}$ and $R_{(16)}$, or obligatory or preferential rules like $R_{(15)}$ and $R_{(17)}$, or some combination of them. It is also possible that $R_{(18)}$ and $R_{(19)}$ are the preferred rules but that women are allowed to be cutesy and men are allowed to use profane language more than women are.

$R_{(18)}$: If one is an adult, then one should not use cutesy phrases (e.g., "adorable," "oh dear," "my goodness").

$R_{(19)}$: If one wishes to be polite, then one should not use profane language (e.g., "I'll be damned").

Thus, the perceived regularities may only represent rule-allowance behavior rather than behavior prescribed by rules. Because Edelsky asked only whether men or women were more likely to say "X," and not whether they should or should not say "X," her research does not provide a measure of prescriptive force. In order to infer rules, researchers must ask if the behaviors are obligated, preferred, or prohibited.

ADVANTAGES VERSUS DISADVANTAGES

For the most part the advantages and disadvantages of the survey method are similar to those of the self-reflection method. This is because the survey method is essentially a self-reflection method which combines the reflections of several communicators. It might be argued that communication scholars may be more consciously aware of communication rules and sophisticated variations, since they are both users and researchers of communication. On the other hand, rules generated from the survey method may have more generalizability than rules created by academicians alone, since the survey method relies on the collective experience of more communicators.

There are, however, a few additional disadvantages to the survey methods. The survey method is slightly less time efficient than the self-reflection method, because the researcher must check out the validity of hypothesized rules with someone besides him/herself and that takes time. Probably the biggest disadvantage of the survey method is that it may produce only rules which are part of the collective conscious or "rules" which are based on folklinguistic beliefs. In addition, since the question-naire or interviewer asks certain questions or ask subjects to choose from a given list of alternatives, the research design may bias the kind of responses one gets. That is, in actual inter-actions, behavior different from the alternatives listed on the questionnaire may occur. Finally, as noted above, researchers need to construct a questionnaire that will allow them to answer two questions: (1) What are the behaviors which are likely to occur under what conditions? and (2) Are these behaviors obli-gated, preferred, or prohibited? The validity of the research findings is dependent on the ability of communicators in general to provide accurate answers on the questionnaire.

Naturalistic Observation

The naturalistic observational method consists of observing and recording (e.g., writing down, tape recording, transcribing) behavioral regularities and inferring rules from these regularities. In the observational method one may actually observe the com-municative behavior as it is orginally executed and/or one may watch a video tape, listen to an audio tape, and/or read a tran-script.

In this method the researcher exerts no control over the en-vironment or communication; s/he observes communication in its natural setting and s/he does not analyze any interaction in which s/he was directly involved. When the researcher's com-munication is part of the analysis, the method may be labeled "participant observation." If the researcher asks the communi-cators questions and if those answers are part of his/her analysis, then the method is either survey research or participant obser-vation. Researchers have not always made it clear whether or not their data included their own participation. Unless the re-searcher specifically indicated that his/her communicative behavior was included in the analysis, the study was counted here as an observational study.

ALTERNATIVE LABELS

Not only have researchers failed to always make their method explicit, but they also have often lumped naturalistic observation and participant observation together. Both methods have been associated with other labels: (1) anthropological case study,[40] (2) ethnography,[41] (3) ethnomethodology,[42] (4) conversational analysis,[43] (4) discourse analysis,[44] (6) survey,[45] and (7) naturalistic.[46]

Case study, which often refers to the investigation of a single person, seems to be an inappropriate reference for observational research because it rarely if ever considers the behavior of one person. Joseph N. Cappella defined anthropological case study as the attempt to develop the rules of one or more groups in their own cultural or social settings.[47] Studies that investigate a group, subculture, or culture are not any more or less case studies than experimental studies that utilize only college students to draw their conclusions. In either situation, the researcher utilizes the rules of a sample group in order to infer the rules of a population. Therefore, case study is a misleading label for observational research. *Anthropology* comes from the root words *antrops* for *man* and *logia* for *to speak*; hence, *anthropology* may be defined as a "discourse upon human nature" or more commonly "the science of man and mankind."[48] Therefore, the phrase *anthropological case study* is not very useful for distinguishing one methodology from another.

Similar problems occur with the labels *ethnography* and *ethnomethodology*. Both come from the Greek root *ethnos*, which means *nation*; in English, *ethno* means cultural group.[49] *Ethnography* is "the scientific description of nations or races of men, with their customs, habits and points of difference."[50] The ethnography of speaking is "concerned with the situations and uses, the patterns and functions, of speaking as an activity in its own right."[51] Harold Garfinkel, probably the most influential scholar of ethnomethodology, defines it as "the investigation of rational properties of indexical expressions and other practical actions as contingent ongoing accomplishments of organized artful practices of everyday life."[52] A slightly more comprehensible definition has been offered by Robert Bogdan and Steven J. Taylor: "Ethnomethodology refers not to research methods but rather to the subject matter of inquiry: How (the methodology by which) people make sense out of the situations in which they find themselves."[53] The definitions of both *ethnography* and *ethnomethodology* focus on the goal or the object of study rather than the method; either could be describing a goal of rules research, but neither specifies a method for getting there. Ethnographers and ethnomethodologists may use naturalistic observation as one of their methods, but they may also use other methods, including (1) interviewing, (2) participant observation, and (3) quasi experiments. Ethnography and ethnomethodology were not chosen as a method to be discussed in this chapter, because these terms are references to entire approaches rather than specific methods.

Conversational analysis and *discourse analysis* have been used fairly interchangeably,[54] though the latter is often thought of as more encompassing, referring to all forms of communication whereas the former is restricted to conversational behavior. Both of these labels were avoided because they refer to the object of study rather than the method. The data utilized in conversational analysis may be acquired by a variety of methods, naturalistic observation being only one of them.

Survey methods of research involve the use of questionnaires or interviews.[55] It is unclear why survey was used to describe naturalistic observation; the scholars who used this label did not provide a justification for their choice.[56] Utilization of questionnaires and interviews are appropriate procedures for survey research, and questions may be utilized less formally in participant observation; but these procedures are not part of naturalistic observation.

Naturalistic is a generic term for any research method which involves the investigation of "people, in the social settings which are part of their normal life activity without the manipulation by the investigator of the antecedent condition of behavior," for the purpose of comparing the consequence of various antecedents.[57] Naturalistic research may refer to observations with or without participation and possibly to studies where researchers compare various antecedents to presumed consequences without manipulating the antecedent (e.g., quasi experiments, which are explored more fully later in the chapter). Therefore, *naturalistic* by itself was considered too broad a term. *Observation* by itself is also too broad inasmuch as all methods involve some observations. However, it was hoped that the phrase *naturalistic observation* would connote the conditions under which the observations took place and that it would serve as a contrast to participant observation, connoting that in naturalistic observation the researcher did not participate in the communication exchanges analyzed.

RESEARCH EXAMPLES

The naturalistic observational method has been utilized to construct a number of different kinds of rules. For example, Emanuel A. Schegloff and Harvey Sacks have investigated the rules for adjacency pairs and preclosings; Schegloff has presented rules for telephone conversations and for summons and responses; Sacks, Schegloff, and Gail Jefferson have identified turn-taking rules; and Thomas S. Frentz and Thomas B. Farrell have explicated rules of propriety for discussing the Watergate affair with then President Richard M. Nixon.[58] All of these researchers utilized transcripts which were taken from audio tapes, and it would seem that none of them was physically present when the original dialogues took place; at least, the researchers did not indicate that they were present. However, researchers using this method could use audiovisual tape recording, and they could have been present. The comparative advantages of these different procedures will be considered in the section on data collection. Below are sample rules from the research examples on the naturalistic observational method listed above. In addition, sample dialogues have been provided to help illustrate the rules.

Dialogue(12):

A: How are you?

B: Fine, and you?

R(20): "Given the recognizable production of a first pair part of an adjacency pair on its first possible completion its speaker *should* stop and a next speaker *should* start and produce a second pair part from the pair type of which the first is recognizaably a member [emphasis added]."[59]

Dialogue(13):

A: Jonny?

B: Yeah.

A: Come home.

$R_{(21)}$: If one answers a summons, then one is *obligated* to listen to the summoner's next remark.[60]

Dialogue$_{(14)}$:

Terry: Pat, what do you think about the plan as outlined?

Pat: Well, I think we need to . . .

$R_{(22)}$: "For any turn, at the initial transition-relevance place of an initial turn constructional unit: If the turn-so-far is so constructed as to involve the use of a 'current speaker selects next' technique, then the party so selected has the right and is *obligated* to take next turn to speak, no others have such rights or obligations, and transfer occurs at that place [emphasis added]."[60]

Dialogue$_{(15)}$:

In the dialogue below, Dean (D) violates $R_{(23)}$ by making implicit knowledge of the President (P) explicit.

D: The reason that I thought we ought to talk this morning is because in our conversations, I have the impression that you don't know everything I know and it makes it very difficult for you to make judgments that only you can make on some of these things and I thought that ——

P: In other words, I have to know why you feel that we shouldn't unravel something?

D: Let me give you my overall first.

P: In other words, your judgment as to where it stands, and where it will go.

D: I think that there is no doubt about the seriousness of the problem we've got. We have a cancer within, close to the Presidency, that is grow. . . .[62]

$R_{(23)}$: "P, as a cooperative actor on a crisis management team, must be presumed to share the same knowledge as other institutional actors. But the knowledge P is presumed to have *can never be* explicitly articulated; for to do so would legally implicate him [emphasis added]."[63]

Not all of the rules were expressed in the if/then format, but each of them could be. Each of them prescribes behavior which is obligated, preferred, or prohibited; words which mark the prescriptive force of the rule have been italicized. One of the rules, ($R_{(22)}$), also described a regularity: "transfer occurs at that place."

If the statement described only a common regularity which is not prescribed by a rule, it should not be part of the rule. If, however, the regularity is related to the rule, then the authors need to insert either "must" or "should" before "occur."

The process of inferring rules from naturalistic observation involves two research phases: (1) data collection and recording and (2) data analysis.[64] Observational data may be collected and recorded by writing down communicative behavior as it occurs, by taping remarks to one's self as one observes the behavior, by recording the interaction via electronic equipment (e.g., video or audio-video tape recorder), by transcribing the behavior which was recorded electronically, or by some combination of these methods. Data analysis involves the process of inferring rules from the data collected.

ADVANTAGES

There are four advantages to inferring rules from behavior collected via naturalistic observation: (1) the rules are inferred from actual interactions, (2) the rules may be more generalizable, (3) tacit rules may be identified, and (4) the data may be quantifiable.

In naturalistic observations, the behavior is actual rather than self-constructed as in the self-reflective method. Hence, it is assumed that the rules inferred from naturalistic observational data are more likely to reflect actual communicative rules than folklinguistic rules. Further, if a naturalistic observation includes actors who are not academicians, the rules inferred may have greater generalizability than the rules generated by a researcher via self-reflection.

Many of the advantages and disadvantages of the self-reflection method are just reversed in the naturalistic observational method. Naturalistic observations are more likely to involve common behavior inasmuch as the researcher must be able to observe it often enough to infer a rule. This aspect of the naturalistic observation method may result in only rules that generalize to many contexts. On the other hand, systematic observation and analysis of this more common data may also reveal regularities which are not part of one's conscious awareness (a necessary factor in self-reflection rules), and, therefore, perhaps less "obvious" rules may be discovered via the naturalistic observational method. For example, Edward T. Hall has identified proxemic rules by observing behavior, but he could not get native communicators to identify these rules.[65]

The naturalistic observational method has the potential for being quantifiable; that is, one can report when and how often a specific behavior occurred, or did not occur, and/or whether nonoccurrences were repaired, sanctioned, or resulted in rule changes. Descriptive and inferential statistics may be part of the research report. For example, Schegloff reports that a particular behavior occurred for all but one case in roughly 500 cases, and Starkey Duncan utilizes inferential statistics to support hypothesized rules. Sacks et al. report how violations of turn-taking rules get repaired, and Frentz and Farrell argue that John Dean's violation of rules for presidential discussions about Watergate both sealed the fate of the Watergate episodes and redefined the power relationships.[66] Information about responses to rule deviations is essential to assessing the prescriptive force, but these reports would have been more useful if the researchers would have demonstrated that the deviations occurred less often than conformity to the rule.

The naturalistic observation method "forces" a researcher to report and hopefully account for conflicting evidence. Although the unscientific researcher may suppress messy data, s/he cannot simply dismiss troublesome examples as the result of faulty memory or poor imagination as s/he might if s/he were constructing rules from self-reference data. Having to contend with conflicting evidence can be useful in refining a rule. Schegloff's work with telephone conversations and summons and responses serves as a good case in point.[67]

Schegloff offered $R_{(24)}$ as a general rule of telephone conversations, but dialogue$_{(16)}$ contradicts this general rule inasmuch as the caller rather than the answer speaks first.

Dialogue$_{(16)}$:

(Police make call.)

(Receiver is lifted, and there is a one second pause.)

Police: Hello.

Other: American Red Cross.

Police: Hello, this is Police Headquarters . . . er, Officer Stratton
etc.[68]

$R_{(24)}$: If one telephones another person, then the answerer speaks
first.[69]

What is important in this example is that rather than dismissing
this case as deviant and offering a separate analysis for it,
Schegloff discussed replacement rules for $R_{(24)}$. $R_{(25)}$ and $R_{(26)}$
prescribe all of the regularities described by $R_{(24)}$, and they prescribe the behavior observed in dialogue$_{(16)}$; thus, the new rules
have greater generalizability than $R_{(24)}$.

$R_{(25)}$: If a summons has been answered, then the summoner must
not repeat the summons.[70]

$R_{(26)}$: If a summons is not answered but the summoner has reason
to believe the summoned person is or will be shortly available
and s/he wants to talk with the summoned person, then s/he
should repeat the summons.[71]

The one second pause may be taken as the police officer's
attempt to comply with $R_{(25)}$; he seems to be waiting for an
answer to his summons (the phone ringing). The lifting of the
receiver sends a mechanical signal to the caller, indicating someone has been summoned, but it does not indicate the person
called is available for talk; hence the police officer repeats a
summons ("hello") in compliance with $R_{(26)}$. The response
"American Red Cross" functions as an answer and the summons-
response sequence is terminated. In self-reflection research,
"deviant" cases may or may not come to mind. In naturalistic
observation, they may or may not occur (note that this example
was one out of approximately 500); but when they do occur, they
may on occasion generate useful rule revisions as the above case
did for Schegloff's work.

The advantages of data analysis in the naturalistic observational method all stem from the method of data collection. One's
analysis may be predicated on naturally recurring behavior; it
may include empirical data, and it may reveal regularities that
are not part of one's conscious awareness but that generalize
across enough situations to result in an observable regularity.
These factors contribute to the quality of the analysis in that
they may reveal tacit rules of naturalistic interaction that are

supported by quantifiable evidence. Naturalistic observations have provided rich and varied data concerning communication.

DISADVANTAGES

In spite of its many advantages, there are also several disadvantages associated with behavioral data acquired via naturalistic observation, including (1) tedious, time-consuming work, (2) poor sampling, (3) incomplete or absent contextual information, (4) selective perception, (5) reactivity, (6) possible absence of evidence of prescriptive force, and (7) absence of control.

Time Consuming. Collecting enough data from naturalistic observations to infer rules can be a long and tedious process. Starkey Duncan reports that the time involved in making two nineteen-minute transcripts was "great, involving the better part of 2 academic years."[72] In explicating the "opening up of closings," Schegloff and Sacks relied on conversational materials they had "collected over the last several years."[73] Using Gail Jefferson's transcription system, which calls for a limited amount of nonverbal data, it may take a minimum of one hour per one minute of conversation for transcription.[74] The lengthy time needed for data collection may discourage researchers from using naturalistic observation, or cause them to take on projects of more limited scope.

Sampling. The amount of data collected for analysis is related to another problem, that of sampling. The more limited the number of conversational behaviors collected, the less confident the researcher can be in his/her inferences about what rules are related to observed regularities; perhaps the regularities observed are due to sampling error or to rule-symptomatic or rule-allowance behavior. Further, researchers have often collected naturalistic observational data in a somewhat haphazard fashion. That is, they collected data wherever and whenever it was convenient to collect data—on talk shows, in group therapy sessions, at police desks, in college classrooms, and so forth. They often fail to provide a rationale for why a particular conversational exchange should be recorded and analyzed.[75] If one assumes that what operates in one dialogue or group of dialogues is likely to occur in others, then any dialogue would suffice, but one

cannot assume universality; it must be demonstrated by specifying the various conditions under which the data were collected.
Sacks et al. claim that their rules hold true for all conversations.[76] This claim is based on their data and limited comparisons
with cross-cultural data. One is told that their data were "assem-
bled out of a substantial number of conversations."[77] But how
many conversations, under what conditions, or who the participants were is not revealed. The reader must accept on faith that
the sample conversations reflect a wide enough range of conversations that the researchers are justified in concluding that
their rules apply to all conversations. Their examples seem
impressive, but the authors offer no total number of occurrences
or comparative statistics, so again the reader must take on faith
that turn-taking behavior occurred with enough regularity to
warrant the rules proposed. If researchers reported the number
of conversations, the conditions surrounding their occurrence,
and the degree of regularity, scholars would be better able to
assess the soundness of the conclusions drawn.

The naturalistic observation method is often associated with
qualitative rather than quantitative procedures, hence very little
attention has been given to sampling procedures or statistical
analyses. However, these procedures need not be mutually exclusive. As already pointed out, some scholars (e.g., Duncan or
Schegloff) provide quantitative data and qualitative analysis.
William Labov's naturalistic observations have been praised for
the quality of his analysis and his ability to quantify the evidence
supporting his assertions and statistical analyses.[78] W. Barnett
Pearce has denounced the dichotomy of naturalistic observations
and statistical analyses.

> There is no inherent reason why the powerful quantitative tools
> of statistics and observation cannot be used in naturalistic study,
> yet those involved in studies of actors' meanings are frequently
> seen offended by quantitative procedures. . . . Obviously, there
> are limitations to the range of phenomena to which a particular
> method may be usefully applied, but such categorical renunci-
> ations are all too common and counterproductive.[79]

Contextual Information. The amount of contextual information about communicators and the specific environment varies
from study to study. For example, Sacks et al. provide no in-

formation about their interlocutors;[80] Schegloff and Sacks indicate that their speakers were adults who spoke American English, but they argue that these factors may be irrelevant.[81] Duncan, on the other hand, offers a five-paragraph description of the actors and the situation, plus a brief justification for the material selected.[82]

Schegloff and Sacks argue that descriptive data about inter-locutors may be misleading, in that they may lead researchers to conclude that rules hold for only certain groups—for example, adults speaking American English when the rule may have nothing to do with these factors. Therefore, they exclude such information from their data and analysis.[83] But such exclusions may give a false impression of universality. Susan U. Philip's research has raised some questions about the universality of turn-taking rules,[84] and Elinor O. Keenan has demonstrated that rules regarding information are not universal.[85] Before their work, it was assumed by some that there were universal rules for these phenomena.

Although it is possible that scholars may misuse contextual information, suppressing such information can only lead one to guess about the generalizability of the data collected, and its absence makes comparisons with other studies more difficult. Perhaps a compromise can be reached. Scholars could report demographic information and caution readers that until more research is done, it is not known whether or not these factors had any impact on the regularities observed. If cross-cultural research continues to demonstrate the same rules, then one may make claims about the degree of universality.

Poor sampling techniques and incomplete data are disadvantages of some of the previous research using the naturalistic observational method, but these disadvantages are not inherent in the method. Researchers can choose their dialogues more systematically, and they can specify the conditions under which the data were collected.

Selective Perception. The self-reflection method is greatly influenced by selective perception and memory. The naturalistic observation method controls for the possible inaccuracies produced by self-perception and memory by relying on observable behavior rather than contrived dialogues. However, naturalistic observation may still be influenced by selective perception. If one is recording the conversation by hand as it occurs, one may record one's perception of what occurred rather than what actually took place, and one will be unable to record all behavior, so selective perception may influence what is recorded. But even if one records the interaction via electronic media, one may overlook some relevant data, or selective perception may influence what is heard or said, or in the process of transcribing the interaction, some data may be left out or transcribed inaccurately.

Transcribing experience has revealed that even the most conscientious transcribers may hear grammatical utterances when the utterances were ungrammatical or they may hear different words or phrases. Transcribers are also sensitive to different aspects of communicative behavior. For example, some hear multiple stresses per utterance, whereas others hear only occasional stresses; some catch all pauses over .2 seconds; others hear only pauses of .9 seconds or more.[86] Further, not all sounds and motions appear on the transcript. It may not be physically feasible to include them; furthermore, the transcript may become unreadable due to the various notations and symbols. Therefore, transcribed versions of interactions represent something less than the total set of communicative behaviors.

The problem of selective perception, however, is not inherent in the naturalistic observational method. Any method that involves conversational data is susceptible to this problem. This disadvantage can be minimized by increasing the number of observers and transcribers and comparing observations and transcriptions for areas of agreement and disagreement. Leonard Hawes's research, for example, utilized three people in order "to insure multiple perspectives for validity checks."[87]

Reactivity. Reactivity to the process of observation itself is also a potential problem. Researchers will undoubtedly not be privy to very private, intimate dialogues; and when observers appear on the scene, the communicative behavior may change to reflect a shift from the rules for private interactions to the rules for more public exchanges. The communicative behavior of some individuals may be particularly affected by the presence of electronic equipment. William Labov describes this problem as the "Observer's Paradox." He explains, "The aim of linguistic research in the community must be to find out how people talk when they are not being systematically observed; yet we can only obtain these data by systematic observation."[88]

Concern about reactivity to the observational process is not an unwarranted concern. William Labov reports that how the observation is conducted may greatly influence the data obtained.[89] Consider the contrasts in dialogue$_{(17)}$, which took place between Clarence (CR), a black adult male, and Leon, a black male child who is eight years old, and in dialogue$_{(18)}$, which also includes Gregory, a friend of Leon. Labov describes four changes that were made in the context from dialogue$_{(17)}$ to dialogue$_{(18)}$:

1. [Clarence] brought along a supply of potato chips, changing the interview into something more in the nature of a party.
2. [Clarence] brought along Leon's best friend, eight-year-old Gregory.
3. [Clarence] reduced the height imbalance (when Clarence got down on the floor of Leon's room, he dropped from 6 ft. 2 in. to 3 ft. 6 in.).
4. [Clarence] introduced taboo words and taboo topics, and proved, to Leon's surprise, that one can say anything into our microphone without any fear of retaliation. The result of these changes is a striking difference in the volume and style of speech.[90]

Dialogue$_{(17)}$:

CR: What if you saw somebody kickin' somebody else on the ground, or was using a stick, what would you do if you saw that?

Leon: Mmmm.

CR: If it was supposed to be a fair fight—

Leon: I don' know.

CR: You don' know? Would you do anything . . . huh? I can't hear you.

Leon: No.

CR: Did you ever see somebody got beat up real bad?

Leon: . . . Nope ? ? ?

CR: Well—uh—did you ever get into a fight with a guy?

Leon: Nope.

CR: That was bigger than you?

Leon: Nope . . .

CR: You never been in a fight?

Leon: Nope.

CR: Nobody ever pick on you?

Leon: Nope.

CR: Nobody ever hit you?

Leon: Nope.

CR: How come?

Leon: Ah 'on' know.

CR: Didn't you ever hit somebody?

Leon: Nope.

CR: (incredulously) You never hit nobody?

Leon: Mhm.

CR: Aww, ba-a-a-be, you ain't gonna tell me that.[91]

Dialogue(18):

CR: Is there anybody who says *your momma drink pee*?

{ Leon: (rapidly and breathlessly) Yee-ah!

{ Greg: Yup!

Leon: And *your father eat doo-doo for breakfas'*!

CR: Ohhh! (laughs)

Leon: And they say your father—*your father eat doo-doo for dinner!*

Greg: When they sound on me, I say *C.B.M.*

CR: What that mean?

{ Leon: Congo booger-snatch! (laughs)

{ Greg: Congo booger-snatcher! (laughs)

Greg: And sometimes I'll curse with *B.B.*

CR: What that?

Greg: Black boy! (Leon crunching on potato chips) Oh that's a *M.B.B.*

CR: *M.B.B.* What's that?

Greg: 'Merican Black Boy!

CR: Ohh . . .

Greg: Anyway, 'Mericans is same like white people, right?

Leon: And they talk about Allah.

CR: Oh year?

Greg: Yeah.

CR: What they say about Allah?

⎰Leon: Allah—Allah is God.

⎱Greg: Allah—

CR: And what else?

Leon: I don' know the res'.

Greg: Allah i—Allah is God, Allah is the only God, Allah—

Leon: Allah is the *son* of God.

Greg: But can he make magic?

Leon: Nope.

Greg: I know who can make magic.

CR: Who can?

Leon: The God, the *real* one.

CR: Who can make magic?

Greg: The son of po'—(CR: Hm?) I'm sayin' the po'k chop God! He only a po'k chop God! (Leon chuckles).

CR: Now, you said you have this fight now; but I wanted you to tell me about the fight that you had.

Leon: I ain't had no fight.

⎰Greg: Yes you did! He said Barry . . .

⎱CR: You said you had one! you had a fight with Butchie.

⎰Greg: An he say Garland! . . . an' Michael!

⎱CR: an' Barry . . .

⎰Leon: I di'n; you said that, Gregory!

⎱Greg: You did!

⎰Leon: You know you said that!

⎱Greg: You said Garland, remember that?

⎰Greg: You said Garland! Yes you did!

⎱CR: You said Garland, that's right.

Greg: He said Mich—an' I say Michael.

⎰CR: Did you have a fight with Garland?

⎱Leon: Uh-Uh.

CR: You had one, and he beat you up, too!

Greg: Yes he did!

Leon: No, I di—I never had a fight with Butch! . . . [92]

The dialogues above involved participant observation, but they illustrate the general principle that the conditions under which the observation takes place affect the data observed. This principle is applicable to the naturalistic observation method as well all other methods involving the recording and observing of communicative behavior, including participant observations, quasi experiments, and experiments.

Researchers should be concerned with the effects of observation on the data collected, but there are ways to minimize the effect. Labov recommends that researchers use a variety of devices which divert attention away from speech, such as: (1) use breaks which lead the subject to assume unconsciously that s/he is not being interviewed at that moment; (2) involve the subject in topics which are so involving that s/he will not think about his/her speech; (3) record peer group interactions; and (4) record public interactions which are easily overheard in such places as trains, buses, lunch counters, ticket lines, and zoos.[93] Reactivity can also be reduced by hiding or disguising equipment. If, for instance, the equipment is placed in an environment where one might expect it to occur naturally (e.g., a tape recorder on a cluttered desk), it may go unnoticed.[94] Stephen Taylor was able to reduce the possible effects of reactivity by acquainting his subjects with the equipment.[95]

On the other hand, reactivity itself may produce data worth analyzing. Robert Nofsinger has pointed out that "the communicative behaviors people employ when others may be watching are genuine behaviors for that setting."[96] Reactive behavior may lead to the production of the most formal, careful speech, and such behaviors may provide the researcher with a sense of what the speakers believe are the most appropriate behaviors or preferred rules.

Prescriptive Force. Data collected by the naturalistic method may contain only behavioral regularities; to infer rules, the researcher must also have evidence of prescriptive force. It is possible that prescriptive force may be indicated by an explicit statement of the rule or by repair and/or explicit sanctioning if rule deviations occur. Or researchers may consciously choose to study situations (e.g., counseling sessions for poor performance) when remediations for previous violations are likely to occur, since the prescriptive force of rules should be particularly evident in these situations.[97] But it is also possible that all the behavior in the data sample may be rule compliant-behavior or that repairs and negative sanctions of noncompliance will not occur for a host of reasons (see Chapter 3 for more details). In order to assess the prescriptive force of a behavioral regularity, one may need to incorporate research techniques utilized by other methods.

One may ask communicators to judge the appropriateness or inappropriateness of certain behaviors just as one might when utilizing the survey method. Or the researcher may purposely violate what s/he believes is the behavior prescribed by the rule and observe whether or not the behavior and/or actor is negatively sanctioned. The latter technique has been called "garfinkeling" after Harold Garfinkel, an ethnomethodologist who uses this technique to explicate rules.[98] It is used by some participants observers, and it has been described as constituting a quasi-experimental methodology inasmuch as the researcher manipulates the antecedent conditions while exercising a minimum control.[99] By combining research techniques which are more common to other methods, researchers utilizing naturalistic observation increase the probability that they will be able to demonstrate prescriptive force.

Control. Limited control is an additional problem for rule analysis which is based on data collected via the naturalistic observational method. When one simply "takes conversation as it comes," one's ability to determine precisely which antecedent conditions are relevant to subsequent behavior is severely hampered. Some scholars mistakenly assume that because rule scholars do not explicate causal mechanisms, they are disinterested in antecedent conditions. Actually, antecedent conditions are an integral part of rules research. The scope conditions of rules are essentially the antecedent conditions which must be met in order for the rule to be relevant. Therefore, rules researchers must be able to determine which variables among those that preceded a behavioral regularity comprise the scope conditions of a rule prescribing that regularity. The greater the researcher's control over the antecedent conditions, the greater the possibility that s/he may be able to state accurately the scope conditions of a rule.

To test their assumptions about the scope conditions of rules, researchers using naturalistic observation may choose to observe particular behaviors in various contexts. However, because they do not manipulate or control the environment, they cannot be certain that all conditions, except those specified by the rule, were the same in situations where the rule seemed to be operant and those where it seemed to be irrelevant. This problem is further complicated by researchers who do not use systematic sampling procedures or by those who fail to state the conditions under which the data were collected. Greater confidence in the accuracy of the scope conditions for a rule may be achieved by utilizing methods that involve greater control, as in quasi-experiments or experiments; however, these methods are not without their disadvantages.

A MATTER OF INTERPRETATION

In addition to the potential disadvantages, naturalistic observers must determine how to interpret the data observed. To infer the rule for openings, closings, summons/responses, turn-taking, and so on from behavior, one must have some notion of what it is to perform these acts, but such knowledge comes from knowing the rules for their performance. Hence, the researcher is caught in a paradox: s/he can use behavioral data to infer the rules, but s/he must some knowledge of the rules in order to interpret the data. Part of this paradox rests in the distinction between social versus physical data, action versus motion, and brute facts versus institutional facts.[100]

Social Versus Physical Data. Romano Harré argues that social data cannot be reduced to physical data. He offered a problem of translation as an illustration. If one assumes a one-to-one correspondence between physical and social data, then one may try to translate "the cat" into another language by partitioning the phrase as "t.h.e. + c.a.t." and then search for a rule which transforms it into another language letter by letter. Such an endeavor would be fruitless. However, one can identify the semantic components "the" and "cat" and seek corresponding elements in another language like Spanish. "El gato" is a Spanish translation of the English "the cat." This translation is predicated on semantic (social) analysis rather than the formal partition of physical elements. Similarly, the physical property of long hair on males has provided different social data in American history. In the 1960s long hair was indicative of the politically left, but in the 1790s those on the extreme left had short hair and those on the extreme right wore long hair.[101] Clearly, then, communication researchers cannot infer rules from physical evidence alone.

Action Versus Motion. The distinction between action and motion has been discussed previously, but it is equally relevant to our discussion here. Romano Harré and Paul Secord offered the following statements as illustrations of mere movement (the a's) versus action (the b's).

    1a. His arm extended straight out through the car window.
    1b. He signalled a left turn.
    2a. Her arm moved rapidly forward and made contact with
        his face.
    2b. She slapped him angrily.[102]

Rules may prescribe how one makes a left turn or how one may slap someone else, but these rules cannot be inferred from only the movements described in 1a and 2a. Researchers need actional as well as motional knowledge.

Brute Versus Institutional Facts. John Searle distinguishes brute facts from institutional facts.[103] Brute facts are physical entities or motions; they are known by empirical observations of sense experiences. Institutional facts become facts because there are rules for performing certain acts and humans use these rules to infer certain facts. For example, paper money is an institutional fact; as a brute fact, it is merely a piece of paper with various gray and green markings; or, football may be viewed as a series of brute facts (e.g., running over lines, clustering, and throwing or kicking a ball) or as being comprised of institutional facts (e.g., touchdowns, huddles, field goals). Clearly, one cannot describe adequately the game of football via brute facts alone; it is institutional facts that constitute the game.

Similarly, communicative behavior is not comprised solely of brute facts; in fact, rule scholars are seeking to discover and identify rules which relate to institutional facts, social data, and human actions. If physical facts are not the same as social facts, then the researcher is faced with the problem of choosing among several alternatives. For example, is a hand extended upward a stretch or a request for permission to speak? The questions that must be answered are: How does one write the rules for an act if one does not know what that act is? Who should decide what constitutes an act? What are the behaviors prescribed by rules for that act? One might look to the above examples for an answer. In the case of long hair and a slap, it may be that communicators informally determined the institutional facts and corresponding rules. In the case of money and football, it may be that those in power (e.g., the government, originators of the game) formally determined the facts and rules. The rules for "the cat" probably involve the collaboration of communicators, prescriptive grammarians, and dictionary writers. One lesson for researchers to learn from these cases is that in not one of them did a researcher determine what constituted a particular institutional fact or social action. To identify institutional facts of a community, researchers must rely on experience beyond their own.

Researcher's Versus Actor's Interpretation. In observational research as well as in quasi-experimental and experimental studies, however, researchers often assume that they know the institutional facts of the communicators; hence, they assume they can write rules for social actions. Leonard C. Hawes describes such assumptions as elitist and ethnocentric "insofar as the researcher assumes, whether implict or explicit, his/her account of other peoples' behavior is superior to the accounts they formulate for themselves."[104] Although elitism and ethnocentrism have become pejorative references, researchers might be willing to live with these labels if they were always correct. But Joan Ganz clearly illustrates that one may erroneously attribute entirely different actions to motions from those intended by the actor. Ganz utilizes a passage from a pastiche on Sir Conan Doyle's Sherlock Holmes by Robert Fish to illustrate her point. In the passage, Watney adjusts a clock, begins to drink a vodka martini, and then shakes his head and pours the liquor back in the bottle. Holmes deduces from these movements that Watney was attempting to have a drink before 5:00 by adjusting the clock to read after 5:00, but his conscience bothered him, so he returned the liquor to the bottle. Watney, however, reports that he adjusted the clock because he had learned it was in error, and that he returned the liquor because given the present political situation his choice of liquor (vodka) might be misinterpreted, and hence, he was going to drink scotch.[105] The point of the illustration is that researchers may provide questionable interpretations of motions.

An alternative solution to researcher-based interpretations is to allow the actors to interpret their behaviors. This procedure is utilized in the survey method when actors are asked to specify the rules or make judgments about appropriateness. It is also part of the participant observation method inasmuch as the researcher is also an actor and hence s/he plays both roles. Using the actor's categories has been advocated by scholars who label their work in various ways: conversational analysis,[106] phenomenology,[107] ethnography,[108] naturalistic,[109] interpretive,[110] constructivism,[111] and symbolic interaction.[112] It has also been recommended by a number of rule scholars.[113]

Given this endorsement, can it be said that actors will always accurately describe their actions and/or rules? Again, the answer must be, not necessarily. As has already been pointed out, actors are not always aware of their regularities or willing to admit the influence of rules; and what is more, they may offer folklinguistics rather than actual behavior as the bases for their rules.

It is possible that researchers may more accurately describe the behavior of actors than the actors themselves? The research of Mark Knapp and associates suggests that in some cases researchers may have more conscious knowledge than the actors and therefore it is possible that the description of researchers may be more accurate.[114] Knapp et al. manipulated status by having undergraduates speak with faculty members for the high-status condition and to a peer for equal status. As a manipulation check, the students were asked whether they perceived any difference in status; the students responded that they did not. However, the researchers offered several behavioral cues to support their hypothesis that status was a factor affecting the interaction: (1) students took longer when departing the company of professors than students (the task was to get an attitudinal reading on the interviewee in the shortest time possible), (2) reinforcement and buffing (e.g., uh, er, well) behaviors were greater in differing status dyads than in peer groups, and (3) professional inquiry was greater between peers than between professor and student.

The researchers interpreted reinforcement as supportive behavior and buffing as acts of deference. The researchers also reasoned that inquiries may be viewed as inappropriate intrusions with the private lives of high-status persons, or that such inquiries may have been avoided because the subject wanted to terminate the interview quickly and professionals often tend to become verbose when responding to questions about their profession. Subjects reported that judgments of status were predicated on perceptions of the friendliness or threatening qualities of the interviewer rather than on the ascribed status of "Dr." or "Professor." The researchers do not report whether the degree of perceived threat and ascribed status correlated. Nor does the reader know whether the subjects and researchers were using *status* to refer to socioeconomic status or superordinate/subordinate status. Are the researchers correct in indicating that different rules are appropriate for leave-taking depending on the relative status of the actors marked by the roles of student and professor, or are the subjects correct in maintaining that degrees of friendliness or threat changed their behavior? One might be better able to assess the answer if the researchers had reported the correlation between status and perceived threat, and if there had been a greater attempt to demonstrate that the researchers and the actors were using *status* in a similar manner. But even with this additional information, the accounts of researchers and actors may be in conflict.

In an attempt to resolve the controversy between utilizing the actor's *or* the researcher's actional labels, several scholars have offered alternative means of differentiating actions from motions. Leonard Hawes's solution is very much like the philosophy of "Why not ask the actors?" But he does not simply ask actors what behaviors constitute which acts or what are the rules for performing those acts. Rather, he observes what motions are named in the act of their performance.[115] He, for example, attempts to learn what the act of providing information is by observing how motions became labeled information in the process of naturalistic conservation. Dialogue(19) was used by Hawes to explicate what one might do to provide information, state a fact, or give an opinion. (References to information, fact, and opinion have been italicized to assist the reader; these words were not italicized in the original dialogue. Hawes does not state corresponding rules for these acts; but given more data, one might assume that he could hypothesize the existence of such rules.)

Dialogue(19):

1 M: project 294 has really broken down. Paul left us and then we had that city hall screw up and well but we're really up against it now.

Another member then said:

2 S: getting back to the agenda what are we going to do for to-morrow's board meeting?

A third member, called an "executive director," took the third turn:

3 H: wait a sec I think uh well the *fact* that M's 294 is well behind and in trouble we should get that straightened out first.

Member S then took a turn.

4 S: the feds are probably well I think its certain they are going to cut off 294 money in mid year so we so could put it on the back burner for a while and M's people could help my people out with my aged housing study we could sure use more staff.

Member H, the "executive director," took the next turn:

5 H: where the hell did you get that *information*? You got contacts in Washington or are you just giving us your *opinion*?[116]

Although Hawes's method offers the researcher an alternative means for utilizing the actors categories, Robert Nofsinger indicates under what conditions the researcher's perception may be valid or invalid:

Accordingly, if the researcher is a member of the same speech-language-talk community as the participants, it may be satisfactory for the researcher to exercise direct judgment of the original data. If, however, the researcher's conservational intuitions and judgments can be expected to differ systematically from those of the participants, it may be wise to obtain interpretations (descriptions) from people who are "plugged into" the same communication system as the participants.[117]

W. Barnett Pearce argues that the solution to this problem is to conduct two kinds of research, one which uses actor's meanings for behaviors, which he calls naturalistic inquiry, and one which involves only the researcher's categories, which he calls objectivistic research.[118] Pearce maintains that "the theorist must use both, realizing that he sacrifices control but gains a greater dependency on the data when he uses naturalistic procedure, and reverses that trade off when he uses objectivistic procedures."[119]

While Pearce describes two different types of research practices regarding the naming of institutional facts, Romano Harré and Paul Secord propose a solution to the problem that could be accommodated in a single study. They call this technique "negotiation."[120] The technique consists of pooling the various viewpoints of an interaction and the subsequent correction of the accounts. All actors and the researcher offer their interpretations of the behaviors; if all are in agreement, the accounts may be viewed as "authentic." If the researcher ultimately agrees with the actors, the negotiation is described as inward resolution; but if the actors change in the direction of the observer, then it is labeled outward resolution. Outward resolution may be the most accurate, but Harré and Secord caution that outward resolutions may also occur simply because the researcher is more persuasive, assertive, dynamic, or because s/he is believed to be the greater expert.

Ultimately, researchers may be forced to accept competing interpretations as legitimate. This is the position of interpretive scholars. After observing behavioral patterns, a researcher may infer actional interpretations and/or rules. S/he should then compare his/her inferences with those of the actors. Even if the actors have different inferences, the actors should recognize the researcher's interpretation as plausible, even if it is not their own.[121] A researcher would be wise to report whether there is immediate agreement, a negotiated agreement, an acceptance of the researcher's interpretation as plausible, or a total rejection of his/her interpretation. Such reports would help the reader assess the probable accuracy of the accounts. Whose institutional facts, the researcher's or the actor's, to use in data analysis is a potential problem for naturalistic observation. It has been usually resolved by using the researcher's classification scheme. This preference may be elitist, ethnocentric, and inaccurate, but using the actor's interpretation can also cause problems. Negotiating the interpretations seems like a viable alternative. This problem is not unique to naturalistic observation. It is also prevalent in quasi experimental and experimental research, and the same solutions could be used in those methods.

QUALITY

Like rules generated via the self-reflection method, the quality of the rules which are inferred from the naturalistic observation method may be judged in terms of intersubjective agreement and the richness of the analysis. In addition, the rules may be compared to empirical evidence; the more the data and the rules agree, the greater the confidence in the rules. The empirical data should include evidence that the behavior is controllable, contextual, and criticizable (See Chapter 3). These three criteria, intersubjective agreement, richness, and empirical support, also hold true for participant observation. All three criteria could be applied to quasi-experiments and experiments, but most often the rules generated by these methods will be evaluated solely in terms of statistical evidence.

SUMMARY

The naturalistic observational method consists of observing and recording naturally occurring regularities and inferring rules from these regularities. The greatest advantage of this method is that rules may be inferred from naturally occurring interactions. The method will probably result in rules for relatively common behaviors. It may also identify implicit rules by using behavior to infer rules. Such rules cannot be identified via the self-reflection or survey methods, which rely on conscious rule knowledge. The rules may be, though they are not always, based on empirical data. Disadvantages of this method will include: (1) time-consuming processes, (2) poor sampling, (3) incomplete data, (4) selective perception, (5) reactivity, (6) no indication of prescriptive force, (7) difficulty in determining precise scope conditions, and (8) institutional facts generated by the researcher. The advantages and disadvantages of this method are not limited to it alone; many of them are also shared by other methods.

Participant Observation

The participant observer seeks to identify communicative regularities and the rules which are relevant to those regularities by observing interactions in which s/he is a participant. The researcher may record his/her observations in field notes or by electronic media. The advantages of each technique are discussed in the previous section on naturalistic observation. Florence Kluckhohn offers the following definition of participant observation and its purposes:

> conscious and systematic sharing, insofar as circumstances permit, in the life-activities, and, on occasion, in the interests and effects of a group of persons. Its purpose is to obtain data about behavior through direct contact and in terms of specific situations in which the distortion that results from the investigators being an outside agent is reduced to a minimum.[122]

Participant observation may involve only observing communicative interaction in which the researcher participates, or it may include interviewing informants (knowledgeable members of a speech community), interviewing other actors, document analysis, and/or limited manipulation of the situation by varying one's behavior and/or the environment. This last technique may include garfinkeling (the violation of presumed rules).[123] Informants may be "native" members of a community, or they may be individuals who are attempting to pass as natives. Studying people who are "passing" in a community may be particularly useful because they often must become conscious of the rules in order to follow them, whereas native members may be unconscious of them. Harold Garfinkel demonstrates the usefulness of this technique by interviewing Agnes, originally a male who succeds in passing as a female.[124] Romano Harré and Paul Secord indicate that a further application of this technique would be to interview "con-men."[125]

The participant observer also has several responsibilities to his/her readers. S/he should describe her own role, status, and personal biases regarding the interaction studied so that others may attempt to assess the accuracy of the judgments made. The researcher should also specify his/her procedures clearly, and in enough detail that other researchers can attempt to replicate the findings.[126]

RESEARCH EXAMPLES

Participant observation to identify communicative rules has been used less often by communication scholars than the self-reflection method or naturalistic observation. Nonetheless, this method has produced some interesting research. For example, Gerry Philipsen has used it to identify the rules for "speaking 'like a man' in Teamsterville," and Donna M. Jurich has explicated the rules involved in the enactment of returning.[127]

Philipsen twice describes the regularities he observed as rules, but he seems to be more comfortable with phrases like: "cultural [i.e., shared, tacit] understandings," "implicit understandings," "tacit understanding about situation appropriateness," and "underlying values about what is appropriate and proper communicative conduct."[129] Nonetheless, these phrases and Philipsen's descriptions of the regularities and sanctions for deviations are consistent with the conception of rule as it is used in this study. Jurick does not use the word *rule* to account for the regularities that she observed; however, she grounds her work in the tradition of other rule scholars such as Labov, Nofsinger, Sacks, Schegloff, and Jefferson,[130] and she talks about appropriate and inappropriate behavior. Formally stated rules do not appear in the research reports of either scholar, but they can be inferred from their generalizations about the behavioral regularities. Below are some of those generalizations, and rules which may be inferred from the generalizations. These rules should be viewed as possible rules and not neccessarily proven rules. (Generalizations which are direct quotations are marked with quotation marks; paraphrases are not so marked.)

Generalization(01):

"In Teamsterville speech is judged appropriate for male self-presentation in assertions of solidarity, but not in assertions of power over another person. . . . If one's addressee is of lower status . . . the power assertion may rely on nonverbal threat or physical combat. When one's addressee is of high status . . . male power assertion may properly employ personal connections with an intermediary who states the resident's case for him."[131]

R(27): If one is a Teamsterville male and wishes to communicate solidarity to one's peer, then one should use a verbal mode of communication.

R(28): If one is a Teamsterville male and wishes to assert power over a subordinate, then one should use a nonverbal mode of communication.

R(29): If one is a Teamsterville male and wishes to assert influence over a superordinate, then one should use an intermediary to speak for him.

Generalization(02):

"Members refuse to allow the interactant, categorized as a returnee, to assume characteristics of the category stranger. . . . members, when answering questions of the returnee, demand the right to take for granted that the questioner will cooperate to understand what is implied instead of what is said. . . . an utterance such as Good morning, you must be the researcher who's here on an interviewing project? by a terminal or permanent member might be responded to by the returnee with Don't you recognize me? or Ah, come off it, or what's got into you?"[132]

R(30): If one is a returnee, then one is prohibited from behaving as a stranger.

R(31): If one is a returnee, then one should allow group members to respond to questions by implications which depend on what is assumed to be the shared knowledge of the group.

R(32): If one is a member of a group and is addressing a returnee, then one's greeting should indicate that one knows the returnee.

ADVANTAGES

Janice H. Rushing has argued that of all of the available methods, participant observation is the most appropriate method

for rules research.[133] Rushing's argument is based on an answer
to the question of whose interpretation of the situation is the
accurate one; she holds that it is the actor's. Believing that actions
are situationally bound, Rushing argues:

> In order for the scientist to understand the meanings that people
> have for their objects, then one must *take the role* of these peo-
> ple—individually or collectively. That is, the scientist must know
> the meanings that the *actors* have for their concepts or objects,
> and must not input his or her own meanings to concepts, if these
> meanings are not gained by interacting with the people under
> study.[134]

The ability to have the interpretation of an actor firsthand
may be viewed as one of the advantages for participant observation. However, it also seems possible that the participant observer might become the smug, elitist, ethnocentric researcher
described by Hawes. That is, s/he might automatically presume
that because s/he is both a researcher and a participant that
his/her interpretation must inherently be correct. Participant
observers might do well to use the negotiation techniques recommended in the section on naturalistic observation.

For the most part, the advantages and disadvantages of naturalistic observation and participant observation are the same,
but the act of participating in the interaction provides a few differences. One of the greatest advantages of participant observation is
the limited control of the researcher. S/he can manipulate some
variables in the situation and note the various effects of the
manipulation, and s/he can violate a hypothesized rule in order
to assess prescriptive force. Or, if the researcher is trying to pass
a member and fails, the reaction to his/her faux pas may provide
useful data.[135] Edward T. Hall also reported that a participant
observer can identify rules by exploring behaviors which make
him/her uncomfortable.[136] Asking actors about appropriateness,
another means of assessing prescriptive force, may be part of
participant observation, but this advantage as well as those above
are not part of naturalistic observation.

The participant observer also has access to one kind of data
which is inaccessible to researchers using other methods. This
data consists of the choices not made. The importance of this
data has been stressed by several rule scholars.[137] Some rules

prohibit behavior. In order to infer these rules from behavior, the researcher must have a sense of what the actors are not doing because they consider it prohibited. As a participant, the researcher has a sense of choices not made.

Typically, though not always, participant observation includes an extended observation of the same group, whereas naturalistic observation involves different groups.[138] Hence, participant observation may reveal information about behavior across time that is not available to methods which observe behavior at one time and place.

Rushing points out that participant observation is often criticized as being unstructured and nonstandardized, and, therefore, not as rigorous as traditional experimental studies. But Rushing turns this criticism around and presents it as an advantage, arguing that the participant observer can revise hypotheses as necessary and can remain flexible enough to allow data to shape themselves rather than force them to conform to a preconceived design or rationalizing them away if they do not conform.[139] This ability seems to be also true of naturalistic observation, though not true of quasi-experiments and experiments.

DISADVANTAGES

Participant observation has all the potential disadvantages of naturalistic observation and three additional ones. The manipulation abilities of the participant observer may reduce the uncertainty about the scope conditions and prescriptive force of rules, but it may also influence behavior of the other actors in such a way as to achieve a self-fulfilling hypothesis. Or the researcher may end up writing rules which are applicable only if s/he or his/her manipulation is present. Personal involvement in the interaction increases the actor's sensitivity to the actor's interpretation of motions, but there is no guarantee that researchers as participants will not be as blind and resistant to regularities and rules as other actors. One way to compensate for these "trade-offs" is to do both naturalistic observation and participant observation research.

SUMMARY

The participant observer seeks to identify communicative regularities and the rules which are relevant to those regularities by observing interaction in which s/he is a participant. The advantages and disadvantages of naturalistic observation and participant observation are largely the same, but there are some differences. The participant observer has more direct knowledge of how at least one actor (him/herself) interpreted the motion and s/he may also ask other actors their opinion. Other advantages include the ability to manipulate antecedent conditions, access to choices not made, longitudinal observation, the ability to revise hypotheses, and the opportunity to allow data to shape themselves. The three disadvantages of participant observation, in addition to those also associated with naturalistic observation are: self-fulfilling hypotheses, the potentially low generalizability of the rules, and blindness and/or resistance to regularities and rules.

Quasi-Experimentation

Quasi-experiments are characterized by three defining features: (1) subjects are drawn from two or more parent populations (e.g., different ages, sexes, or races), (2) all subjects are exposed to essentially the same antecedent conditions, and (3) a particular response is measured to determine whether subjects drawn from different populations will respond differently to the same antecedent conditions.

ALTERNATIVE LABELS

Sometimes quasi-experiments are labeled experiments, but experiments differ from quasi-experiments on all three dimensions. (The characteristics of experiments are discussed in the next section.) The distinguishing features of quasi-experiments and experiments are taken from the work of Gerald R. Miller.[140] Miller uses the term *investigation* rather than *quasi experiment*. The label *investigation* was not used here because it is often used as a generic substitute for *study*. Therefore, it was believed that the term quasi-experiment more clearly connoted the particular method than *investigation*.

RESEARCH EXAMPLES

The quasi-experimental method has been used by Paul D. Krivonos and Mark L. Knapp to study behaviors for initiating communication and by Mark L. Knapp and associates to explicate the "rhetoric of good-bye."[141] For research projects, Krivonos and Knapp compare greeting behaviors of acquaintances with those of strangers in a waiting room. Knapp et al. compare the leave-taking behavior among acquaintance, stranger, equal status, and differential status dyads. These researchers do not use the term *rule*, but they attribute the observed regularities to norms of appropriateness, and they argue that violations of these norms may affect the perceived effectiveness; hence, it is reasonable to assume they are using the term *norm* in the same way that *rule* is used in the present study. There are no formal rules in the research reports, but possible rules may be inferred from generalizations.

Generalization(03):

"*Reference to Other* provides a means of signalling maintenance of the relationship." [It occurred significantly more often among acquaintances than strangers]. . . . "*External References* in this situation also seemed to be a possible way of indicating maintenance of the relationship . . . by reintroducing a past aspect of the relationship." [External references occurred significantly more often among acquaintances than strangers].[142]

R(33): If one is greeting an acquaintance and wishes to maintain the relationship, then one's greeting should include references to the other and external references.

Generalization(04):

"When status differences obtain in communication, apparently significantly more Reinforcement and Buffing is demanded of the communicative partner of lower status."[Both behaviors occurred significantly more often if the subject was talking to someone of higher status than someone of equal status].[143]

R(34): If one is taking leave of someone of higher status, then one should reinforce the remarks of the higher status persons and demonstrate deference by using buffing (e.g., "huh," "er," or "well").

ADVANTAGES

The major advantage of the quasi-experimental method is control. By specifying precisely which behaviors under what circumstances will be measured, the researcher is more assured that his/her comparisons between or among groups is accurate. The researcher attempts to hold all conditions similar so that s/he can determine whether different rules hold for different populations (e.g., acquaintance versus stranger, status equals or status differentials). Hence, the quasi-experimental method facilitates the development of scope conditions for rules as they apply to different populations (e.g., blacks, whites, males, females, children, adults, high status, low status, friends, strangers). However, because people are not randomly assigned to these populations, it is difficult to determine absolutely that behavioral differences are due to these different populations and not other factors. For example, if one observes that children behave differently from adults, one might conclude that there are different rules for adults and children, but it is also possible that the observed differences are due to biological or experiential differences. The quasi-experimental method offers some control over antecedent conditions and thus improves the accuracy of the rules it produces, but it does not provide as much control as the experimental method.

DISADVANTAGES

Artificiality. While control is the greatest advantage of the quasi-experimental method, it is also its greatest disadvantage. Data from quasi-experiments may be more "artificial" than data collected via naturalistic observations or participant observations. This artificiality may reduce the generalizability of the rules. The "artificiality" may stem from the unusualness of the task (e.g., finding another experimental subject in a research waiting room or interviewing a professor for less than five minutes in order to get an attitudinal reading),[144] or from the knowledge that one's behavior is being studied. These problems can be minimized by choosing common tasks and diverting the subject's attention away from the behavior under investigation. In both of the examples given above, the researchers were fairly successful at attempting the latter. In the greeting study, subjects did not know they were being observed, and in the leave-taking study, subjects thought they were being judged on their ability to get an accurate attitude measure quickly rather than having their leave-taking behavior observed.

Controlling all the antecedent conditions may result in a rather sterile study. That is, one may talk about the rules for greeting experimental subjects in research waiting rooms, but one does not know whether those rules are applicable to other environments. The quasi-experimental study considers one context at a time, whereas naturalistic observations and participant observations may make comparisons across contexts. Further, the antecedent conditions chosen for quasi-experiments may be chosen for facilitating control or convenience (e.g., research waiting rooms, professors, and students), rather than for interest or theoretical import.

Response Versus Initiation. What is more, controlling all of the antecedent conditions allows the researcher only to report the responses of subjects. The initiating behaviors of communicators who are not constrained by predetermined environments cannot be studied by this method.[145] By predetermining the context and the instructions to subjects, researchers are faced with the problem that they, rather than their subjects, are determining the rules and their scope conditions.[146] Hence one is left with the question: Does quasi-experimental research identify the rules of the researcher or the actor?

Quasi-experimental research often uses preconceived categories to measure responses. This has two disadvantages. First, it presumes the researcher's categories are inherently accurate and it ignores the actor's interpretation. Second, it presumes the researcher is aware of all of the relevant variables. This presumption may be an error.[147] The alternative method of participant observation allows for greater flexibility, and it takes the actor's perspective into account.

Time. Time is also a comparative advantage/disadvantage for studying rules from a quasi-experimental method. By limiting the context in which data will be collected, the researcher controls precisely how long his/her period of data collection will be. The naturalistic observer or participant observer will stop collecting data at some indeterminate time, that is, whenever s/he believes that s/he has collected enough data. The precision of the time dimension in quasi-experimental research indicates that the researcher's personal bias did not influence when to observe and when to stop observing; thus one is inclined to view his/her conclusion as more objective. On the other hand, the time limit may be arbitrarily chosen and hence valuable data may be excluded. In addition, observing behavior at one point in time minimizes one's ability to explicate variables across time. Rule negotation, change, and renegotiation may be processes which quasi experimentation cannot measure, and relational rules may require the kind of longitudinal observation available to participant observation, but which is precluded by one-shot experiments.

Reactivity. If communicators believe they are part of an experiment, they may try to conform to whatever behavior they believe the researcher wants to observe, or they may deliberately try to invalidate the research, depending on their attitude toward research. This problem is minimized when communicators are unaware that they are being observed.

In addition to the above problems, quasi-experiments may be subject to all of the same problems of observational studies related to data recording and transcribing. However, problems of reactivity due to the process of observation will probably be even greater in quasi experiments and experiments where subjects are more likely to know that their behavior is being observed for scientific purposes. Further, like naturalistic observation, the quasi-experimental method may not result in any rule deviation, thus making it impossible to determine if the behavioral regularity is criticizable. Therefore, a follow-up study in which rule compliance/noncompliance is a variable may be needed in order to infer a rule.

SUMMARY

A quasi-experiment seeks to determine if the rules for different populations (e.g., males versus females or children versus adults) are similar or different under the same conditions. The relative control of variables provides the greatest advantages and disadvantages of this method. The quality of the rules generated by this method are usually judged in terms of empirical fit.

Experimentation

Experimental research is characterized by four qualities: (1) all subjects are drawn from the same parent population, (2) all subjects are randomly assigned to treatment groups (stimuli conditions) which are systematically manipulated, (3) all other variables are held constant, and (4) a particular response is specified and measured in order to determine whether stimulus variations are systematically related to response differences.[148]

RESEARCH EXAMPLES

The use of experimental methods for rules research is relatively new. To the present author's knowledge, they have all been paper and pencil tests on which the participants are asked to rate messages and actors on specific scales; they have not involved the manipulation of contextual variables in order to observe subsequent interaction. Charlene Edna O'Brien has studied company rules in task and social settings, Janet Lynn Weathers has investigated rules for the use of assertive and nonassertive communication by students, and W. Barnett Pearce and Forrest Conklin have explored rules related to indirect answers in various settings.[149] Although all three research investigations were grounded in a rules approach to communication, Weathers is the only one who provided a formal statement of the rules identified or confirmed. But, in the absence of formal rules, rules may be inferred from generalizations provided by the researcher. Below are examples of some of the generalizations and inferred rules.

O'Brien first identified two rules by interviewing company members. She then hypothesized that if these rules were actually operable, those who complied with them should be perceived as more promotable than deviators. Generalizations$_{(05)}$ and $_{(06)}$ are taken from O'Brien's research. These generalizations can be used to infer $R_{(35)}$ which applied to all subordinates and $R_{(36)}$ which applied to managers, but not subordinates.

Generalization$_{(05)}$:

"Successful people in the company accepted assignments that their bosses felt were important. They did not initially express reservations about the assignment."[150]

$R_{(35)}$: If one's superordinate gives one an assignment, then one must not express reservations about it.

Generalization(06):

"In the rule consistent version of the [social episode] dialogue, both the supervisor and subordinate discuss an impending work related topic. Neither shifts the topic. . . . In the rule inconsistent version of the dialogue, a female or male supervisor shifts from the work-related topic to a social topic. . . . Rule inconsistent behavior for managers was always penalized (in task and social episodes), but subordinates were only penalized in the task episode."[151]

R(36): If one is a manager and in a dialogue about an impending work related topic, then one must not shift the topic to recreation.

Weathers had students and teachers evaluate assertive and nonassertive messages attributed to a student addressing a teacher in one of three audience conditions: in the presence of other students, in the presence of another teacher, and in private. Since teachers and students did not demonstrate a preference for assertive or nonassertive messages, Weathers concluded it was not possible to generate a rule regarding perceptions for the use of assertive communication in the classroom.[152] In addition to the ratings on the scales, Weathers asked her participants to describe the message and their reaction to the actor in writing, and she also informally interviewed them. These data indicate that rather than a preferential rule for assertive or nonassertive communication, there may be a prohibitive rule that prescribes the absence of aggressive communication. However, since aggressive communication was not directly manipulated in the study, Weathers indicates that additional research is needed in order to infer a rule.[153]

The comparisons across the three audience conditions proved to be more fruitful for identifying a rule. Using both the pencil and paper evaluations, and the interviews, Weathers indentifies four preferential rules. R(37) is one of them.

R(37): When a student interacts with a teacher about a disputed test answer, it is preferable for the student to communicate with the teacher in private or in the presence of another teacher rather than in the presence of other students.[154]

Pearce and Conklin compared direct and indirect responses in six different settings: coworkers, close friends, enemies, just introduced, subordinate to asker, and superior to asker. Direct responses were perceived as more appropriate, friendly, and respectful; indirect responses were least appropriate between persons who had just been introduced.[155] From these findings, two rules can be inferred:

R$_{(38)}$: If one has been asked a question, then one should give a direct response rather than an indirect one.

R$_{(39)}$: If one has been asked a question by someone to whom s/he has just been introduced, then one must not respond with an indirect answer.

ADVANTAGES VERSUS DISADVANTAGES

The comaprative advantages/disadvantages of the experimental method are generally the same as the quasi-experimental method, only magnified because of the additional control. For example, the added control of the experimental method, offered by manipulating the antecedent conditions, increases the probable accuracy of the scope conditions of a particular rule. This same control increases the probability that the specific antecedents which were manipulated in an experimental study may not recur in the nonexperimental setting; hence, the rule may lack generality.

Prescriptive Force. As with each of the other methods, experimental studies must provide evidence of prescriptive force. In measuring prescriptive force, experimenters typically restrict the response of their participants to rating a message and/or actors on prearranged scales. However, there seems to be no standard set of scales for trying to assess the prescriptive force of rules, as evidenced by the diversity of scales used in the three example studies. O'Brien's scales included measures of promotability, effectiveness, willingness to work for the person, and so on. Weather's scales focused on frequency, appropriateness, comfortableness, and positive/negative evaluation. Pearce and Conklin measured usualness, humor, appropriateness, friendliness, and respect. The diversity of scales chosen may lead one to question whether they could all be measuring the same phenomena, that is, prescriptive force. But, as it was demonstrated in Chapter 3, prescriptive force may manifest itself in various ways, so situation-specific scales are probably appropriate. It is important, however, that the researchers justify their choice of scales.

Further, if multiple scales are used, researchers need to indicate what they will take as evidence of prescriptive force. For example, in O'Brien's research, the same behavior was rated positively on some scales, negatively on others, and neutral on still others. Given this diversity, a researcher needs to establish criteria for making sense out of the data obtained. Weather's study provides a good example of how this might be done. She eventually dropped her scale on appropriateness because it did not factor with the other scales, and through the interview process she found that the participants had assigned divergent meanings to that scale, making it ineffectual as a measuring device. The combination of qualitative and statistical analyses strengthens one's confidence in the decision to drop this scale.

Force-Choice. Finally, using predetermined, force-choice scales may result in inaccurate or incomplete data. When participants are limited to using the researcher's scales, the investigation may result in judgments not typically made in natural settings, or it may fail to uncover the richness of responses that occur naturally. The utility of open-ended questions and the interview process used by Weathers illustrates the importance of combining force-choice answers with other methods. It was only through these procedures that she was able to acquire evidence about the possibility of a prohibitive rule for aggressive behavior. Further, this data confirmed the results obtained from the scales, thus lending greater confidence to the arguments that the scales were well chosen, that the conclusions drawn were warranted, and that the rules inferred were accurate.

Folklinguistics. Instead of having the problems associated with analyzing communication interaction, the above experimental studies are faced with the potential problems of inferring rules from self-report data (i.e., folklinguistics) like that used in the survey method. Actors may be unwilling or unable to make accurate judgments about behavior. Getting actors to make judgments did not seem to be a problem, however, for the three studies highlighted above. All three got actors to make judgments. O'Brien and Weathers confirmed these judgments in interviews. Our confidence in the accuracy of these judgments would be even greater if the presumed rules were confirmed through observation of naturalistic interactions.

Organismic Variables. Some rules pertain to particular classes of persons (e.g., students, friends, enemies, subordinates). Such rules cannot be inferred from experimental studies that randomly assign persons from the *same* population to different conditions (e.g., environments or messages). Methods other than experimentation may be used to study such rules. A mixed design study (multiple populations and experimental procedures) as well as other methods discussed in this chapter may be used to study the role organismic variables play in the scope conditions of various rules. In the three studies highlighted in this section, the researchers were able to infer rules that contained organismic variables by asking the participants to judge the behavior of different persons. But the accuracy of these inferences is limited to the accuracy of the participants' folklinguistics.

Mechanistic Causation. One of the reasons rules researchers may have shied away from the experimental method is its association with mechanistic causation, which is antithetical to the philosophical assumptions of the rules perspective. This assumption, however, is false.

Experimental research allows one to conclude with greater accuracy than other methods that a given antecedent will be followed by a given consequence, but it does not determine the precise nature of that relationship. These antecedents may constitute the scope conditions for different rules, and hence different behavior may be prescribed, or they may be the causal mechanisms for different laws. In order to demonstrate that given antecedents mechanistically determined given consequences, one must establish the impossibility of willful deviation. In the research examples above, this is clearly not the case. Students, company members, coworkers, and so on could violate the rules proposed. Therefore, the antecedents in these studies may more appropriately be thought of as the scope conditions for different rules. This distinction has two important implications for rules researchers: (1) researchers cannot claim causal explanations simply by doing an experimental study, and (2) they need not avoid the experimental method on the grounds that it is appropriate only for testing causal relationships; the experimental method may be appropriate whenever one wishes to maximize control and one is primarily concerned with the accuracy of scope conditions for particular rules or in determining if different antecedents mean that different rules are salient.

In the studies summarized here, the researchers assessed both the contextuality (regularity) and the criticizability of the behavior. Both types of judgments are necessary to infer rules. If researchers ask only how common or usual is this behavior, they may identify norms or habits that are not prescribed by rules. If researchers manipulate antecedent behaviors and then observe behavior, they must demonstrate the contextuality and criticizability of the behavior, which means they may have to make sure rule deviations occur. Such research studies would also be subject to problems related to data recording and transcribing, and reactivity.

SUMMARY

An experiment seeks to determine if different antecedents lead to different or similar consequences. In rules research this means trying to determine the scope conditions for a rule; that is, as the antecedents change, are different rules salient? The comparative advantages of an experimental study are generally similar to those for quasi-experiments; only they are magnified. Using the experimental method will not guarantee causal explanations, and rules researchers should not assume that the method is inherently inconsistent with the philosophical assumptions of a rules perspective.

Combining Methods

Since different methods tend to be associated with different advantages and disadvantages, one may maximize the accuracy and quality of the rules inferred if one utilizes multiple means of data collection and analysis. Combining methods has been utilized and advocated by several scholars.[156]

In choosing which methods to combine when, it is useful to compare the primary advantages of each. Self-reflection and survey methods may be used to develop and to refine hypothe-

sized rules; but if one is to establish rules of naturalistic interactions, then the behavioral implications of rules must be tested
by either naturalistic observation or participant observation.
Similarly, the quasi-experimental and experimental methods can
be used to refine rules, and these methods improve one's confidence in the accuracy of a rule. However, unless it is demonstrated
that these rules operate in naturalistic interactions, they are of
little value to a theory about naturalistic communication. Although the other methods offer definite advantages, naturalistic
observation and participant observation should be the primary
methods of rules research. The trade-offs between naturalistic
observation and participant observation make them a useful
combination. The self-reflective method may also be used in
combination with all other methods. By comparing their own
experiences with what they observe via other methods, researchers have a "built-in" check system. The resolution of any
discrepancies between their own experience and what they observe may reveal some interesting findings that would otherwise
be ignored.

The primary focus of this chapter has been to compare the
relative merits of six methods for identifying rules. Having
identified rules, researchers will want to construct research that
will allow them to determine when and to what degree rules may
be used to explain behavior. As argued in Chapter 4 rules may be
related to behavior in a number of ways, but only certain types
of relations can be used to explain behavior in terms of rules. The
next section will consider the comparative advantages of the six
methods for determining the nature of a rule-behavior relationship.

Determining the Nature of
a Rule-Behavior Relationship

In Chapter 4 it was argued that behavior may be related to
rules in a number of ways. Behavior may be described as positive-
rule-reflective, rule-following, rule-conforming, rule-fulfilling,
rule-absent, rule-ignorant, rule-error, rule-violation, negative-
rule-reflective, rule-governed, rule-guided, rule-symptomatic, or
rule-allowance. Rules research has focused primarily on inferring

rules from behavior, rather than attempting to specify the relationship between particular behaviors and the level of rule compliance/noncompliance. Further, since the above taxonomy appears for the first time in this study, it would be unrealistic to look for an example of research which demonstrates each type of association. Nonetheless, it is possible to ask whether the different methods can provide the necessary evidence for confirming various rule/behavior relationships and to what degree can they provide that kind of evidence. This section will seek to answer these questions.

The survey method and pencil and paper experimental designs can answer questions about which rules govern which situations, and they can tap into attitudes regarding the relative value of a rule. Since it is only in rare cases that an actor, without being asked, will explicitly state what rules s/he values and/or believes govern a situation, these methods may be the only means of making these associations. However, since surveys and paper and pencil experiments do not involve communicative interaction, they cannot be used to assess the degree to which rules influence particular behaviors.

The naturalistic observational method may provide enough data for any level of rule-behavior associations, but it is also quite possible that the data will lack evidence or criticizability (repairs or explicit sanctions, explicit references to the rules, or overt evaluation of the rules). Without such evidence, one cannot claim rule-guided relationships such as rule-conforming, rule-erroring, rule-following, or rule-reflective behavior. S/he may also have difficulty distinguishing rule-symptomatic and rule-allowance behavior from other types of rule-generated behavior. The participant observer and experimenter may maximize his/her ability to claim that the behavior was rule-guided by maximizing the possibility that rule-deviation will occur or by interviewing the participants. If the behavior is rule-governed but there is no evidence of the actor's knowledge of the rule, then the behavior should be described as rule-fulfilling if it is compliant, and rule-ignorant if noncompliant. To use any of the other labels in the taxonomy is to attribute greater rule knowledge and utilization of the rule than is warranted by the data.

Research aimed at determining what kind of rule-behavior association exists begins with a presumed rule. The research of Stephen Taylor is an example of this method.[157] He begins with what he believes to be adult rules, and asks at what age children display adherence to adult rules. In terms of the taxonomy offered here, Taylor essentially attempts to determine when the behavior of children *fulfills* adult rules. Taylor describes the behavior of the children as rule-conforming, but he does not provide evidence that the children have a sense of the prescriptive force of the rule. He does not have them judge the appropriateness of certain behaviors, nor does he report repairs or sanctions which would be consistent with the rules. It is possible that the observed behavioral differences for children of different ages are due to biological factors or differential rules for children of different ages more so than to more conscious rule knowledge. More evidence is needed to call it rule-conforming behavior. For the most part, the behavior of the children is best described as rule-fulfilling. At one point, however, Taylor offered one example of rule-related behavior that could be labeled rule-following behavior. This behavior consisted of third grades stating a turn-taking rule and following it.

Taylor utilizes two methods in explicating the relationships between rules and behavior: naturalistic observation and quasi-experimentation. (He describes his method as experimental, but he draws his samples from different populations, i.e., different age groups, and holds the stimulus constant; thus the method meets the requirements of a quasi-experiment, as it has been defined here.) He argues that each method provided him with different advantages. The observational method provided information regarding the functions of talk, the initiation of talk, the role of setting, and the effect of the number of participants on talk. The quasi-experimental method did not provide this information, because all of these variables were held constant. It would be possible, however, to manipulate each of these variables in an experimental study in order to compare the effects of the different variations.

The quasi-experimental method provided greater control over extraneous variables than the naturalistic observation so that the relevance of age could be more accurately judged. In addition, by choosing to tape and transcribe all of the communicative interaction occurring in his quasi-experimental study, Taylor had more precise empirical data in that phase of his research than he did in his more informal observational stage. However, he could have taped and transcribed the observational data as well, since there is nothing inherent in the method to preclude it.

Taylor's method demonstrates that multiple methods are useful in improving the accuracy of and confidence in conclusions regarding the relationships between rules and behavior. If theorists are to explain behavior as well as identify rules for behavior, more emphasis needs to be placed on doing this kind of research and the use of multiple methods encouraged.

Summary

This chapter was concerned with comparing six methods for inferring rules from behavior and identifying different rule-behavior associations. The six methods were self-reflection, survey, naturalistic observation, participant observation, quasi-experimentation, and experimentation. The comparative advantages and disadvantages of each method were described. An attempt was made to discuss typical and inherent differences. It was argued that combined methods increased the probable accuracy and quality of the conclusions drawn.

Chapter 6

COMMUNICATION THEORY
FROM A RULES PERSPECTIVE

This chapter will be concerned with constructing communication theories from a rules perspective. It will address four questions: (1) What must be the structure of a communication theory from a rules perspective? (2) What are the potential constituents of a theory of communication from a rules perspective? (3) To what degree would such a theory meet criteria of scientific knowledge? (4) How does a communication theory predicated on a rules perspective differ from a communication theory based on a laws or systems view of human interaction.

Structure of Communication Theories from a Rules Perspective

A theory may be defined as "a set of interrelated constructs (concepts), definitions, and propositions that present a systematic view of phenomena by specifying relations among variables."[1] These specified relationships must be in the form of: laws, axiomatic statements, or causal process statements.[2] Rules theory is concerned with regularities which are prescribed, not those which are caused. Therefore, rules theory cannot take the form of causal statements.

COVERING LAWS

Since it has been argued by at least one communication scholar that rules research should be subsumed under a covering law theory, the utility of a covering law model to communication will be explored further. Charles R. Berger has been the most ardent supporter of the covering law approach to communication theory.[3] In defining the covering law model, Berger utilizes William Dray's definition:

> To put it in a summary way, what the theory maintains is that explanation is achieved, and only achieved, by subsuming what is to be explained under a general law. Such an account of the basic structure of explanation is sometimes referred to as "the regulatory analysis"; but because it makes use of the notion of bringing a case under a law, i.e., "covering" it with a law, I shall often speak of it hereafter as "the covering law model."[4]

The above definition seems to tell one more about "covering" than about the nature of laws, so a definition of laws will have to be found elsewhere. Law is often conceptualized in communication literature as a universal generalization about phenomena which are invariant through time and space.[5] Berger rejects this definition, arguing that laws are bound in space and time by their scope condition, and are therefore not universal.[6] By deleting these qualities from the definition, one is left with the statement that laws are generalizations about phenomena. If one accepts this definition, then laws cannot be distinguished from other theoretical statements which are generalizations about phenomena.

Berger also rejects two other qualities commonly associated with laws, namely, causation and determination. He draws upon Carl G. Hempel's *Aspects of Scientific Explanation* to support his arguments.[7]

Hempel indicates that all laws are not causal; some laws describe coexistence relationships. He offers Ohm's law as an example of a law of coexistence. Berger describes the relationship in the following manner:

> Thus, when Ohm's law asserts that the amount of voltage or potential in an electrical circuit (E) can be determined by multi-

plying the current flowing through circuit (I) by the resistance of the circuit (R) or E = I·R; we cannot say that the various products of current (I) and the resistence (R) cause variations in voltage (E). The equation E = I·R simply states a relationship among three variables, but says nothing about temporal order.[8]

While Berger argues that E = I·R is not a causal realtionship, he does not provide any alternative means for describing the relationship. It would seem, however, that it might be best described as a mechanistic relationship, one devoid of choice. It is meaningless to talk about voltage choosing from among available alternatives how it will respond to current flowing through a circuit and the resistance of that circuit. Given certain amounts of current and resistance, the amount of voltage is determined mechanistically, and it will always be the same amount given the same conditions.

Both Hempel and Berger argue that all laws are not 100 percent deterministic; that is, some are probabilistic. Hempel provides several examples of probablistic laws, including the effects penicillin has on curing streptococcus infections, Mendelian genetic principles, radioactive decay of radon, kinetic theory of heat, and weather patterns. Not one of these probablistic relationships identified by Hempel involves the notion of choice.[9] Rather, the effects of penicillin are only probablistic, because some infections are penicillin-resistant or some hosts are unreceptive to penicillin; Mendel's law is probabilistic, because parents can give their offspring various genes and one can therefore only estimate which genes will combine with which others, and so forth. It is meaningless to talk about penicillin choosing to affect some infections and not others, or about specific genes choosing to combine to form new life. The above laws are only probablistic, because the knowledge of the relationship is incomplete. For example, if we knew which infections were resistant, which hosts were receptive, and so on, it is conceivable that one would be able to write laws which could indicate precisely which infections in which hosts could be cured by penicillin.[10]

Berger offers the following as a probablistic law in communication: "Perceived similarity of attitudes between persons has the high probability of producing a high level of attraction between two persons."[11] In determining the nature of laws, one may ask whether Hemple's laws and Berger's law describe the same kind of relationship. For example, is the relationship between penicillin and infectious diseases the same as the relationship between perceived attitude similarity and attraction? Berger would answer this question in the affirmative by arguing that they both describe probable relationships. Rule scholars, on the other hand, would argue that Hemple's laws and Berger's law constitute different types of probable relationships, and hence they should be distinguished from each other. Actors may choose who they will be attracted to; they can violate Berger's law. Some actors may find those with similar attitudes to be boring, or they may pride themselves in being open-minded and thus surround themselves with people of various persuasions. But penicillin, genetic materials, the weather, and the like cannot choose to act in certain ways; their impact is determined mechanistically, that is, without volition.

Kaplan argues that free-will behavior may be described by laws, because laws are concerned simply with consistent behavior.[12] Rule theorists concur that humans may choose to exhibit behavioral consistencies, but they maintain that regularities based on choice are sufficiently different from mechanistic consistencies to warrant their being described by different terms.

In order to illustrate the differences that rule theorists believe are important, the following four generalizations will be compared:

(1) Objects which are falling freely near the earth will fall at 32 feet per second squared.

(2) Language development is partially dependent on the nervous system.

(3) Profane language does not appear in presidential addresses.

(4) When addressing higher-status persons, lower-status speakers address them using title plus last name, whereas higher-status speakers address lower-status persons by their first names.

Rule theorists would maintain that generalizations (1) and (2) are laws, whereas (3) and (4) are derived from rules. That these are different types of generalizations can be demonstrated by rewriting all four, the first two as if they were derived from rules and the last two as if they were laws. The asterisks indicate that the laws are unacceptable as rules and that the rules are now laws.

(*1) It is desirable that objects which are falling freely near the earth fall at 32 feet per second squared.

(*2) It is desirable that in developing language, children utilize their nervous system, though they are capable of ignoring it.

(*3) Presidents are physically incapable of cursing.

(*4) Higher-status speakers are physically incapable of addressing lower-status persons by their title plus last name, and lower-status speakers are physically incapable of addressing higher-status persons by their first name.

The major distinction that can be made between laws and rule-related descriptions is that relationships are determined in laws and prescribed by rules. It is meaningless to talk about laws describing behavior which will be evaluated positively if fulfilled, and negatively if not. For example, it is nonsensical to talk about punishing objects which do not obey the laws of gravity. In rules theory, phenomena and their interconnectedness are patterned in accordance with rules which have prescriptive, not absolute, force. Therefore, the concepts of choice and evaluation are very meaningful notions to rules theorists. The distinction between mechanistic and prescriptive phenomena is a distinction rule theorists believe worth making. Hence, they argue that the term *law* should be reserved to describe mechanistic relationships; it should not be used to describe rule-related phenomena.

The competing positions on the viability of a communication theory in the form of laws can be summarized briefly. Proponents of covering laws define them as generalizations about phenômena which are probablistic, not invariant in time and space and not necessarily universal or causal. Further, these scholars argue that communication may be described by these generalizations. Rules theorists view laws as universal generalizations which are invariant in time and space and which describe causal mechanisms. Rules theorist would probably concur that Hempel's examples of probablistic laws are laws, and, therefore, there should seem to be a contradiction between their definition of law and some relationships that are thought to be law-related. How can this contradiction be resolved?

First, rule scholars should admit that laws may be bound by scope conditions and are therefore in this sense not universal, but that laws are universal statements for the phenomena which fall under their scope conditions. Second, rules scholars can acknowledge that some laws are probablistic. They can, however, also maintain their distinction between laws and other theoretical statements by indicating that laws describe particular kinds of relationships, that is, relationships which are determined mechanistically. Rules scholars can then argue that the set-of-laws form is an inappropriate structure for communication theory from a rules perspective because laws describe mechanistic rather than prescriptive relationships.

What are scholars giving up when they reject the covering law model? Laws have been touted as the pinnacle of scientific knowledge. By not describing generalizations as laws, communication scholars run the risk of not having their truisms treated as true as the truisms of natural science, where laws describe mechanistic relationships. But this advantage is meaningless if in using the term *law*, one misrepresents the phenomena and relationships described in the theoretical statement. It is interesting to note that Dray, from whom Berger draws his definition of covering law, rejects covering law explanations for history on the grounds that it misdescribes phenomena. In fact, he argues that it is "so misleading that it ought to be abandoned as a basic account of what it is to give an explanation."[13] It is precisely because the term *law* misrepresents communication phenomena that rule scholars in general and the present author in particular reject the covering law model as the theoretical form for communication theory.

Other scholars, including Abraham Kaplan, have distinguished laws from other theoretical statements by arguing that laws are more general in scope and are supported by more empirical evidence than other theoretical statements.[14] Some may argue, therefore, that the label "law" facilitates distinguishing general from specific statements, and well-supported from less-supported claims. But such an argument does not warrant keeping the covering law model, because there are alternative classifications of theoretical statements which will allow one to organize theoretical statements hierarchically according to the degree of generality and assumed truth. Theories cast in the axiomatic form provide these advantages. Further, axiomatic theories may refer to mechanistic or prescriptive regularities. Thus, by adopting the axiomatic form, rule scholars can accrue the advantages of the law model without misrepresenting the phenomena described.

AXIOMATIC FORM

Axiomatic theory is most commonly associated with mathematical theories, such as geometry theories, but the form has also been associated with covering laws theory and causal relationships, but it need not be limited to either. In fact, Kenneth D. Bailey argues that assuming axiomatic theories must express causal relationships will result in either distorted theories or the absence of theories about noncausal relationships.[16] He maintains that axiomatic theories may describe causal, correlational, or teleological relationships. The axiomatic form can be used by rule theorists to test empirically hypothesized relationships that are derived from assumed truths.

An axiomatic theory from a rules perspective may include six types of theoretical statements. These statements may be hierarchically ordered from the most global to the most specific: axiom, postulate, proposition, theorem, hypothesis, and fact.[17] They are also ordered in terms of their dependency on direct empirical evidence. A fact is a statement applying to a particular time and place. A hypothesis is a statement which proposes a relationship between two or more different facts. Axioms, postulates, and propositions are primary statements of a theory. They differ in terms of observability. In axioms, none of the concepts are directly observable; in propositions, all are observable; and in postulates, some concepts are observable. Theorems are secondary statements which are derived from primary statements or rules, and all of their concepts are observable.

Given the prescriptive force and contextuality of rules, one can expect to observe the behavioral regularities prescribed under conditions specified by a given rule. Therefore, rules for behavior may be used to formulate theorems that explain and predict behavioral regularities given certain conditions. Facts and hypotheses can be used to test a theorem and hence its corresponding rule. Hypotheses are confirmed or disconfirmed by facts; in turn, the confirmation or disconfirmation of hypotheses is used to formulate theorems and so on up the ladder of abstraction until one reaches axioms.

Working from the opposite direction axioms are used to derive the theoretical statements below them. Axioms are like laws in that they are general in scope and they are assumed to be true, but they are different from laws in that they are not restricted to mechanistic relationships. Postulates are derived from axioms. Propositions are derived from postulates; axioms, in the absence of postulates; or definitions. Theorems may be derived from propositions. Having identified the structure rules theory may take, it is now possible to explore the nature or content of such theories.

Nature of Communication Theories from a Rules Perspective

Rules theories may relate to a variety of phenomena, such as rules for behavior, rule-related behavior, rule sanctions, meta-rule processes (e.g., development, maintenance, negotiation, change of rules), rule manipulation, and the relationship of rules and sociological-psychological variables. Theory construction from the rules perspective is too young in its development to have established axiomatic theories for these phenomena. However, in an effort to support the assertion that such theories could be developed, hypothetical examples of each will be presented below. The purpose of these examples is to demonstrate the form these theories might take and to identify possible areas of concern for rules scholars. In each case, there are many more theoretical statements which might have been made; thus, the ones listed below should be taken only as illustrative. Further, one may note that propositions have been inferred directly from axioms rather than from postulates. As rules theory becomes more advanced, theorists may wish to make more refined distinctions and thus use all three levels (axioms, postulates, and propositions) of primary statements; but given the present state of knowledge, the two part division seems more appropriate.

RULES FOR BEHAVIOR

The axioms in rules theory of communication articulate the basic assumptions of the theorists; they are not directly testable. While their validity is assumed, they are also indirectly supported by propositions that are in turn supported by theorems that are susceptible to empirical verification. Below are three axioms that would be part of a rules theory.

Axiom 1: Human beings are choice-making animals.

Axiom 2: When given a choice, human beings will choose socially acceptable behavior over behavior that is negatively evaluated.

Axiom 3: Behavior that complies with rules will be evaluated more positively than non-compliant behavior.

Propositions are derived from axioms. Given the assumptions that humans will choose positively evaluated behavior over negatively evaluated behavior and that rule-compliant behavior will be evaluated more positively than noncompliant behavior, one would expect the relationship described in proposition 1.

Proposition 1: The behavior of human beings will more often be compliant with rules than noncompliant.

Proposition 1 is not directly testable because the terms *behavior, compliant, rule,* and *noncompliant* are too general. In rules theory various theorems define these terms more specifically. Each theorem is predicated on a different rule. For example, $R_{(01)}$ is used to generate theorem 1, which in turn may be viewed as one implication of proposition 1.

$R_{(01)}$: If one wishes to take one's turn at talk, then one should wait to speak until other speakers have finished their turn. One must not interrupt another speaker.[18]

Theorem 1: Given $R_{(01)}$, speakers will exchange turns speaking more often without interruption than with interruption.

Although rules may be used to generate theorems, rules themselves are not theoretical statements, and thus are not part of the theory itself. Theoretical statements must be confirmable. (The term confirmable is used here to refer to a statement that may be confirmed or disconfirmed.) Rules are not confirmable; therefore, they cannot be theoretical statements. Rules are prescriptive statements; they express value and moral judgments. They are not statements about what exists or what will exist. Theoretical statements, on the other hand, describe relationships. If there is evidence to support the relationship described, the theoretical statement is thought to be true; if the evidence fails to support the relationship, then it is thought to be false. But the same cannot be said for rules. For example, suppose one observed a child interrupting others. This observation would not allow one to conclude that the statement "A child is morally prohibited from interrupting others" is false. The observation might, however, be used to support the description that "the child does not know the rule," and this statement is confirmable. Or similar data might be used to test the assertion that "a rule exists which prohibits interrupting another speaker."

While the prescriptions of rules are not confirmable, theorems that are derived from rules are confirmable and whether or not a rule exists is confirmable. Theorems describe the relationships expected given certain rules. Whether the relationships or behavior predicted occurs can be used to test theorems. In short, theoretical statements indicate what will happen; rules indicate what should (in a moral sense) happen. Rules express value judgments; theoretical statements do not.

Theorems are tested in specific cases in the form of hypotheses. Hypothesis 1 and 2 represent one way a researcher might seek to test theorem 1. Fact 1 represents the kind of data which might be used to confirm hypothesis 1, and fact 2 supports hypothesis 2. Since status, desire to dominate, and sex may all mitigate against rule compliance (see the section on rule-allowance behavior in Chapter 3), these factors may be controlled in a specific test of theorem 1. Note that both hypotheses are needed in order to confirm theorem 1. Hypothesis 1 tests whether or not a behavior recurs in a similar context, but all behavioral regularities are not rule-generated (see Chapter 3). Hypothesis 2 tests the criticizability of the behavior. Since behavior may be evaluated for reasons other than rule compliance, both hypotheses 1 and 2 are needed.

> Hypothesis 1: In groups where communicators are of equal status
> and equal desire to dominate, speaking turns will be exchanged
> more often without interruption than with interruption.

Hypothesis 2: The exchange of turns without interruption will be evaluated more positively than those with interruptions.

Fact 1: In an all-male, leaderless group, 90 percent of the turns at speaking were exchanged without interruption.

Fact 2: The exchange of turns without interruption was rated significantly more positive than those with interruption.

The above format could be used to write theoretical statements for any rule. The axioms and propositions would remain the same, but theorems would vary according to their corresponding rules, and hence different hypotheses would be generated and different empirical regularities tested. To illustrate this possibility, statements for a rule for summons and response are outlined below; axioms 1 through 3 and proposition 1 would remain the same.

$R_{(02)}$: If one is summoned and one hears that summons, then one is obligated to respond to that summons.[19]

Theorem 2: Given $R_{(02)}$, speakers will respond to a summons more often than not.

Hypothesis 3: If a communicator hears his/her name called, s/he will answer the call more often than not.

Hypothesis 4: Speakers who hear their names called and answer the summons will be evaluated more positively than those who do not.

Fact 3: In the 500 cases observed, all calls were answered.

Fact 4: Native speakers indicated that not answering a summons that is heard is rude.

RULE-RELATED BEHAVIOR

Theoretical statements for rule-related behavior may indicate when a particular kind of rule-related behavior is most likely to occur. Because the rule taxonomy in Chapter 4 has never appeared in print before, one cannot expect to find previous theoretical statements based on that taxonomy. However, it is possible to envision potential theoretical statements based on that taxonomy.

Rule-Fulfilling and Rule-Ignorant Behavior.

Definition 1: Rule-fulfilling and rule-ignorant behavior involve an absence of rule knowledge.

Axiom 4: Rule awareness is dependent on rule exposure; the more the exposure, the greater the awareness.

Proposition 2: Children, newcomers, and foreigners are less likely to be exposed to the rules; therefore, they are less likely to know the rules of interaction in a given culture than native adults.

Theorem 3: Since children, newcomers, and foreigners are less likely to know the rules than native adults, and since rule-fulfilling and rule-ignorant behavior occur when the actor is unaware of the rule, the behaviors of children, newcomers, and foreigners are more likely to be rule-fulfilling and/or rule-ignorant than the behavior of native adults.

Rule-Conforming and Rule-Error Behavior.

Definition 2: Rule-conforming and rule-error behavior involve a tacit sense of a rule.

Axiom 5: The more often rule-related behavior is repeated, the more likely the rule will become part of the actor's tacit knowledge.

Proposition 3: Since behaviors which occur everyday are repeated often (e.g., turn-taking, greeting), rules for everyday behaviors are more likely to be part of one's tacit rule knowledge than rules for more formal, less common, rituals (e.g., formal table setting, flag folding, addressing wedding invitations).

Theorem 4: Since rules for everyday behaviors are likely to be known tacitly and since rule-conforming and rule-error behaviors involve tacit knowledge, then in performing common behaviors, one's behavior is more likely to involve rule-conforming or rule-error behavior than more conscious adherence to the rules.

Rule-Following and Rule-Violation Behavior.

Definition 3: Rule-following behavior and rule-violation behavior involve explicit reference to the rules in acting in a given situation.

Axiom 6: The less often a given behavior is repeated, the less likely the rule will become part of the actor's subconscious knowledge.

Proposition 4: Since behaviors which occur less often are repeated less, actors will need to refer to rules explicitly more often when performing less common behaviors than everyday behaviors.

Theorem 5: Therefore, rule-following and rule-violation behavior are more likely to occur in performing less common behaviors than common ones.

Rule-Reflective Behavior.

Definition 4: Positive and negative rule-reflective behavior involve judgments about the quality of a rule as well as whether to enact the rule.

Axiom 7: Actors typically take rules for granted unless changes occur or they experience dissatisfaction.

Proposition 5: Therefore, assessments of rules are more likely to occur at transitional times, such as during changes in roles, relationships, and social institutions, than when these factors are in a stable state.[20]

Theorem 6: Therefore, positive and negative rule-reflective behaviors are more likely to occur in times of change than in times of stability.

RULE-SANCTIONS

Chapter 3 included a discussion of when behavior that does not comply with a rule is or is not likely to be sanctioned. From the generalizations presented in Chapter 3, some theoretical statements regarding rule-related sanctions can be proposed:

Axiom 3: Behavior that complies with rules will be evaluated more positively than noncompliant behavior.

Proposition 6: Noncompliant behavior will be negatively sanctioned most of the time, but there are some circumstances that mitigate against negatively sanctioning noncompliant behavior.

Theorem 7: Persons who are thought to be ignorant of a rule are less likely to be negatively sanctioned for noncompliance than those who are thought to be knowledgeable.

Theorem 8: Minor deviations from a rule that fail to reach one's threshold for deviation tolerance are less likely to be negatively sanctioned than major deviations which cross over the threshold.

Theorem 9: If a negative sanction is violation of politeness rules and is thought, in a particular case, to be a greater violation than the original violation, the negative sanction is less likely to occur.

Theorem 10: If there is little agreement about a rule and/or the conditions for which it applies (low crystallization), negative sanctions are less likely than if there is high agreement.

Theorem 11: If a rule is considered trivial (low intensity), noncompliance is less likely to result in sanctions than if the rule is considered vital.

META-RULE PROCESSES

In addition to identifying rules and various relationships between rules and behavior, rule scholars are interested in how rules are developed, maintained, negotiated and changed. Theoretical statements relative to rule-reflective behavior and rule-sanctions are relevant to meta-rule processes inasmuch as rule-reflectivity may result in developing, maintaining, negotiating, or changing the rules, and sanctioning or not sanctioning behavior may result in the same processes. Below are some additional examples of possible theoretical statements regarding meta-rule processes.[21]

Axiom 8: Rules do not exist in nature; rather, they are developed by humans.

Axiom 9: Although rules are developed by humans, communicators do not typically begin interactions by developing rules; rather, actors of the same culture will asume that they share the same rules unless given contrary evidence.

Proposition 7: Therefore, actors will behave as if they share rules until the behavior of one indicates that they do not share the same rules.

Proposition 8: If behavior is viewed as a deviation from the rule, actors will attribute an explanation to the deviation.

Proposition 9: Noncompliant behavior with an assumed rule may be perceived as rule-ignorant, rule-error, rule-violation, or negative-rule-reflective behavior, or nonagreement on rules.

Theorem 12: If a noncompliance is viewed as rule-ignorant behavior the actor who knows the rule will either ignore the deviation or s/he will inform the deviator of the rule and ask the deviator to comply.

Theorem 13: If the noncompliance is viewed as an error by both actors and the deviation is acknowledged, the behavior will be corrected and the rule maintained.

Theorem 14: If the noncompliance is a rule-violation and the deviation is sufficiently disturbing, the deviator will be expected to justify his/her behavior.

Theorem 15: If the noncompliance is the result of conflicting rules, and the actors wish to continue interacting, the rules will be negotiated.

Theorem 16: If previous rules seem outdated, inappropriate, or in conflict with other rules, they will be negotiated and changed.

RULE MANIPULATION

All conscious uses of rules could be described as rule manipulation, but the phrase is used here to refer to the manipulating of rules in such a way as to benefit oneself at the expense of others. For example, one may manipulate self-disclosure rules to maximize power rather than intimacy,[22] one may use politeness rules to exercise power over others to get one's way at the expense of others,[23] or one may exploit conversational maxims in order to deceive others.[24] (For a more detailed discussion of this type of manipulation, see the section on negative sanctions of manipulative rule-violation and the section on rule-allowance behavior in Chapter 3.) Theories related to rule manipulation may contain theoretical statements similar to the following ones:

Axiom 10: The manipulative nature of a given behavior must not be apparent if it is to be a successful manipulation, because actors do not like to be manipulated.

Proposition 10.: Behavior which manipulates the rules must, on the surface (i.e., exclusive of motives, intentions, and so on), be rule-compliant behavior if it is to be successful.

Theorem 17: A person who wishes to increase intimacy will self-disclose private information.

Theorem 18: A person who wishes to manipulate others via self-disclosure will give the appearance of sharing private information in order to encourage another person to self-disclosure; this, in turn, will make the second person vulnerable to the first.

Theorem 19: A person who wishes to be polite will provide options for his/her listeners.

Theorem 20: A person who wishes to manipulate others via politeness will provide the appearance of giving options, while obli-
gating the hearer to comply with the speaker's request.

Theorem 21: Indirect answers to questions will often be viewed as
legitimate answers.

Theorem 22: Devious speakers will dodge accountability by answering questions indirectly.

RULES AND SOCIOLOGICAL AND PSYCHOLOGICAL VARIABLES

Sociological factors—culture, status, class, race, sex, age,
roles, and so forth—are related to rules as part of the scope conditions of rules. Therefore, theoretical statements in a communication theory from a rules perspective may include references to
sociological variables. These theoretical statements would be
similar to those for rules in general, with the addition of sociological factors. Below is one possible example of such statements:

Axiom 11: The applicability of some rules is dependent on actor
variables.

Proposition 11: Status is one actor variable which influences rules;
different rules are applicable for high-status and low-status
speakers.

Theorem 23: Higher-status communicators will be addressed more
often by their title plus last name by lower-status speakers than
by their first name.

$R_{(03)}$: If one is addressing a higher-status person, then one should use
that person's title plus last name.[25]

Theorem 24: Lower-status communicators will be addressed more
often by their first name by higher-status speakers than by their
title plus last name.

$R_{(04)}$: If one is addressing a lower-status person, then one should use
that person's first name.[26]

Psychological variables, like dogmatism, ego-involvement,
introversion, extroversion, and attraction, may also be part of the
scope conditions of rules if one is concerned with rules of how one
communicates that one is dogmatic, ego-involved, extroverted,
attracted, and so on. In these cases, the theoretical statements

should look something like the sociological statements only with the variables and relationships changed.

Psychological variables may be related to rules in other ways.[27] Since psychological variables have not been the focus of rules research, the following hypothetical statements should be viewed as illustrative but highly speculative as to what some of these theoretical statements might be.

Axiom 12: Dogmatic individuals have a greater respect for authority than nondogmatic individuals.

Proposition 12: Since rules may be symbols of authority, dogmatic individuals will have a lower tolerance for rule-violation than nondogmatic individuals.

Theorem 25: Since the expression of negative sanctions is negatively correlated with a tolerance for rule-violation, dogmatic individuals will more often negatively sanction rule-violation than nondogmatic individuals.

Axiom 13: Communicators differ in their ego-involvement with rules.

Proposition 13: The degree to which one is ego-involved with a rule will affect his/her compliance with the rule.

Theorem 26: Those who are highly ego-involved with a rule will comply with the prescription of the rule more often than those who are lowly ego-involved.

Axiom 14: Extroverted persons are more likely to confront others with disagreements than introverted persons.

Proposition 14: Introverted and extroverted persons will differ in their methods for the resolution of rule conflict among other persons.

Theorem 27: Introverted persons are more likely to adopt the rules of others to avoid conflict than extroverted persons; extroverted persons are more likely to negotiate which rules should apply in a given situation than introverted persons.

Axiom 15: People who comply with rules are perceived more positively than those who do not comply with rules.

Proposition 15: Since different persons in a given situation may comply with different rules and since compliance may increase positive evaluations and attractions, attraction may be affected by the degree of rule agreement.

Theorem 28. As rule agreement increases, attraction will increase; as rule agreement decreases, attraction will decrease.

These examples illustrate that communication theory from a rules perspective may include sociological and psychological variables which have appeared in previous communication theories and research. However, to be included in a communication theory from a rules perspective, such variables must be related to rules.

SUMMARY

The purposes of this section have been to illustrate what theories of communication from a rules perspective might look like and to highlight a variety of theoretical issues with which theories might be concerned. Rules theory may be concerned with such phenomena as rules for behavior, rule-related behavior, rule sanctions, meta-rule processes, rule manipulations, and the relationship of rules to sociological and psychological variables. Communication theory from a rules perspective may be expressed in an axiomatic form with axioms stating what is assumed to be true about humans as communicators and theorems describing specific relationships predicted by rules. Theoretical statements from axioms to theorems increase in their specificity. The next section will consider how these statements can be used to explain, predict, and control phenomena.

Criteria for Scientific Knowledge

Theory construction is a basic aim of science.[28] Theories may be evaluated in regard to their ability to explain, predict, and control behavior.[29] The relative merits of two other theoretical approaches, covering laws and systems, have been compared recently with the rules perspective.[30] This section will be concerned with two questions: (1) Does the rules perspective provide explanation, prediction, and control in relation to communication behavior? and (2) Does the rules perspective provide advantages over the covering laws or systems approaches in respect to the three criteria for scientific theory?

EXPLANATION

To provide an explanation is "to make intelligible facts which have already been recorded."[31] Explanation may take many forms: (1) what, (2) mental-concept, (3) reason-giving, and (4) causal.[32] Each type of explanation will be defined and the relationship of a rules theory to these various forms of explanation will be explored in this section. After the explanatory power of rules theory has been presented, it will be compared with the explanatory functions of covering laws theories and systems theories. Before beginning, however, it must be made clear that rules do not in themselves explain behavior; rather, it is theoretical statements inferred from rules which explain phenomena.

What Explanations. What explanations classify and categorize phenomena. They answer questions like: What is it? and What is going on? Such explanations may constitute the definitions in theory construction. The nine-part taxonomy of rule-related behavior explicated in chapter 4 is a what explanation. In addition, theorists may use rules to explain what a particular behavior or role is. For example, if one were to ask, "What is statement B in dialogue$_{(01)}$?" a rules theorist might respond, "B is an indirect answer to A"; B can be explained as an indirect answer by appealing to a rule for producing indirect answers, like R$_{(05)}$.

Dialogue$_{(01)}$:

A: Going to be working at the office?

B: Do I dress up like this to mow the lawn?[33]

R$_{(05)}$: If one wishes to answer a question indirectly, then one should utter a statement or question for which the existential value is known to the original questioner.

Or in answering the question "What is a given act (e.g., promise)?" theorists might say that X (e.g., a promise) is an act which occurs when all the rules for X (e.g., John Searle's five rules for making a promise)[34] are honored. For role-related questions like "What is a lady?" theorists may answer that a lady is a woman who follows the rules which apply to ladies. Finally, to questions like "What is going on?" rule theorists might respond that X (e.g., lecturing, arguing, gossiping) is happening because the actors are fulfilling the rules for X.

Peter R. Monge claims that "what explanations can be scientifically useful for classifying phenomena, but they do little to advance our knowledge and understanding of communication."[35] Monge does not elaborate on this assertion, and there seems to be little reason to accept his criticism of what explanations. What explanations are valuable in telling us what constitutes certain communicative acts (e.g., promises, greetings, answers), roles (e.g., lady, subordinate, leader), and episodes (e.g., fighting, loving, chatting). In specifying what constitutes an act, role, or episode, one may have a better sense of what communication behaviors are and how they are enacted. What explanations can provide important insights into the process of communication.

Mental-Concept Explanations. If behavior is explained in terms of some mental states, such as attitude, attraction, knowledge, or personality factors, it can be labeled a mental-concept explanation. A mental state is measured by some form of behavior such as answering direct questions, making comparisons, performing certain tasks, and filling out scales. This behavior is then compared with other behaviors and/or other variables. For example, individuals may indicate how ego-involved they are with certain rules, and then one could investigate whether the degree of reported ego-involvement influenced rule-compliance. If reported ego-involvement did have an impact, then rule-compliance could be at least partially explained by appealing to the mental state of ego-involvement.

All of the theoretical statements regarding rule-related behavior presented in this chapter may be viewed as having the potential to provide mental-concept explanations. All are concerned with the level of rule knowledge and rule consciousness. Rule-reflective behavior is also related to attitudes, another mental concept. Similarly, the statments regarding psychological variables and rules may provide mental-concept explanations. Mental-concept explanations may answer questions such as "Why does rule-reflective behavior occur at certain times and not others?" or "Why do some people seem less tolerant of rule violations than others?" The answer to the first question may utilize a mental-concept of changing values, whereas an answer to the second might appeal to individual differences in dogmatism or ego-involvement.

Monge maintains that "mental-concepts are what-explanations. They do not attempt to relate two things in such a way that one could be predicted from the other."[36] From the examples above and the theoretical statements, it should be clear that mental-concepts can be used to predict other phenomena (e.g., increases in ego-involvement lead to greater rule conformity). Further, mental-concept explanations can answer why questions such as those identified above, and they can be used to predict future behavior.

Reason-Giving Explanations. Teleological or reason-giving explanations have been the type most often associated with the rules perspective.[37] A reason-giving explanation answers questions about why someone or some group acted in a certain way by offering a justification for that behavior. As the concept of a rules-based theory of communication implies, behavioral regularities are explained in terms of rules; that is, such questions as "Why did s/he do that?" may be answered, "Because a rule prescribed that behavior."

With regard to dialogue$_{(02)}$, for example, one can answer the question "Why did Chris say 'Yes?'" by referring to rules. The explanation might be as follows: Pat summoned Chris; summons-and-response rules obligate Chris to respond to Pat's summons; "Yes?"—is an acceptable response to a summons; therefore, Chris said "Yes?" because a rule obligates one to respond to a summons.

Dialogue$_{(02)}$:

Pat: Chris?
Chris: Yes?
Pat: Did you see . . . ?

The practical syllogism has been offered as the primary model for teleological explanation for the rules perspective.[38] The practical syllogism explains actions in terms of reasons. It represents what was "practical" from the actor's point of view by indicating that an actor behaved in a certain way because s/he believed that the behavior was necessary to bring about a desired goal. In its simplest form, the practical syllogism is constructed in this way.[39]

A person intends to bring about p.

S/he considers that p cannot be brought about unless s/he does a.

Therefore, the person sets him/herself to do a.

Although the practical syllogism is the most popular explanatory model for rules research, it has several weaknesses: (1) it implies that rules can only explain intentional behavior, (2) it fails to incorporate the prescriptive force of rules, and (3) it does not include explicit statements of rules or evidence of their existence.

The emphasis on intentions in the practical syllogism may have contributed to the assumption that rules can be used to explain only intentional behavior. This assumption has been one of the major criticisms of the paradigm.[40] But as discussed in previous chapters (2-4), rules may be known tacitly and actors may comply with rules consciously or subconsciously. An adequate explanatory model of rule-related behavior must be able to accomodate both intentional and unintentional behavior.

Another inadequacy of the practical syllogism as a model for rule-related explanations is that it may be used to describe any relationship between a goal and a behavior or set of behaviors. Rule-related explanations, however, are not appropriate for all behaviors. As argued in Chapter 3, rule-generated behavior is a particular type of behavior.

The practical syllogism may lead to explanations of behavior that is not the result of a rule. Consider, for example, this practical syllogism:

A person intends to become wealthy.

This person considers that in order to become wealthy, s/he must rob a bank.

Therefore, this person proceeds to rob a bank.

W. Barnett Pearce argues that rules are the warrants that justify the second premise of the practical syllogism.[41] Therefore, if the behavior in the above syllogism is to be taken as an explanation of rule-generated behavior, some understanding of the operative

rule is necessary. The second premise of the syllogism implies a rule
something like $*R_{(06)}$.

> $*R_{(06)}$: If one wishes to become wealthy, then one is obligated (preferred) to rob a bank.

Such a rule is theoretically possible, but it does not represent the
legal position of this country, nor, for that matter, the moral perspective of most Americans. Robbing banks to become wealthy
may be a rule of bank robbers. but it is also possible that they
would prefer to be independently wealthy. But my primary point
is not that a rule like $*R_{(06)}$ does not or could not exist but rather
that the practical syllogism does not state that a behavior is obligated, preferred, or prohibited, nor does it provide evidence of a
rule prescribing that behavior.

In fairness to rule scholars who use the practical syllogism, it
should be said that they would probably not generate syllogisms
like the bank robbing example. Rather, they would probably
begin with evidence of a rule's existence and then use the syllogism to explain only rule-related behavior. However, the practical
syllogism itself does not focus on prescriptive behavior or evidence of a rule, and these qualities should be explicit components
of any explanatory model of rule-generated behavior.

Explanations for behavior on the basis of rules is further restricted by the nature of the relationship between a rule and a
behavior. Rules may be used to explain rule-compliant behavior.
They cannot explain noncompliant behavior, except when noncompliance is due to negative-rule-reflection (e.g., feminist rejection of rules for traditional heterosexual relationships) or when
noncompliance occurs because one rule supersedes another (e.g.,
when one's disagreement with another person violates a preferential rule for agreement in order to honor a rule regarding honesty).
In all other cases, noncompliant behavior must be explained by
other constructs, including ignorance, inattention, noise, frustration, anger, and manipulation. Further, rules cannot be used to
explain rule-fulfilling behavior because the actor does not know
the rule. To explain behavior in terms of a rule, researchers must
also demonstrate that an actor had at least tacit knowledge of it.
An adequate model of rule-related explanations must take into

account the prescriptive quality of rules and the actor's knowledge of the rule.

The prescriptive force of rules is consonant with the assumption that human beings seek to maximize rewards and minimize punishments. Since deviations from rule prescriptions may result in negative sanctions, actors comply with the rule in order to minimize punishment. Further, complying with preferential rules may increase the actor's rewards (e.g., the polite speaker may be liked more than the impolite or minimally polite speaker). An explanatory model for communicative rules should include references to the desire of humans to maximize rewards and minimize punishments.

In summary, then, a model for rule-related explanation should include the following features: (1) specification of the behavior observed, (2) identification of the operative rules, (3) evidence of the existence of the rule, (4) notation that rule explanations are limited to situations where the actor has at least tacit knowledge of the rule, and (5) a statement accounting for the original behavior in terms of the prescriptive force of rules and the desire of humans to maximize rewards and minimize punishments.

Walter R. Fisher and the present author have argued that Stephen E. Toulmin's model of argument meets these requirements more satisfactorily than the practical syllogism.[42] Below are two graphic representations of this model. Figure 6.1 is an abstract model, and Figure 6.2 is an application of the model to a specific case.

In the model, the actor's behavior is the data. The rule serves as the warrant for the claim that the behavior can be explained in terms of the rule, and the rule is backed by evidence of the rule's existence. The "unless" statement qualifies an explanation rendering it invalid if the actor has no knowledge of the rule. The model represents explanations for behaviors resulting from obligatory or preferential rules. It can, however, be easily modified for prohibitive rules. In the abstract model for the data, one may substitute "did not to Y" for "did Y"; the first warrant may replace "required (preferred)" with "prohibited"; for the backing, the rule could read "If X, then Y is prohibited" and the evidence should then indicate that Y is regularly absent in context X; and, for the claim, substitute "not doing Y" for "Y."

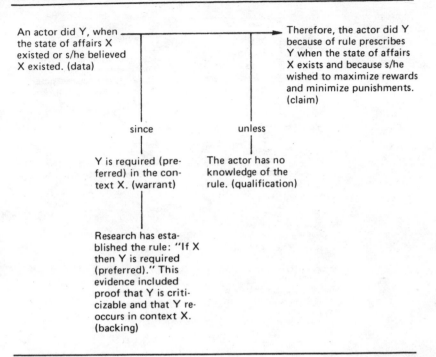

An actor did Y, when the state of affairs X existed or s/he believed X existed. (data)

Therefore, the actor did Y because of rule prescribes Y when the state of affairs X exists and because s/he wished to maximize rewards and minimize punishments. (claim)

since

unless

Y is required (preferred) in the context X. (warrant)

The actor has no knowledge of the rule. (qualification)

Research has established the rule: "If X then Y is required (preferred)." This evidence included proof that Y is criticizable and that Y reoccurs in context X. (backing)

FIGURE 6.1:   Explanatory Model—Abstract Version

This model specifies the relationships among behavior, rules, and their prescriptive force. It requires that researchers establish the operative rules and provide evidence of their existence. The qualification clause indicates that rule explanations are valid only if the actor has at least tacit knowledge of the rule, but unlike the practical syllogism, it is not limited to intentional behavior. In short, the model meets all of the needs of a rule-related explanation without incurring any of the disadvantages of the practical syllogism. Using this model, researchers can use rules to provide reason-giving explanations for rule-generated behavior.

Causal Explanation. Rules, by definition, cannot provide causal/mechanistic explanation. Rules prescribe behavior which is followable and breakable; hence, theoretical statements

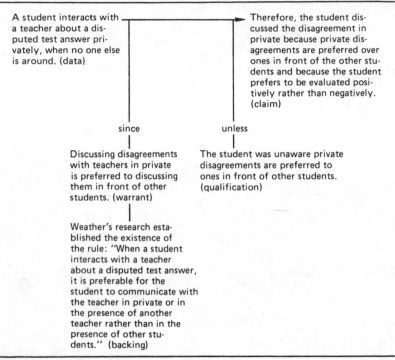

A student interacts with a teacher about a disputed test answer privately, when no one else is around. (data)

Therefore, the student discussed the disagreement in private because private disagreements are preferred over ones in front of the other students and because the student prefers to be evaluated positively rather than negatively. (claim)

since

unless

Discussing disagreements with teachers in private is preferred to discussing them in front of other students. (warrant)

The student was unaware private disagreements are preferred to ones in front of other students. (qualification)

Weather's research established the existence of the rule: "When a student interacts with a teacher about a disputed test answer, it is preferable for the student to communicate with the teacher in private or in the presence of another teacher rather than in the presence of other students." (backing)

FIGURE 6.2: Explanatory Model—Specific Example

generated from rules cannot describe mechanistic relationships. Because rules do not provide causal explanations, it has been argued that rules theory cannot explain phenomena. But this position assumes that there is only one kind of explanation.

Charles R. Berger has been critical of the rules perspective on the grounds that it does not explain *why* a particular behavior occurred.[43] But, it has already been demonstrated that rules research can provide two kinds of why answers: either in terms of mental-concept explanations or in terms of teleological explanations. To argue that rules lack the ability to explain why something happened is to assume mistakenly that all explanations are causal.

To illustrate how causal and teleological explanations differ, examples of these two forms of explanations are provided below. In the reason-giving explanation, the actor plays an active role in determining the outcome. In the causal explanation, the actor is the passive medium through which something occurs.

Reason-giving explanation: The actor did X because s/he chose to follow rule A, which prescribes X.

Causal explanation: Y caused the actor to do X.

Some of Berger's other criticisms are at least partially predicated on a misunderstanding of the concept "rule." For example, he assumes that rules cannot provide an explanation of why certain rules are chosen over other rules (In fairness to Berger, it should be pointed out that two rule scholars, Romano Harré and Paul Secord, make the same error.)[44] Scope conditions are part of the structure of a rule. Scope conditions indicate when a particular rule is applicable and when it is not. Hence, in complying with rules, an actor matches the scope conditions of a given rule with his/her desires, the context, the other actors, and so forth and makes his/her choice of rules accordingly. For instance, whether one follows the address rules indicating that first names or last names plus title are appropriate will depend on a number of factors outlined in various address rules. Whether an actor would follow $R_{(07)}$ and $R_{(08)}$, for example, would depend on whether or not the situation matched the if clause of $R_{(07)}$ or $R_{(08)}$.

$R_{(07)}$: If one is addressing superordinates, then one should address them by title plus last name.[45].

$R_{(08)}$: If one is addressing subordinates or status equals, then one should address them by first names.[46]

The above description of how the scope conditions of rules can be used to explain why certain rules are chosen implies only a one-way relationship between rules and situations; that is, it assumes a situation exists and the actor simply complies with rules that are appropriate for that situation. But one may also use rule-compliance behavior to create a situation; for example, if one wants to escalate the intimacy of a relationship, one may behave according to rules appropriate for friends rather than strangers on the hope that the behavior will change the definition of the situation (relaship). One's desires may be part of the scope condition of the rules (e.g., if one wishes to escalate the intimacy of a stranger/ stranger relationship, then one . . .), but if one asks why the actor wishes to escalate the relationship, then it is possible that s/he may have to seek an explanation outside of the rules paradigm and appeal to such things as need states. On the other hand, it is possible that the desire to escalate the relationship is based on the fact that s/he perceived that s/he and the other person share similar rules. The point here is that why an actor wants to create a certain situation may be beyond the power of rules to explain, but why s/he behaves in certain ways given his/her desires can be explained in terms of rules.

Berger also argues that rules will not explain why one culture abides by one set of rules and another culture follows other rules. At times, however, rules may be explained at least in part by referring to other rules. This procedure is illustrated below by using the maxim-and-rule format suggested in Chapter 2. The rules may be explained in terms of the maxims, which may be viewed as higher-order rules. The maxims and rules have been inferred from comparisons of Indian and non-Indian communities and classrooms reported by Susan U. Philips.[47]

Non-Indian Community

Maxim: If a single individual has been officially designated a leader, then that individual should direct and control the activity of the group as long as that person retains his/her official position. (For example, a teacher should direct his/her students.)

$R_{(09)}$: If one is a teacher, then one should decide when a student will be allowed to speak and to whom.

Indian Community

Maxim: If one is a member of a group, then s/he should chose his/ her degree of participation in any activity.

$R_{(10)}$: If one wishes to speak, then one should speak when s/he is able to get the floor in accordance with turn-taking rules but s/he should not wait to be chosen by someone else to speak.

$R_{(11)}$: If a member of a group does not wish to speak, then other members of the group are prohibited from forcing that person to speak.

Using rules (maxims) to explain other rules is characterized by Berger as follows: "Resort to such notions as meta-rules, meta-meta rules, and meta-meta-meta rules with the hope of subsuming more particular rules under more general ones seems little different from the logic of the covering law approach."[48] In this statement, Berger is not using meta-rule in the same way as it was defined in Chapter 2, where it was defined as a rule which prescribes other rules; rather, his meta-rule seems similar to maxim, and meta-meta rule seems similar to principle, as maxim and principle were defined in Chapter 2. His description of meta-rules, meta-meta rules, and meta-meta-meta rules implies the same hierarchy implied by the principle to maxim to rule relationship; maxims are derived from principles, and rules are derived from maxims. As one moves from rules to principles, the statements become more general in scope. Thus, principles share the quality of greater generality with laws, but they are distinct from laws in three ways: (1) they express cultural values, (2) they are not theoretical statements, and (3) they do not describe mechanistic relationships. The principle-rule hierarchy and the axiom-fact hierarchy make it possible to explain cultural differences in rules without appealing to laws.

Ultimately, however, one may ask why do certain cultures have different maxims. If one answers "Because they have different principles and values," then one might ask why this is true. One may try to explain such relationships by appealing to historical, geographical, and/or physiological evidence, but these particular relationships cannot be explained by referring to rules. This, then, is a limitation of rules theory in general.

In addition to not answering why questions requiring historical, geographical, and physiological explanations, rules do not provide explanations which are predicated on the nature of humans. For example one cannot use rules to answer such questions as "Why are humans symbol-using animals?" or "Why do actors seek to avoid punishment and maximize rewards (if in fact they do)?" The answers to these questions are relevant to rules research, inasmuch as rule theorists assume that humans are symbol users, that they must develop rules in order to use those symbols for communicative purposes, and that the avoidance of punishment is the primary motivation for following rules. However, these questions are concerned with psychological or biological matters rather than symbolic interaction itself. Therefore, by not providing such explanations, rules theory does not present a significant hindrance to the development of communication theories qua communication.[49]

This does not mean that answers to historical, geographical, physiological, or psychological questions are irrelevant to communication processes or theory. Such information can improve our understanding of communicators and their symbolic interaction. For example, communication scholars may feel a greater sense of understanding if they can relate communication theory to theories regarding such factors as (1) physiological development and decay, (2) physical limitations of memory and sensory processing, and (3) respiratory and sound processes—all relative to communicative behavior. For example, in addition to asking when and how children acquire certain communicative rules, we may want to know what physical development must occur in order to make the acquisition process possible. Or, while we know that the rules of grammar permit infinitely long sentences, it may be useful to know the physical limitations for processing utterances in order to explain rules regarding practical or preferred limitations on length and complexity. Or, in trying to assess whether voice differences between males and females are solely biological or a combination of social rules and biological factors, one needs to know the range of biological possibilities.

Communication theories can profit from knowledge gained from research based on the assumptions of laws, but this knowledge should not comprise the primary focus of communication theories, because laws do not explain symbolic interaction itself; they do not explain what happens when two or more individuals interact symbolically or why they are able to orchestrate and make sense out of their symbolic interaction. Theory from a rules perspective can provide this kind of explanation. Therefore, a rules perspective should play a central role in the development of communication theories.

Communication theory from a rules perspective can provide what, mental-concept, and reason-giving explanations; it cannot provide causal explanations. This limitation does not seem to be very serious inasmuch as mechanistic relationships do not appear to play a central role in explaining symbolic interaction. However, rules theory is predicated on certain assumptions about the inherent nature of human beings, and these assumptions cannot be explained by appealing to rules.

One may, then, ask whether a covering law or systems theory offers a more complete explanation of communication. Theory from a laws perspective is concerned with mechanistic relationships. Communication theory from a laws perspective assumes that there is a necessary relationship between the antecedents and consequences; they do not use prescriptive force to explain behavioral regularities. Systems theory involves constructs, definitions, and theoretical statements which focus on a holistic approach to a system. A system may be defined as "a whole that functions as a whole by virtue of the interdependence of its parts."[50]

Rules, Laws, and Systems Explanations. All three types of theories can provide what explanations. For example, a cognitive dissonance law might be used to answer the question "What is cognitive dissonance?" and system statements about feedback might be used to answer the question "What is feedback?" However, some what explanations in rules theory may differ from what explanations in covering laws. In rules theory, one may appeal to rules to answer what some act is (e.g., promise, greeting, request), but in covering laws theory, what explanations may be a function of formal definitions, equations, or mechanistic relationships. Laws cannot answer what is a symbolic act inasmuch as such acts are prescribed by rules.

Some scholars have assumed that laws do not deal with mental states because mental states can only be measured indirectly via behavior. However, this has not been the position of many communication theorists from a law perspective. In fact, quite the opposite has been the case; their research has been dominated by constructs related to mental states such as attitudes, attribution, cognitive dissonance, communication apprehension, and ego-involvement.[51] The utilization of mental-concept explanations has been more typical of communication research from a laws perspective than either the systems or rules approach, but it is not inherent to the covering law paradigm. It has already been demonstrated how rules theory might involve mental-concept explanations. There is some disagreement among systems scholars about whether or not systems theories should include mental-concepts.[52] But if system theories include mental-concepts, then they can provide mental-concept explanations.

It would be nonsensical to talk about laws providing reason-giving explanations; it does not make sense to say the earth chooses to circle the sun because it believes that is the appropriate thing to do. Peter R. Monge argues that systems theory could include teleological explanations.[53] Donald Cushman and W. Barnett Pearce, on the other hand, maintain that relationships in systems theories are determined by logical rather than prescriptive force.[54] In response to Cushman and Pearce's argument, Vernon E. Cronen and Leslie K. Davis argue that Cushman and Pearce confuse open systems with closed systems; that while closed systems are not affected by prescriptive force, open systems could be susceptible to this influence.[55] If systems theorists view teleological explanations as relevant to their analysis and include it in their research, then systems theory can provide reason-giving explanations. However, even though reason-giving explanations may be provided by systems theory, reason-giving explanations have not been typical of systems research.[56]

Laws provide causal explanations. If a system theorist is investigating mechanistic relationships (e.g., functions of a biological system), then s/he may provide causal explanations. Rules theory does not provide causal explanations.

A summary of the types of explanations that can be provided by the various theoretical perspectives is presented in Table 6.1.

Of the conceptual approaches covered here, systems theory is the only one that offers all four types of explanation. It would appear, therefore, that systems theory is more heuristic than rules theory. However, systems theory can only explain rule-generated acts and various levels of rule-related behavior if it incorporates theoretical statements from rule theory. Because symbolic interaction (communication) requires the use of rules in order to make sense out of otherwise arbitrary representations, rules are central in communicative processes; therefore, above all else, a theory of communication must involve rule-related explanations if it is to account fully for symbolic interaction. Although some scholars have argued that systems theory can include such explanations, these explanations have not appeared in most communication studies from a systems perspective.[57] Whether or not systems

TABLE 6.1   *Explanatory Potential of Laws, Rules, and Systems Approaches*

Theory Type	What	Mental-Concept	Reason-Giving	Causal
		Type of Explanation		
Law	X	X		X
Rule	X	X	X	
System	X	X	X	X

theory embraces rules theory, the dimensions, criteria, and implications of rules theory must be clearly stated if scholars are to provide accurate explanations of communication.

PREDICTION

There has been some question over the degree to which rules theory can predict behavior.[58] With the exception of highly ritualized routines, such as "Thank you/ You're welcome," "How are you?/Fine," "Do you solemnly swear to tell the whole truth and nothing but the truth?/ I do," rules theory will not predict specific behaviors; but, then, neither can the covering law or systems approaches to communication theory.

Based on the theorems offered in the first part of this chapter, rules theory may be able to offer predictions regarding (1) what type of behavior will occur if the desires of actors and/or environmental factors (linguistic and nonlinguistic) that influence rule choice are known, (2) when certain levels of rule-conscious behavior will occur, (3) when negative sanctions for noncompliant-rule behavior are most and least likely to occur, (4) how and when various meta-rule processes will occur, (5) how rule manipulation will occur and when it is most likely to be successful, and (6) the interdependence of psychological variables and rule-related behavior. There may well be other predictive relationships that involve rules, but these six illustrate the wide range of behavior rules theory might predict.

If one talks about predicting certain classes of behavior, paired groups like "questions/answers," "summons/response," "greeting/greeting," then given the first member of the pair, rules theory can predict the second pair-part with relatively high success.[59] Or, given a preact (e.g., preoffer, preannouncement, preclosing) and the response to the preact, rules theory can predict whether the act will occur or be aborted.[60] Rules theory can also predict patterns like turn-taking behaviors.

The ability to predict a rule-related behavior is related to the range, specificity, intensity, and crystallization of a rule. As the range of a rule increases, the potential for general prediction in multiple situations increases. As the specificity of a rule increases, the possibility for more precise predictions about behavior in a few situations increases. As the degree of prescriptive force (intensity) and agreement about rules (crystallization) increase, one's ability to predict also increases, because greater rule-compliance is expected under these conditions.

In addition to the range, specificity, intensity, and crystallization of a rule, several other factors may influence the ability to predict behavior on the basis of the rule. For instance, if an actor has no knowledge of a rule, the relevant rule will not be a good predictor of his/her behavior. Or, if a second rule supersedes a first, then the first rule will not be an effective predictor. Although rules may guide one's behavior, there are other motivating factors that influence behavior, such as graft, the desire to protect oneself, or anger, Further, actors may deviate inadvertently from a rule because they are tired or distracted. Because Toulmin's model makes allowances for qualifications, it can accommodate these factors. Graphic representation of how rules, based on Toulmin's model, can be used to predict behavior are presented in Figure 6.3, which is an abstract, general presentation of the model, and in Figure 6.4, which illustrates how one can predict a specific behavior using the model.[61]

In the predictive model, the context is the data (context may include previous behavior as it does in the specific example). A rule serves as the warrant for the prediction (claim) that a behavior will occur, and the rule is backed by evidence of the rule's existence. The "unless" clause identifies some of the factors that may invalidate the prediction. Using this model, researchers can predict behavior on the basis of rules. The present model is written for obligated or preferred rules, but like the explanatory model, it can be adapted for prohibitive rules. The data and the qualifications would remain the same, but the warrant and back-

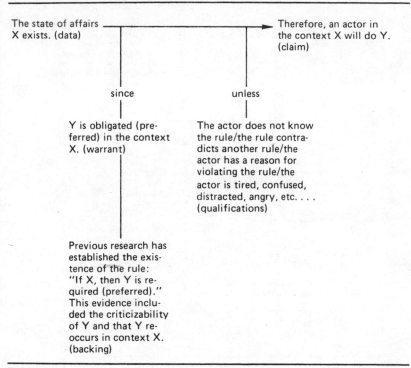

The state of affairs X exists. (data) ——————→ Therefore, an actor in the context X will do Y. (claim)

since

unless

Y is obligated (preferred) in the context X. (warrant)

The actor does not know the rule/the rule contradicts another rule/the actor has a reason for violating the rule/the actor is tired, confused, distracted, angry, etc. . . . (qualifications)

Previous research has established the existence of the rule: "If X, then Y is required (preferred)." This evidence included the criticizability of Y and that Y reoccurs in context X. (backing)

FIGURE 6.3: Predictive Model—Abstract Version

ing would need to indicate that Y is prohibited and does not occur in context X and the prediction would be that the actor would not do Y.

Rules, Laws, and Systems Predictions. Covering laws theories will not predict any of the behavior predicted by rules theories inasmuch as they each refer to different types of behavior. Predictions from covering laws are more likely to be accurate than those stemming from rules theory, because rules theory assumes actors can violate rules, but actors cannot violate laws. Laws predict mechanistic relationships between antecedents and consequences; rules theorists predict relationships on the basis of prescriptive force. If systems theory includes both law- and rule-related phenomena, then it will be able to predict both mechanistic and prescriptive relationships.

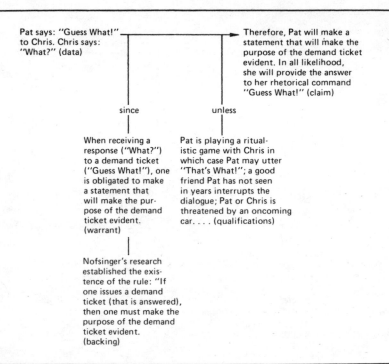

Pat says: "Guess What!" to Chris. Chris says: "What?" (data)

Therefore, Pat will make a statement that will make the purpose of the demand ticket evident. In all likelihood, she will provide the answer to her rhetorical command "Guess What!" (claim)

since

unless

When receiving a response ("What?") to a demand ticket ("Guess What!"), one is obligated to make a statement that will make the purpose of the demand ticket evident. (warrant)

Pat is playing a ritualistic game with Chris in which case Pat may utter "That's What!"; a good friend Pat has not seen in years interrupts the dialogue; Pat or Chris is threatened by an oncoming car. . . . (qualifications)

Nofsinger's research established the existence of the rule: "If one issues a demand ticket (that is answered), then one must make the purpose of the demand ticket evident. (backing)

FIGURE 6.4:   Predictive Model—Specific Example

CONTROL

Although control is sometimes listed as a goal of scientific knowledge,[62] all scholars do not consider it to be a criterion for judging the value of scientific theory. They argue that the issue of control is a practical concern rather than a scientific issue. Fred N. Kerlinger maintains that "the basic aim of science is not the betterment of mankind. It is theory."[63] The concern seems to be that practical application might get in the way of good theory, that is, full explanation and prediction. But a theory which has explanatory and predictive value and a theory which has high practical payoff need not be different theories. In fact, the ability to explain and predict may be positively correlated with the ability to control. Besides, when there are so many questions that will go unanswered, why not answer questions that not only improve one's ability to explain and predict phenomena but also offer an opportunity to control phenomena for the betterment of humanity. Rules theory can be used to explain, predict, and control phenomena. The discussion of what we might control to what end will be organized around the six groups of theoretical statements presented in the first part of this chapter: rules for behavior, rule-related behavior, rule sanctions, meta-rule processes, rule manipulation, and rules and sociological-psychological variables.

Rules for Behavior. If actors fail to comply with rules, their behavior may be subject to criticism and they may be negatively evaluated; they may be viewed as "mad or bad," insulting, less promotable, and so on.[64] But if the rules for communicative interaction are known, then presumably these rules can be taught and followed. If noncompliance is due to rule-reflective or rule-violation behavior, then the actor may be reasonably held accountable for his/her action. If the noncompliance is due to rule-error behavior, then the actor would have chosen to act differently if s/he had "remembered" the rule or if the circumstances had been different. Perhaps methods could be worked out that would help the actor maximize the possibility for rule compliance. In rule-ignorant behavior, actors need to "know" the rules in order to be able to comply with them by some means other than chance.

If rule theorists are to disseminate their knowledge about rules with communicators in general, then they must determine the best means for sharing this knowledge. Stephen Krashen argues that actors come to know rules in two ways: acquisition and learning.[65] Acquisition is an unconscious process, whereas learning is a conscious process. Acquisition is enhanced by good intake (behavior that is useful to language acquisition) that is comprised of (1) language that is understood, (2) language that is at or just beyond the speaker's own ability to follow the rules, (3) behavior that represents progressive stages, moving to more complex uses of the rules, and (4) natural communication. Learning involves exposure to the rules and error correction of noncompliant rule behavior.

Besides maintaining that some rules are acquired and that others are learned, Krashen has argued that different teaching strategies may be required for rules that are acquired and those that are learned.[66] Krashen's model has been applied to syntactical and phonological rules; more work is needed to know if it is applicable to pragmatic rules. If it holds, then researchers will not only have to know what the given rules are but they will also need to know the best strategies for helping communicators acquire or learn them.

Researching and laying out teaching strategies is way beyond the scope of this book. The point to be made here is that it may be possible to help others acquire or learn the rules. Since noncompliant behaviors and actors may be negatively sanctioned, then knowing the rules and sharing that knowledge with others so that they may choose to comply with rules is one useful application of rules theory in terms of control.

Rule-related Behavior. Knowledge about rule-related behavior may also assist in identifying problems and possible solutions to noncompliant-rule behavior. Theorems about rule-related behavior identify target audiences who may be most in need of rule knowledge (e.g., children, newcomers, and foreigners), and they identify the kinds of behaviors that are most likely to be related to implicit and explicit rule knowledge. This latter type of knowledge may be helpful in identifying rules that are acquired and rules that are learned, in that it is possible that implicit rules are acquired and rules that can be stated explicitly are learned.[67] If different teaching methods are appropriate for each type of rule knowledge, then such information may help one choose a method for teaching the different rules. If one knows when the value of rules are most likely to be questioned (rule-reflective behavior), then one may be able to know when it would be most important to offer assistance to those who would like to change the rules, those who would like to cope with the changes, and those who would like to resist those changes. What kind of assistance might be offered will be discussed further in the section on controlling meta-rule processes.

Rule Sanctions. Knowing under what circumstances deviations from rules are more or less likely to get negative sanctions may help a person in choosing between competing rules. Researchers may be able to help actors identify rules that are high and low in deviation tolerance, crystallization (agreement), and intensity (strength of prescriptive force) in order that they may choose among rules. Or, researchers may identify what are considered minor and major deviations from the rule. Or, scholars may be able to demonstrate how actors might be able to make judgments regarding the likelihood of negative sanctions for themselves.

Meta-Rule Processes. Knowing how to maintain, negotiate, and change rules effectively is valuable information regarding meta-rule processes. Effective meta-rule processes may be those that are most expedient, most democratic, least controversial, etc., depending on one's goal. Understanding meta-rule processes may also assist a person in coping with changes that may increase uncertainty and discomfort. Virginia McDermott describes this problem with regard to retired persons, and Gail Fairhurst explores the possible impact of changing rules on divorced women.[68] Knowing that some people will assume different rules are applicable when interacting with people whose roles have changed (e.g., an employed versus retired person or a married versus divorced person) may help individuals understand why and how they are being treated differently. In addition to understanding why and how rules change, knowledge about meta-rule processes will allow actors to identify new rules, and then actors can evaluate, maintain, negotiate, and change them.

Rule-Manipulation. Rules can be manipulated for one's self-interest at the expense of others, but rule-manipulation knowledge can also be useful in recognizing and preempting a manipulation. In addition, there may be times when one wants to manipulate a rule for the benefit of someone else, for instance, to tell the polite or kind lie. Knowing how to perform these kinds of manipulations is valuable rule knowledge.

Rules and Sociological-Psychological Variables. Knowing what rules are appropriate for which actors in what context (sociological scope conditions of a rule) is as important rule knowledge as is knowing how to communicate the importance of a rule or one's attraction for another (possible psychological scope conditions of a rule). Knowledge about rules may also help one to create roles or to be recognized as performing a specific role. For example, if we can identify the rules for leaders or high-status persons, then by following those rules one may be viewed as a high-status person or leader. This is not to say that rule-related behavior alone creates a leader or status. Certainly, other factors, like intelligence, who s/he knows, who his/her friends are, and personality, may affect the perception of leadership or status. But these factors do not emphasize the role of symbolic interaction (communication) in influencing leadership. Communication rules for the leadership role would indicate appropriate communicative behavior for leaders. Thus, following certain rules may be one way in which self-initiated *communication* may contribute to one's being perceived as a leader or a person of high status.

If one knows which psychological variables are likely to increase rule-compliance, one might try to control rule-compliance by manipulating these variables. For example, if it can be established that rule-compliance and ego-involvement are positively correlated, and if one believes that rules against littering are valuable rules, then one might try to increase rule compliance by increasing ego-involvement. Or, if one believes rule-negotiation is a valuable communication skill and if introverted persons use this skill less often, one might try to improve negotiation skills and to reduce negotiation apprehension. Or, if one wants to increase one's attraction to another person, and one knows that attraction and shared rules are positively correlated, then one may seek to determine and adopt the rules of the person to whom s/he wishes to increase attraction.

Our ability to control rule-related phenomena is directly related to the ability to explain and predict it. This section has considered the various ways in which rule-related knowledge may be used to control phenomena. Those ways illustrate a potentially rich payoff for communication theory from a rules perspective; they demonstrate the possibility of varied, useful, and significant uses for rules-knowledge.

Rules, Laws, and Systems Control. Laws theory cannot be used to control the same phenomena as rules theory; rules theory cannot be used to control the same phenomena as laws theory. Systems knowledge can be used to control law-related and rule-related phenomena if the theoretical statements provide explanations and predictions for both types of relationship. Law-related phenomena can be controlled with greater accuracy than rule-related phenomena. For example, if the volume of a gas in a container is held constant, then by increasing the temperature, we can increase the pressure. There is no question that we can control the pressure. On the other hand, even if one follows the rules for a person of higher status, we cannot be sure that s/he can control his/her perceived status, not only because so many other factors influence that perception but also because actors may choose whether or not they will grant someone status; pressure cannot choose whether to increase or decrease based on temperature.

Communication scholars may reasonably object to comparing rules theory about status-related behavior to natural laws about pressure, volume, and temperature. One may ask how do rules theory and laws theory for *communication* differ? The problem in trying to make such a comparison is that scholars do not often explictly state that they are researching a *communication law*. For example, Charles R. Berger, the leading proponent of covering law theory in communication, casts his theory of interpersonal communication in the axiomatic form rather than in sets of laws.[69] However, given Berger's support for the covering law perspective, it seems reasonable to assume that he considers his axioms as laws. Further, Berger's research is based on the general covering law model which assumes a necessary relationship between antecedents and consequences. This kind of assumption leads Berger to the following type of generalization: "High levels of uncertainty *cause* increases in information seeking behavior [emphasis added]."[70] If one takes a covering law perspective, then one would assume that by manipulating the levels of uncertainty, one could automatically control the amount of information-seeking behavior. If the relationship between uncertainty and information-seeking behavior is mechanistically determined, as with other laws, then control based on this relationship would be more consistent than control based on rules theory, because the relationship is presumed to be automatic rather than prescriptive.

SUMMARY

Rules theories meet three criteria for scientific knowledge; they can be used to explain, predict, and control communication phenomena. Rules and covering-law theories make different contributions to communication theory because they are concerned with different relationships; rules theories are concerned with prescriptive relationships, whereas laws describe mechanistic relationships. Laws provide the opportunity for more accurate predictions and controls, but these advantages are limited to mechanistic relationships. Symbolic interaction is dependent on rules, and hence prescriptive relationships. Laws are not concerned with prescriptive force; therefore, they lack the ability to address phenomena which are central to communicative interaction. Rules theory is specifically concerned with prescriptive relationships; thus it can provide insights not covered by laws. Systems theory may explain, predict, and control both rule and law-related phenomena if the theoretical statements include references to both.

Comparative Analysis of Laws, Systems, and Rules Research

Laws, systems, and rules theories have been compared and contrasted in general with regard to their ability to explain, predict, and control communicative behavior. Since research provides data which may be used to construct theories, it is useful to consider how laws, systems, and rules research compare. They may be compared and contrasted in terms of (1) the questions asked, (2) the data analyzed, (3) the conclusions drawn, and (4) the theoretical statements that are inferred. Rather than talk about such research in the abstract, this section examines a representative research example from each paradigm. It was reasoned that specific examples might illustrate the differences and similarities more clearly than abstract statements. In addition to comparing and contrasting research in terms of the above four criteria, some suggestions are made for how these research studies might have been approached differently. Specifically, the covering law and systems studies are discussed in terms of how they might have been done from a rules perspective, and the rules study is considered in terms of laws and systems approaches. These comparisons illustrate the similarities and differences in communication research and theory approached from a rules, systems, or laws perspective.

COVERING LAW RESEARCH

The clearest examples of covering law research in communication would be those studies which are concerned with physiological processes such as the physics of sound production or physiological developments as they relate to language acquisition and decay. From this research, it would be possible to write laws which would describe mechanistic relationships. However, a comparison of such research to rules research in communication would have limited utility because (1) communication is not limited to physiological variables, (2) it would ignore a great deal of communication research which has clearly not been done from either a system or rules perspective but which looks at processes which are at least not immediately explainable in terms of physical laws, and (3) causally determined relationships could never be studied from the rules perspective; thus, the comparison would yield no interesting information for rules theory.

All proponents of the covering law model have not been concerned exclusively with physiological processes. Some advocates of the covering law perspective, like Berger, have denied that laws are universal, deterministic, and necessarily causal, but they do not explicitly state what a law is.[71] Nonetheless, the research of scholars in the covering law tradition can be differentiated from rules research in a number of ways: (1) researchers tacitly, if not explicitly, assume a necessary relationship between antecedents and consequences; (2) the actors' reasons and prescriptive force are not part of their explanatory model; (3) researchers typically measure the response of subjects to pencil and paper tests; (4) communication is typically an independent or mediating variable; (5) researchers do not typically study communication interaction; (6) they rarely study encoding behavior, and when they do so, subjects are asked to choose responses from those provided by the researcher; and (7) statistics are the most typical means of interpreting the data and supporting the conclusions drawn.[72]

Because Charles R. Berger has been the most vocal defender of the covering law perspective in communication, and because his research on proactive and retroactive attribution exhibits the typical features of covering law research identified above, his attribution research has been chosen as the example of communication research from a covering law perspective.[73] Berger does not label any of his empirical generalization "laws." But, it is also clear that he is not taking a systems or rules perspective, and he does explain his research findings in terms of causal relationships. Given his support of the covering law perspective and his search for empirical generalizations which were caused, it seems reasonable to conclude that Berger approaches proactive and retroactive attribution from a laws perspective.

Berger's research report on proactive and retroactive attribution includes three studies: one on proactive attribution and two on retroactive attribution. In the proactive attribution study, the apparent research question was: Is biographic and demographic information used to make predictions about attitudes held? Retroactive studies were primarily designed to answer the question: Is early information (biographic and demographic data) used to explain later information?

In the proactive attribution study, subjects were asked to predict the attitudes of fictitious persons who had backgrounds like or unlike their own. These predictions were compared with what they had indicated were their own attitudes. The discrepancy score between their attitudes and their predicted attitudes of the similar or dissimilar fictitious persons constituted the data analyzed. The discrepancy score for the similar-other condition was 21.02, whereas for the dissimilar-other condition it was 28.80 (theoretically, scores could have ranged from 0 to 105). This difference was statistically significant. It was concluded that subjects predicted that those with similar backgrounds were more likely to share their attitudes than those with different backgrounds.

In the two studies investigating retroactive attribution, subjects either listened to or read what they believed to be two portions of a conversation. In the first portion, the communicators exchanged background information which showed them to be similar to or different from one another. In the second portion they discussed issues upon which they agreed or disagreed. Subjects were then asked to explain the attitude agreement or disagreement. They were asked in an open-ended question to write down all the possible factors that influenced the attitude agreement or disagreement. These responses were classified according to nine categories: (1) demographic given, (2) demographic inferred, (3) attitudes, (4) personality, (5) conversation style, (6) interaction characteristics, (7) conversation setting, (8) film related (one of the issues was the film *The Exorcist*), and (9) political opinions (the other issue was whether Richard Nixon should be impeached). The total number of responses was counted, and then a percentage score was assigned to each category on the basis of what percentage of the total explanations fell in that category. The subjects were also directly asked to indicate the percentage that personality, background characteristics, communication, and other factors contributed to the agreement/disagreement. Finally, the subjects were asked to rate the conversation on nine semantic differential scores: good-bad, friendly-unfriendly, fast-slow, pleasant-unpleasant, warm-cold, active-passive, honest-dishonest, nice-awful, and simple-complex.

When the early information was consistent with the attitude agreement/disagreement (i.e., similar background/similar attitudes; different backgrounds/different attitudes), it was used to explain attitude agreement/disagreement. When it was inconsistent (i.e., similar background/different attitudes; different backgrounds/similar attitudes), then alternative explanations were given; most notably differences were attributed to specific attitude differences. Disagreements were also attributed to the conversational setting and personality more often than agreements were.

The primary questions in this study regarding attribution would not be questions in a study from a rules perspective. The questions were not concerned with prescribed behavior or relationships between rules and attribution or sociological and psychological variables. In addition, the questions were not primarily concerned with communication. It is true that the sociological and psychological variables (demographic background and attitudes) were communicated; but if the mere presence of a message is one's definition of communication research, then any study using symbols in any capacity would be a communication study. Berger's study does not identify how or when or with what success communicators exchange background, demographic, or attitude information; rather, it is designed to control these variables in order to measure the effects of sociological information on psychological prediction and explanation.[74] B. Aubrey Fisher has characterized such research as not studying communication but using it as a mediating variable.[75]

A rules scholar might have asked: "Are there obligatory, preferential, or prohibitive rules for disclosing demographic background and attitudinal data? If there are rules, what are the scope conditions for these rules? How are these rules generated, negotiated, changed, and so on? What happens when the rules are violated? Or a rules scholar might have asked, "What are the rules for communicating or checking out one's attributions?"

Berger does not offer a theoretical explanation for having the subjects rate the conversations on the semantic differential scales. Nor does he demonstrate the relevance of these ratings to his primary questions about proactive or retroactive attribution. Nonetheless, the data collected in this manner may be at least partially explained by appealing to conversational rules.

In conversations where actors disagreed, the conversation was heard as more unpleasant, cold, unfriendly, active, honest, awful, and complex than in conversations in which actors agreed. In addition, when there was an inconsistency between background and attitude similarity/difference, the conversation was perceived to be more honest than when the information was consistent.

This data may be related to $R_{(12)}$ and $R_{(13)}$.

$R_{(12)}$: If one is in a conversation, then one must not say what one believes to be false.[76]

$R_{(13)}$: If one is involved in a conversation, then one should try to agree rather than disagree.[77]

If it was assumed, for the moment, that Berger's subjects adhered to these rules, then one may use them to interpret the subjects' ratings. One can easily see that $R_{(12)}$ and $R_{(13)}$ come into conflict whenever there is a legitimate disagreement. In complying with one rule, a person violates the other rule. Hence, if one openly disagrees with another person, one may try to explain his/her behavior by assuming that s/he had to violate $R_{(13)}$ in order to be honest and honor $R_{(12)}$. On the other hand, if the communicators agree, then one is less sure that they are following $R_{(12)}$; rather, it may be reasoned that they may be violating $R_{(12)}$ in order to follow $R_{(13)}$. Thus, it is reasonable that disagreeing is viewed as more honest than agreeing.

Disagreeing with someone violates $R_{(13)}$; hence it is reasonable that such a conversation may be viewed negatively and thus rated as unpleasant, cold, unfriendly, and awful. The present author cannot think of a law that would explain these phenomena and Berger himself attributes the evaluations of the paragraphs to what is socially desirable, which is an indirect appeal to prescriptive rules. There may also be rules that will help explain why conversations involving disagreements are viewed as more active and complex than those involving agreements, but the present author is unaware of such rules.

Summary. If one assumes that Berger's results would be replicated, then one might offer the following theorems:

Theorem 29: Actors will use sociological information to predict attitudes.

Theorem 30: If the sociological and psychological information about a person is consistent, then sociological information will be used to explain the psychological information.

Theorem 31. Conversion with disagreements will be rated as more unpleasant, cold, unfriendly, active, honest, awful, and complex than conversations with only agreements.

Rule scholars would have approached the variables studied by Berger by focusing on how the disclosure of background, demographic, and attitude similarity/difference actually occur in naturalistic conversations, what are the rules regarding such disclosures, and how one appropriately communicates one's attribution. Secondary data collected by Berger on the rating of conversations involving agreements or disagreements can be at least partially interpreted by appealing to rules, and covering laws will not explain the ratings obtained.

Rules research also differs from covering law research in other ways. Berger assumes his findings represent a causal relationship between antecedents and consequences; rule scholars would search for prescriptive rather than causal relationships. The subjects in Berger's study responded to his stimuli by means of paper and pencil; he did not observe communication interactions, which serve as the primary data for rules scholars.

SYSTEMS RESEARCH

Communication theory from a systems perspective should take into account certain assumptions about systems theory in general, and it should meet some general guidelines. Peter R. Monge describes four general assumptions of systems theory: (1) the whole is irreducible to the parts, (2) systems maintain themselves, (3) systems have the ability to adapt, and (4) systems are hierarchically imbedded.[78] B. Aubrey Fisher identifies five guidelines for communication research from a systems perspective: (1) variables for study should come from a communication system paradigm (in his model, this excludes mental-concepts), (2) research should embody a process focus, (3) a search for interactive features which characterize communicative behavior should be carried out, (4) interaction analysis should be the primary measurement technique, and (5) qualitative analyses should be utilized.[79] The quality of systems research may be judged in terms of whether it meets assumptions of a systems theory in general and the degree to which it adheres to the above guidelines.

Systems research in communication may be characterized by a number of features: (1) a holistic perspective is adopted, (2) the unit of analysis is minimally an interact (two turns at speaking), or the group interaction is assessed as a whole at a given point in time, (3) interaction is measured across time, and (4) there is an attempt to identify various system states or phases. Some researchers also address themselves to the issues of equilibrium (stability) and entropy (uncertainty). Unlike covering law research, systems research is primarily concerned with the interaction process itself. As already stated, system researchers could incorporate rules analysis in their research, but this is not typical. Even when systems researchers use the term *rule*, it is not clear that they are referring to a prescription for behavior that is obligated, preferred, or prohibited. Rather, they seem to be referring to any empirical regularity as a rule. They do not provide evidence of prescriptive force; they do not write formal rules in the form "If X, then Y is obligated (preferred or prohibited)"; and they do not give dialogue examples illustrating the regularity or prescriptive force. Rather than dialogue examples, statistics serve as the primary source for interpreting the data and justifying conclusions.[80]

The research of Donald G. Ellis and B. Aubrey Fisher on the phases of conflict in small group development was chosen as the example of systems research for four reasons: (1) it is one of the more recent communication studies from a systems perspective, (2) it describes several systems variables, (3) it is consistent with the general characteristics of systems research in communication, and (4) Fisher has been one of the most prolific systems researchers in communication.[81]

Ellis and Fisher sought to answer the question, What is the nature of conflict interaction across time leading groups to consensus? They sought to answer this question by comparing the communicative behavior of group members across time. Specifically, they were interested in comments that provide insight into conflict processes. Interacts (the immediately adjacent utterances of two speakers) were coded as a disagreeing interact, a positive reinforcement interact, or an ambiguous interact. These interacts were submitted to a Markov statistical analysis in order to determine the probability of one act or interact following another. After analyzing the interaction patterns, the authors concluded that there are three phases of small group conflict: interpersonal conflict, confrontation conflict, and substantive conflict.

The research focused on descriptive data. The authors reported and classified regularities. They provided what-explanations for the questions, What are the phases of small group conflict? and What characterizes these phases? By estimating interacts, the researchers believed they were getting a more holistic view of the small group process than a single act-by-act analysis. The authors discussed conflict management techniques that may be viewed as adaptive processes for the maintenance of a system. The acts may be thought to be hierarchically embedded in the interacts and the interacts embedded in the phases. These phases may be viewed as different systems states just as movement from one act to another may be viewed as mini-shifts in system states.

The information provided by this study is interesting. It could be incorporated in rules research, but it is insufficient for developing communication theory from a rules perspective.

Regularities may be law- or rule-related; information about prescriptive force is necessary in order to determine if the behavioral regularities are the result of rules. Rules researchers could build upon Ellis and Fisher's findings and ask such questions as: Do different rules operate during different phases of group interaction? How and why do actors shift from one set of rules to another? What happens if one group member follows rules which are appropriate for one phase while other group members are following other rules? Can the use of ambiguity reported in phases I and III be related to politeness or face-saving rules? What are the rules for conflict management?

Summary. Systems research focuses on interacting components with an emphasis on a holistic perspective. Ellis and Fisher's work confirms general systems notions regarding the adaptive, maintenance, and embedded qualities of systems. The primary contribution of their work is the description of the three phases of group conflict which may be generally viewed as three system states. If one assumes their observations are accurate for most small groups, one might offer the following theorem:

Theorem 32: Small groups will go through three phases of conflict: interpersonal, confrontational, and substantive conflict.

The philosophical perspectives of systems and rules research are compatible. Because the data of each are symbolic interaction, it may be possible to generate rules questions based on systems findings. However, rules and systems researchers typically differ in the kinds of regularities they identify. Systems researchers seek to identify systems states, whereas rule researchers seek to identify rules. Statistics has been the primary means of interpreting data and justifying conclusions from a systems perspective. Rule theorists typically support their conclusions with dialogue examples.

RULES RESEARCH

Rules research may focus on a number of different relationships (e.g., rules for behavior, rule-related behavior, and rule sanctions). Some of these relationships are identified in the first part of this chapter. Most of the rules research has focused on developing the first kind of theoretical statements, that is, those related to specific rules. Therefore, it seems appropriate that the example of rule research be concerned with identifying rules.

Research which is designed to identify rules may be characterized by the following features: (1) behavioral regularities are specified, (2) the prescriptive force of a hypothesized rule is demonstrated, (3) dialogue examples are used as the major source of evidence, and (4) the research is designed to explicate symbolic *interaction*. For a more detailed description of rules research and additional examples, the reader should consult other chapters, particularly Chapter 5.

William Labov's research on ritual insults was chosen as the example of rules research for four reasons: (1) it identifies behavioral regularities which are controllable, criticizable and contextual; (2) it reports negative sanction for rule violations; (3) it uses rules to make important distinctions between different types of behavior; (4) it offers what and reason-giving explanations; and (5) the data suggest that the rules that are identified have high predictability.[82]

Labov's primary question was, What are the rules for producing, interpreting, and answering ritual insults (sounding)?[83] Of secondary importance was the question, How do the rules for ritual insults differ from the rules for personal insults?

The data for Labov's report on ritual insults were collected over a four-year period. They consist of transcriptions from tape recordings made of black adolescent peer groups. Most of the dialogues are spontaneous, but occasionally the researchers try to stimulate verbal behavior by asking the adolescents to role-play (Example: "What would you say if Boot said, 'Your father look like Fungi?'")[84] In addition to behavioral regularities, Labov reports the spontaneous evaluations of ritual insults and negative sanctions for deviations from rules for ritual insults. Further, some ritual insults were more positively evaluated than others.

From the above data, Labov wrote two formal rules:

*$R_{(14)}$: "If A makes an utterance S in the presence of B and an au-
dience C, which includes reference to a target related to B,
T(B), in a proposition P, and (a) B believes that A believes that
P is not true and (b) B believes that A believes that B knows
that P is not true . . . then S is a sound, heard as T(B) is so X that
P, where X is a pejorative attribute, and A is said to have
sounded on B."[85]

$R_{(15)}$: "If A has sounded on B, B sounds on A by asserting a new
proposition P' which includes reference to a target related to
A, T(A), and such that it is an AB-event that P' is untrue.
P' may be embedded in a sentence as a quantification of a
pejorative attribute X' of T(A)."[86]

$R_{(15)}$ is the rule for answering a ritual insult. *$R_{(14)}$ is an explanation for what must hold true for a statement to be interpreted as a ritual insult. It is possible to rewrite this explanation
into the production rule, $R_{(16)}$, which conforms to the format and
constituent of rules outlined in the present study.

$R_{(16)}$: If A wishes to ritually insult B, then A should utter a proposition P about a target related to B, T(B), that expresses a
pejorative attribute about T(B) that is obviously not true.

Although Labov only wrote two formal rules, his research
report is full of generalizations that may warrant additional rules.
Of particular importance is the difference between rules for
personal insults and those for ritual insults. Below are just some
of the generalizations from Labov's research from which possible
rules may be inferred:

Generalization$_{(01)}$:

While ritual insults involve references which are obviously not true,
personal insults allege things which may be true.[87]

$R_{(17)}$: If one wants to utter a personal insult rather than a ritualistic
one, then s/he must make pejorative remarks which may be
true. (Example: "His father got a big bald spot with a gray
head right down there, and one long string. . . .")[88]

$R_{(18)}$: If one wants to avoid having a ritual insult interpreted as a
personal insult, then s/he must make sure that the pejorative
reference could not be true. (Example: "Your father got teeth
growin' out his behind.")[89]

Generalization (02):

Ritual insults are usually answered with a ritual insult; personal insults are usually answered with a personal insult.[90]

$R_{(19)}$: If one has been the target of a ritual insult, then one should ritually insult the original insulter.

$R_{(20)}$: If one has been the target of a personal insult, then one should personally insult or physically attack the original insulter.

Generalization(03):

The following ritual insults were more complex than the preceding ones; the reverse order of complexity was not found.[91]

$R_{(21)}$: If one is answering a ritual insult, then one is obligated to escalate the complexity of the insult.

Generalization(04):

Substituting one relative for another is considered a very weak response which is acceptable only from children. (Example: "Your mother got four lips" is an unacceptble response to "Your father got four lips.")[92]

$R_{(22)}$: If one is answering a ritual insult, then one should escalate the insult beyond mere substitution of one target person for another.

Generalization(05):

Ritual insults require negative references to middle-class norms. "Many ritual insults are 'good' because they are bad—because the speakers know that they would arouse disgust and revulsion among those committed to good standards of middle class society."[93]

$R_{(23)}$: If one wishes to utter a ritual insult, then it is preferable that the pejorative reference violate middle class rules of decorum.

Labov's conclusions are supported with examples of dialogue exchanges throughout his research report. The use of naturalistic dialogue to illustrate rules is the most typical form of supporting evidence in rules research. It has not commonly appeared in laws or systems research. On the other hand, Labov's report does not make use of statistics to support his conclusions, but statistical analyses are common to laws and systems research. This is not to say rules researchers cannot use statistical evidence or that laws and systems scholars must leave dialogues out of their reports; rather, these differences are simply indicative of common practice. Statistical analyses may strengthen the conclusions of rules scholars, and dialogue examples may make the relevance of laws and systems findings to communication behavior clearer. The explication of ritual and personal insults provides two kinds of explanations. It provides what explanations for the questions: What is a ritual insult? What is a personal insult? and What distinguishes effective ritual insults from ineffective ones? Rules may be used to offer reason-giving explanations for why ritual insults follow ritual insults, why personal insults follow personal insults, or why some attempts at insults are evaluated positively whereas others are negatively sanctioned. Each of the explanations can be provided by appealing to rules for insults and their prescriptive force, and each of the generalizations that were used to generate rules could become theorems in a theory about rules for behavior.

How would a covering law or systems perspective approach the study of ritual insults? The production and dynamics of ritual insults cannot be studied from a covering law perspective. The regularities reported by Labov are controllable, restricted to certain conditions, and linked to prescriptive force. Covering laws cannot account for these regularities, because they describe behavior which is not controllable and not prescribed. If one were interested in ritual insults from a systems perspective, one could ask such questions as: How does a system develop, maintain, and change its rules? and What happens when two or more systems that abide by different rules interact?

Summary. The most common type of rules research is concerned with inferring rules from behavior. Such research reports behavioral regularities and evidence of prescriptive force. Symbolic interaction serves as the primary source of evidence, and dialogue examples are used to support conclusions. Labov's analysis of ritual insults yields several generalizations that can be formulated into rules for behavior. In turn, support for these rules can lead to theorems like theorems 30 through 34.

Theorem 33: Ritual insults will involve improbable or impossible references more often than probable ones.

Theorem 34: Ritual insults will be more often answered with other ritual insults than personal ones.

Theorem 35: Responses to ritual insults will be more complex than the ritual insult that preceded it.

Theorem 36: Substituting one relative for another in a ritual insult is less likely to occur among adults than children.

Theorem 37: Ritual insults will involve a violation of middle class standards of decorum more often than honor them.

A covering law perspective cannot address the issues in Labov's study. His findings can, however, be used to generate questions that are appropriately answered by a systems approach to communication.

SUMMARY

In examining these three research reports, several generalizations become apparent: (1) laws, systems, and rules researchers have asked different questions; (2) they have focused on different kinds of variables; (3) they have tended to use different kinds of data; and (4) they have used different means to interpret the data and justify their conclusions. Covering law and rules research have little in common. It is often difficult to demonstrate how either paradigm could be used to explicate the relationships identified by the other paradigm, because each is concerned with different kinds of phenomena and relationships. Systems research and rules research seem to have more in common. The focus of each has been different, but the data of each can be utilized by the other to generate questions. Nonetheless, because each paradigm asks different questions, which require different data, additional research would be needed in order to answer the new questions. The data of one paradigm will not answer the questions of the other. For example, more research is needed to answer the rules questions generated by Ellis and Fisher's systems research, and more is needed to answer the systems questions generated by Labov's work. Systems research and rules research are compatible with each other, and each can be used with the other to develop communication theory.

Conclusion

Communication theory from a rules perspective can take an axiomatic form; the axioms should state assumed truisms, theorems should describe specific relationships which are predicted by rules, and theoretical statements from axioms to theorems should increase in specificity while decreasing in scope. The potential constituents of a communication theory from a rules approach are numerous, but many may be expected to fall into six categories: (1) rules for behavior, (2) rule-related behavior, (3) rule sanctions, (4) meta-rule processes, (5) rule-manipulation, and (6) the relationship of rules and sociological-psychological variables.

Rules theories can meet the criteria of scientific knowledge; it can be used to explain, predict, and control communicative behavior. Rules theories can provide what, mental concept, and reason-giving explanations, but they do not account for causal relationships. They predict relationships between rules and other phenomena, and these relationships may fall into the same six categories identified above. The utility of a rules theory with regard to controlling phenomena is directly related to its ability to predict accurately certain relationships.

Communication research from a laws approach differs in many ways from rules research: (1) laws research is concerned with identifying mechanistic relationships; rules research focuses on prescriptive relationships, (2) responses on paper and pencil tests typically serve as the data for laws research; dialogues are the most common data for rules research, (3) laws research does not typically investigate symbolic *interaction*; interaction is the primary focus of rules research, and (4) statistical analyses are the primary means of supporting conclusions in laws research; in rules research dialogues are the most typical form of support.

Systems research and rules research have more in common. They are both concerned with interaction and data from one paradigm can be used to generate questions for the other. Typically, rules and systems research have differed in five ways: (1) systems research focuses on changing system states; rules research has not, (2) systems research includes analyses of interacting systems; this has not been a primary concern in rules research, (3) rules research is concerned with prescriptive relationships; systems research has described empirical regularities without noting the nature of those regularities, (4) statistical analyses are the primary means of supporting systems conclusions, whereas dialogues are the most common form of support in rules research, and (5) system research does not typically identify rules, whereas identifying rules is central to rules research.

Rules and covering law theories make different contributions to communication theory because they are concerned with different relationships; rules theories are concerned with prescriptive relationships, whereas laws describe mechanistic relationships. Laws provide opportunity for more accurate predictions and controls, but these advantages are limited to mechanistic relationships. Symbolic interaction is dependent on rules and hence prescriptive relationships. Laws are not concerned with prescriptive force; therefore, they lack the ability to address some phenomena that are central to communicative interaction. Rules theory is specifically concerned with prescriptive relationships; thus, it can provide insights not covered by laws. Systems theory can explain, predict, and control both rule and law-related phenomena only if the theoretical statements include references to both. Since symbolic interaction (communication) requires rules in order to orchestrate and to make sense out of otherwise arbitrary representations, communication theory, above all else, must include rule-related phenomena and relationships.

Chapter 7

FUTURE TASKS

The preceding chapters have addressed the major issues that have concerned both advocates and critics of a rules approach to communication. These concerns include questions like: What is a rule? (Chapter 2) How can rules be inferred accurately from behavior? (Chapter 3) What are the various ways in which rules and behavior may be related? (Chapter 4) Can rules research be conducted with sufficient rigor to be scientific? Are some methods more appropriate than others? (Chapter 5) What contributions can rules research make to communication theory? Is rules research really different from traditional research? (Chapter 6) Having answered these questions in the previous chapters, it seems fitting that this final chapter identify some possible directions for future research. The list that will be offered is by no means exhaustive; it is meant only to demonstrate the heuristic value of a rules approach to the study of human communication. Other scholars may identify other projects that they believe have more theoretical or practical importance. The suggestions that will be offered can be organized around three general purposes: (1) the identification of communication rules, (2) the construction and confirmation of communication theories, and (3) the development of pedagogical strategies.

Identification of Communication Rules

One of the first steps rule scholars should take is to transform statements about norms, rule-related generalizations, rule interpretations and explanations, presuppositions, statements of empirical regularities, and statement of beliefs (e.g., self-concept "rules") into the form "If X, then Y is obligated (preferred or prohibited)." These transformations could then be tested to determine if they are in fact rules. Sometimes the original research report will provide sufficient information; but in other cases, researchers may need to do additional research. These transformations and tests are important because some researchers have labeled phenomena rules which are probably not rules (this matter is discussed in detail in Chapter 2); and if one is to build theories from rules, one must have confidence in the rules. Further, there are numerous rules for behavior that have not been explicated. With knowledge about the nature and structure of rules, of inferring rules from behavior, and of maximizing the accuracy and generalizability of rules via various methods, researchers will be able to identify additional rules for symbiotic interaction.

Additional rules may be identified for specific acts (e.g., confessions, rejections, and acknowledgements), for persons (e.g., student/teacher, male/female, superordinate/subordinate), for episodes (e.g., getting acquainted, price negotiations, and "trading credentials") for stylistic variations (e.g., politeness, assertiveness, and closeness).[1] Or the identification of rules may be related to more traditional content areas in communication research, such as mass media, public speaking, organizational, small group and interpersonal communication. There are numerous research projects that could be undertaken. A few examples will illustrate the posibilities.

A mass media scholar might compare what seems to be a writer's assumptions about conversational rules (inferred from the dialogue in the story, script, or the like) with the rules of naturalistic conversation. Or, one could study the effect of implicit or explicit communicative rules presented by the media on communicative rules in general.

Scholars might want to compare rules of public speaking with those of conversation to learn how similar or different they are.

This may have utility for the person who wants to appear as if his/her remarks are "off the cuff," when, in fact, s/he had actually planned them very carefully. This person may be a politician wishing to appear knowledgeable on the sopt, a teacher wanting to impart accurate information in a friendly style, or a potential lover not wanting to appear too anxious.

From time to time, organizations find it necessary to make new policy decisions—in effect, to change the rules. Knowing how to best negotiate, implement, and cope with new rules with the least amount of confusion, hostility, and at the lowest cost could be valuable information to organizations. Further, intra- and inter-organizational conflict may arise because actors assume different rules are operable. Future research may be aimed at means for identifying rule conflict and for eliminating the source of conflict. Charlene O'Brien has demonstrated the importance of complying with two organizational rules in terms of promotion.[2] Given the practical importance of rule-compliance in an organizational setting, there is much to be gained from identifying other informal rules.

Since individual group members may come to a group assuming its members should abide by different rules, small group researchers may wish to explore how different aggregates of individuals, and hence, possibly different aggregates of personal rules, result in different or similar group rules and the process by which those rules are determined. Or, researchers may wish to explore the effect of turn-taking rules on the development of group goals and roles. After all, one cannot get one's ideas accepted unless one has had at least an opportunity for them to be heard, and research has indicated that higher-status members speak more and are addressed more than other group members.[3] Rules questions might address issues such as by whom, how, and when turn-taking rules are established.

Some scholars have argued that the intimacy of interpersonal communications is characterized by increasing personal rules.[4] If this assumption is true, then explicating the specific rules of one interpersonal relationship may be useful in therapy, but it will have little utility to theory. On the other hand, future research may indicate that most interpersonal relationships in a given culture have a number of rules in common.[5] Or since it would seem that different rules are applicable for intimate and non-intimate relationships,[6] and since intimate relations must evolve, rules researchers might investigate how communicators indicate that they want to escalate the relationship and concomitantly change the rules. Or rules researchers may contribute to the study of self-disclosure. It has been demonstrated that the target, personalness, and valence of a potential disclosure influences whether or not it will be disclosed.[7] One problem for communicators is to determine the personalness and valence of a particular disclosure in a given context. Perhaps the rules literature on preacts[8] is applicable to this issue; that is, it is possible that communicators preannounce their disclosures to test out the potential response to a disclosure, and then on the basis of the response to the preannouncement, decide whether or not to make the disclosure. Future research might investigate this possibility.

Scholars have just begun to demonstrate the utility of a rules approach to study family communication, communication during transitional periods (e.g., retirement, divorce, the absence of a spouse), undesired repetitive patterns, communication between students and teachers, and doctor/patient communication.[9] The excellence of this research could be continued and expanded to include other significant interactions.

Clearly, rules research can be integrated into traditional concerns in communication research and theory. The potential applications seem limitless; their quantity and quality are restricted only by the creativity and skill of communication scholars.

Construction and Confirmation of Theory

Rules research in the past has given little attention to the construction and/or confirmation of theory. One possible objective of future research might be to test the theoretical statements presented in Chapter 6. Some of the research implications of these statements are discussed below.

Rules for Behavior. By testing theorems via hypotheses. researchers may seek to establish the existence of a rule. By accumulating evidence that confirms various theorems, one might argue for the viability of proposition 1 and axioms 1 through 3 (in Chapter 6). On the other hand, using axioms 1 through 3, proposition 1, and the observation of a behavioral regularity as a basis, one might deduce that the behavior is rule-generated and write a theorem, the validity of which can be tested by hypotheses.

Rule-Related Behavior. When actual behavior is compared with the rule/behavior taxonomy presented in Chapter 4, it is possible that researchers will discover a rule-behavior relationship not covered by the taxonomy, or that they will be able to refine the kind of evidence needed to make claims about the level of rule knowledge and consciousness. The propositions and theorems presented for rule-related behavior are all empirically testable. Researchers can verify or falsify the assumptions that levels of rule-related behavior may vary according to the actors, activities, and environments. As researchers begin to explore rule-related behavior and other phenomena, it is quite likely that they will be able to identify and research other types of relationships. The confirmation or disconfirmation of axioms 4 through 7 (in Chapter 6) is dependent on the validity of the theoretical statements derived from them.

Negative Sanctions. The propositions and theorems offered regarding negative sanctions of rule deviations have received limited empirical support, and future research could futher test their validity. When deviations occur and negative sanctions do not, researchers need to know whether the regularity was prescribed by a rule and something mitigated against a negative sanction, or if the regularity was not prescribed by a rule. Since negative sanctions are one of the primary means rule scholars have for assessing the prescriptive force of a behavioral regularity, understanding how they function can facilitate the accuracy of rules research.

Meta-rule Processes. Although there are theoretical discussions which support the axioms, propositions, and theorems about meta-rule processes offered in Chapter 6,[10] the present researcher does not know of any empirical studies which test these assumptions. Future research might be concerned with the validation of those theoretical statements.

Rule-manipulation. Several scholars have maintained that rule violations may be used to manipulate others and to gain power.[11] It has been further argued in this study that these increases in power may be related to rule-allowance behavior, in that those of higher status are allowed to violate the rules more often than those of lower status and thus the deviator who is not negatively sanctioned may be perceived to be of higher status. At this point these assumptions have not been empirically tested.

Axiom 10 and proposition 10 (Chapter 6) indicate that the surface structure of manipulative behavior appears to be rule-compliant behavior. This assumption needs to be investigated; and if it is determined that manipulative and nonmanipulative actors comply with similar rules, research is needed to discover if and how manipulative behavior may be distinguished from nonmanipulative behavior.

Rules and Psychological Variables. The relation of psychological variables and rules has been largely ignored. Aside from one research proposal on ego-involvement, shared rules, and attraction,[12] the present researcher knows of no attempts to integrate psychological variables and rules.[13] Future research, however, could be designed to investigate various relationships between rules and psychological variables. The theoretical statements proposed under this heading were speculative, but they are testable, and others could be proposed and studied.

Exploring the viability of the axioms, propositions, and theorems proposed in Chapter 6 is one possible starting point for scholars interested in constructing a theory of communication from a rules perspective. Others may choose to treat the statements as models for constructing their own theoretical statements, and still others may begin elsewhere. But whatever the impetus, rule scholars need to demonstrate the interconnectedness of individual research findings by constructing theories. Without such integration, the rules approach will merely be a collection of individual studies. The construction and confirmation of communication theory from a rules perspective can help to give the approach direction and coherence.

Development of Pedagogical Strategies

It is presumed that if rules are known, it is possible to help actors learn or acquire those rules. For communication scholars, this may include the rules for speech acts, episode enactment, public speaking, small group dynamics, conflict management, escalation of intimacy, and so forth. Since noncompliant actors may be viewed as "mad or bad," insulting, and less promotable,[14] knowledge about rules is of practical importance. If actors are taught how to determine which rules have the greatest salience to a given person or group, they may be better able to choose among competing rules. If one can teach communicators how to recognize rule manipulation, they will be better able to protect themselves from being exploited. Teaching actors about meta-rule process can be useful information for those who must maintain, negotiate, develop, change, or adopt rules.

If communication scholars are to teach how to comply with the prescription of rules; how to identify various rules, their relative importance, and rule manipulations; and how to implement and cope with rule changes or resist them; we need to determine the relative merits of various methods for accomplishing these tasks. As pointed out in Chapter 6, Stephen Krashen's work indicates that different types of rules or actors may be better taught by different methods;[15] future research could be directed toward identifying the best teaching strategies for different types of actors and rules. (See also the section on control in Chapter 6 for an additional discussion of practical applications of rules research.)

Conclusion

Rules research is concerned with explicating symbolic regularities in communicative behavior. The utiltity of rules research to the development of communication theory has recently received much attention from both advocates and critics.[16] Advocates have maintained that because rules theory focuses on symbolic interaction (communication) itself, communication research and theory should be approached from a rules perspective. Critics have raised a number of questions regarding the epistemological quality of rules research (e.g., How does one identify a rule? Can rule research meet the standards of scientific inquiry?) If how rule scholars come to know is questionable, then the quality of what they know is suspect; and if rules research is invalid, then its findings are of no value, even if they focus on what is central to communicative processes.

This study demonstrated, however, that the construct rule can be defined with the precision required for theory construction and scientific research; that rules can be inferred accurately from behavior; that various methods can be used to discover and validate them; that a rules approach can make a significant contribution to the development of communication theory; that there are practical implications for rules theory and research; and that this approach is heuristic; in essence, that rules have an important place in human communication inquiry.

Notes to Chapter 1

1. Lewis Carroll, *Alice's Adventures in Wonderland* and *Through the Looking-Glass*, ed. Roger Lancelyn Green (New York: Oxford Univ. Press, 1971), p. 190; Peter Farb, *Word Play: What Happens When People Talk* (New York: Bantam, 1973), pp. 222-23; Dorothy Hage, "There's Glory for You," *Aphra*, 3 (1972), 2; Paul Watzlawick, Janet H. Beavin, and Don J. Jackson, *Pragmatics of Human Communication: A Study of Interactional Patterns, Pathologies and Paradoxes* (New York: Norton, 1967), p. 83.

2. Peter Collett, "The Rules of Conduct," in *Social Rules and Social Behavior*, ed. Peter Collett (Totowa, N.J.: Rowman and Littlefield, 1977), pp. 1-27; Romano Harré and Paul Secord, *The Explanation of Social Behavior* (Totowa, N.J.: Littlefield, Adams, 1973); Theodore Mischel, "Scientific and Philosophical Psychology: A Historical Introduction," in *Human Action*, ed. Theodore Mischel (New York: Academic Press, 1969), pp. 1-40. Donald P. Cushman, "Draft: Rules Article for Handbook of Communication, Part #1" (unpublished manuscript, State University of New York, Albany, 1978).

3. See, for example, Harré and Secord; Thomas S. Frentz and Thomas B. Farrell, "Language-Action: A Paradigm for Communication," *Q. J. of Speech*, 62 (1976), 333-49.

4. Mischel; Horaces M. Kallen, "Behaviorism," *Encyclopedia of the Social Sciences*, I, 495-98; Daniel J. O'Keefe, "Logical Empiricism and the Study of Human Communication," *Speech Monographs*, 42 (1975), 169-83.

5. Mischel, pp. 28, 33.

6. An effort was made in this study to avoid sexist language. As a result, the following pronoun system was adopted: nominative case "s/he," objective case "him/her," and possessive case "his/her."

7. See for example, Harré and Secord; Frentz and Farrell.

8. See, for example, Kenneth Burke, *The Rhetoric of Religion* (Boston: Beacon, 1961); Kenneth Burke, "(Nonsymbolic) Motion/(Symbolic) Action," *Critical Inquiry*, 4 (1978), 809-38.

9. Burke, *The Rhetoric of Religion*, pp. 40-41.

10. Harré and Secord, pp. 27-43, 84-100.

11. John J. Gumperz, "Verbal Strategies in Multilingual Communication," in *Georgetown University Round Table on Language and Linguistics, Nov. 23*, ed. James E. Alatis (Washington, D.C.: Georgetown Univ. Press, 1970), 129-48; John J. Gumperz, "Dialect and Conversational Inference in Urban Communication," *Language in Society*, 7 (1978), 393-409; John J. Gumperz and Dell Hymes, *The Ethnography of Communication* (Washington, D. C.: American Anthropological Association, 1964; issued as Part 2 of the *American Anthropologist*, 66 [1964]); John J. Gumperz and Dell Hymes, *Directions in Sociolinguistics: The Ethnography of Communication* (New York: Holt, Rinehart & Winston, 1972); Dell Hymes, "The Ethnography of Speaking," in *Anthropology and Human Behavior*, eds. Thomas Gladwin and Williams C. Sturtevant (Washington, D.C.: Anthropological Society of Washington, 1962), pp. 13-53; Dell Hymes "Introduction," in *Functions of Language in the Classroom*, eds. Courtney B. Cazden, Vera P. John, and Dell Hymes (New York: Teachers College Press, 1972); Dell Hymes "On Communicative Competence," in *Sociolinguistics: Selected Readings*, (Harmondsworth: Penguin, 1972), pp. 269-93; Dell Hymes, *Foundations in Sociolinguistics: An Ethnographic Approach* (Philadelphia: Univ. of Pennsylvania Press, 1974).

12. Donald P. Cushman and Gordon C. Whiting, "An Approach to Communication Theory: Towards Consensus on Rules," *J. of Communication*, 22 (1972), 217-38; Donald

P. Cushman and Robert T. Craig, "Communication Systems: Interpersonal Implications," in *Explorations in Interpersonal Communication*, ed. Gerald R. Miller (Beverly Hills: Sage, 1976), pp. 37-58; Donald P. Cushman, "The Rules Perspective as a Theoretical Basis for the Study of Human Communication," *Communication Q.*, 25, 1 (1977), 30-45; Donald P. Cushman and W. Barnett Pearce, "Generality and Necessity in Three Types of Human Communication Theory: Special Attention to Rules Theory," *Human Communication Research*, 3 (1977), 344-53; Thomas B. Farrell and Thomas S. Frentz, "Communication and Meaning: A Language-Action Synthesis," *Philosophy and Rhetoric*, forthcoming; Thomas S. Frentz and Thomas B. Farrell, "Language-Action: A Paradigm for Communication, *Q. J. of Speech*, 62 (1976), 333-49; Thomas S. Frentz, "A Generative Approach to Episodic Structure," presented at Western Speech Communication Association Convention, San Francisco, 1976; Thomas S. Frentz and Robert E. Nofsinger, "Some Preliminaries to Language-Action," presented at Western Speech Communication Association Convention, Phoenix, 1977; Robert E. Nofsinger, "The Demand Ticket: A Conversational Device for Getting the Floor," *Speech Monographs*, 42 (1975), 1-9; Robert E. Nofsinger, "Answering Questions Indirectly," *Human Communication Research*, 2 (1976), 172-81; W. Barnett Pearce, "The Coordinate Management of Meaning: A Rules-Based Theory of Interpersonal Communication," in *Explorations in Interpersonal Communication*, pp. 17-36; W. Barnett Pearce, "Naturalistic Study of Communication: Its Function and Form," *Communication Q.*, 25, 3 (1977), 51-56; W. Barnett Pearce, "Consensual Rules in Interpersonal Communication: A Reply to Cushman and Whiting," *J. of Communication*, 23 (1973), 160-68; W. Barnett Pearce and Forrest Conklin, "A Model of Hierarchical Meanings in Coherent Conversation and a Study of 'Indirect Responses,'" *Communication Monographs*, 46 (1979), 75-87.

13. Noam Chomsky, *Aspects of the Theory of Syntax* (Cambridge, Mass.: Massachusetts Institute of Technology, 1965); Noam Chomsky, *Language and Mind* (New York: Harcourt, Brace & Jovanovich, 1968); Noam Chomsky, "Problems in Linguistics," in *Explanation in the Behavioral Sciences*, eds. Robert Borger and Frank Cioffi (Cambridge: Cambridge Univ. Press, 1970), pp. 425-51. William Labov, *Sociolinguistic Patterns* (Philadelphia: Univ. of Pennsylvania, 1972); William Labov, "Rules for Ritual Insults," in *Studies in Social Interaction*, ed. David Sudnow (New York: Free Press, 1972), pp. 120-69.

14. J. L. Austin, *How To Do Things With Words* (Oxford: Oxford Univ. Press, 1962); Joan Safron Ganz, *Rules: A Systematic Study* (Paris: Mouton, 1971); H. Paul Grice, "The Logic of Conversation," in *Syntax and Semantics, Volume 3: Speech Acts*, eds. Peter Cole and Jerry L. Morgan (New York: Academic Press, 1975), pp. 41-58; Harré and Secord; Romano Harré, "Some Remarks on 'Rule' As a Scientific Concept," in *Understanding Other People*, ed. Theodore Mischel (Oxford: Blackwell, 1974), pp. 143-84; Romano Harré, "Rules in the Explanation of Social Behavior," in *Social Rules and Social Behavior*, ed. Peter Collett (Totowa, N.J.: Rowman and Littlefield, 1977); John R. Searle, *Speech Acts: An Essay in the Philosophy of Language* (Cambridge: Cambridge Univ. Press, 1969; John R. Searle, "What is a Speech Act," in *Language and Social Context*, ed. Pier Paolo Giglioli (Middlesex, England: Penguin, 1972), pp. 136-54; John R. Searle, "Indirect Speech Acts," in *Syntax and Semantics*, pp. 58-82; Stephen E. Toulmin, "Concepts and the Explanation of Behavior," in *Human Action*, pp. 71-104; Stephen E. Toulmin, Rules and Their Relevance for Understanding Human Behavior," in *Understanding Other People*, pp. 185-215; Ludwig Wittgenstein, *Philosophical Investigations* (Oxford: Blackwell, 1953).

15. Peter Collett (ed.), *Social Rules and Social Behavior* (Totowa, N.J.: Rowman and Littlefield, 1977); Susan Ervin-Tripp, "Sociolinguistics," in *Advances in Experimental Social Psychology*, ed. L. Berkowitz (New York: Academic Press, 1969), pp. 91-165;

Susan Ervin-Tripp, "On Sociolinguistic Rules: Alternation and Co-occurrence," in *Directions*, pp. 213-250; Harré and Secord; Dan I. Slobin, *Psycholinguistics* (Glenview, Ill.: Scott, Foresman).

16. Erving Goffman, *Encounters* (Indianapolis: Bobbs-Merrill, 1961); Ervin Goffman, *Behavior in Public Places* (New York: Free Press, 1963); Erving Goffman, *Relations in Public: Microstudies in the Public Order* (New York: Harper & Row, 1971); Harold Garfinkel, *Studies in Ethnomethodology* (Englewood Cliffs, N.J.: Prentice-Hall, 1967); Gail Jefferson, "A Case of Precision Timing in Ordinary Conversation: Overlapped Tag-Positioned Address Terms in Closing Sequences," *Semiotica*, 9 (1973), 47-96; Gail Jefferson, "Sequential Aspects of Storytelling in Conversation," in *Studies in the Organization of Conversational Interaction*, ed. Jim Schenkein (New York: Academic Press, 1978), pp. 219-48; Harvey Sacks, "An Analysis of the Course of a Joke's Telling in Conversation," in *Explorations in the Ethnography of Speaking*, eds. Richard Bauman and Joel Sherzer (London: Cambridge Univ. Press, 1974), pp. 337-43; Emanuel A. Schegloff, "Sequencing in Conversational Openings," in *Directions in Sociolinguistics: The Ethnography of Communication*, ed. John J. Gumperz and Dell Hymes (New York: Holt, Rinehart & Winston, 1972), pp. 346-80 (originally appeared in *American Anthropologist*, 70, 6 [1968]); Emanuel A. Schegloff and Harvey Sacks, "Opening Up Closings," *Semiotica*, 8 (1973), 289-327; Harvey Sacks, Emanuel A. Schegloff and Gail Jefferson, "A Simplest Systematics for the Organization of Turn-Taking in Conversation," *Language*, 50 (1974), 696-735.

17. See references in notes 11 through 16. For other examples, see: George Psathas (ed.), *Everyday Language: Studies in Ethnomethodology* (New York: John Wiley, 1979); Jim Schenkein (ed.), *Studies in the Organization of Conversational Interaction* (New York: Academic Press, 1978); David Sudnow (ed.), *Studies in Social Interaction* (New York: Free Press, 1972); Richard Bauman and Joel Sherzer (eds.), *Explorations in the Ethnography of Speaking* (London: Cambridge Univ. Press, 1974); Lawrence W. Rosenfield, "A Game Model of Human Communication" (Minnesota Symposium in Speech Communication, 1968), pp. 26-41; Robert E. Sanders and Larry W. Martin, "Grammatical Rules and Explanation of Behavior," *Inquiry*, 18 (1975), 65-82; Paul D. Krivonos and Mark L. Knapp, "Initiating Communication: What Do You Say When You Say Hello?" *Central States Speech J.*, 26 (1975), 115-25; Gerry Philipsen, "Speaking 'Like a Man' in Teamsterville: Culture and Patterns of Role Enactment in an Urban Neighborhood," *Q. J. of Speech*, 51 (1975), 13-22; Leonard C. Hawes, "How Writing Is Used in Talk: A Study of Communicative Logic-In-Use," *Q. J. of Speech*, 62 (1976), 350-60; James Heringer, "Pre-Sequences and Indirect Speech Acts," in *Discourse Across Time and Space*, eds. Elinor O. Keenan and Tina L. Bennett (Los Angeles: Univ. of Southern California Press, 1977), pp. 169-80; Starkey Duncan, Jr., "Some Signals and Rules for Taking Speaking Turns in Conversation," *J. of Personality and Social Psychology*, 23 (1972), 283-92; Starkey Duncan, Jr., "Toward A Grammar for Dyadic Conversation," *Semiotica*, 9 (1973), 29-46; Donna M. Jurick, "The Enactment of Returning: A Naturalistic Study of Talk," *Communication Q.*, 25 (1977), 21-29; Elinor Ochs Keenan, "The Universality of Conversational Postulates," *Language in Society*, 5 (1975), 67-80; John W. Wiemann and Mark L. Knapp, "Turn-Taking in Conversations," *J. of Communication*, 25 (1975), 72-95.

18. Watzlawick, Beavin, and Jackson; Hymes, "Introduction," p. xxxix; Charlene Edna O'Brien, "A Rules-Based Approach to Communication Within A Formal Organization: Theory and Case Studies" unpublished manuscript, n.d., based on her dissertation at the University of Massachusetts, Amherst, 1978; Sanders and Martin, p. 68.

19. Pearce and Conklin, p. 75.

20. Gidon Gottlieb, *Logic of Choice: An Investigation of the Concepts of Rules and Rationality* (New York: Macmillan, 1968), p. 11; Art Bochner, "On Taking Ourselves Seriously: An Analysis of Some Persistent Problems and Promising Directions in Interpersonal Research," *Human Communication Research*, 4 (1978), 188-89; Jesse G. Delia, "Alternative Perspectives for the Study of Human Communication: Critique and Response," *Communication Q.*, 25, 1 (1977), 54; Nofsinger, "Demand Ticket"; Cushman and Pearce, "Generality and Necessity in Communication Theory," p. 177; Dean E. Hewes, "A Critique of 'An Elaboration of the Concept of "Rule": A Case Study with the Military' by Kathleen Boynton and Gail Fairhurst," presented at International Communication Association Convention, Chicago, 1978, pp. 6-7.

Notes to Chapter 2

1. *Logic of Choice: An Investigation of the Concepts of Rule and Rationality* (New York: Macmillan, 1968), p. 11.

2. Art Bochner, "On Taking Ourselves Seriously: An Analysis of Some Persistent Problems and Promising Directions in Interpersonal Research," *Human Communication Research*, 4 (1978), 188-89.

3. Jesse G. Delia, "Alternative Perspectives for the Study of Human Communication: Critique and Response," *Communication Q.*, 25, 1 (1977), 54.

4. For example, see Robert E. Nofsinger, "The Demand Ticket: A Conversational Device for Getting the Floor," *Speech Monographs*, 42 (1975), 1; Donald P. Cushman and W. Barnett Pearce, "Generality and Necessity in Three Types of Human Communication Theory: Special Attention to Rules Theory," *Human Communication Research*, 3 (1977), 348; Dean E. Hewes, "A Critique of 'An Elaboration of the Concept of "Rule": A Case Study with the Military' by Kathleen Boynton and Gail Fairhurst," presented at International Communication Association Convention, Chicago, 1978, pp. 6-7.

5. Stephen E. Toulmin, "Concepts and the Explanation of Behavior," in *Human Action*, ed. Theodore Mischel (New York: Academic Press, 1969), pp. 71-104; Joan Safron Ganz, *Rules: A Systematic Study* (Paris: Mouton, 1971); Aaron Snyder, "Rules of Language," *Mind*, 80 (1971), 161-78; Donald P. Cushman and Gordon C. Whiting, "An Approach to Communication Theory: Towards Consensus on Rules," *J. of Communication*, 22 (1972), 217-38; Raymond D. Gumb, *Rule-Governed Linguistic Behavior* (Paris: Mouton, 1972); John Fisher, "Knowledge of Rules," *Rev. of Metaphysics*, 28 (1974), 237-60; Romano Harré, "Some Remarks on 'Rule' As A Scientific Concept," in *Understanding Other People*, ed. Theodore Mischel (Oxford: Blackwell, 1974), pp. 143-84; Stephen E. Toulmin, "Rules and Their Relevance for Understanding Human Behavior," in *Understanding Other People*, pp. 185-215; W. Barnett Pearce, "The Coordinate Management of Meaning: A Rules-Based Theory of Interpersonal Communication," in *Explorations in Interpersonal Communication*, ed. Gerald R. Miller (Beverly Hills: Sage, 1976), pp. 17-36; Thomas S. Frentz and Thomas B. Farrell, "Language-Action: A Paradigm for Communication," *Q. J. of Speech*, 62 (1976), 333-49; Donald P. Cushman, "The Rules Perspective as a Theoretical Basis for the Study of Human Communication," *Communication Q.*, 25, 1 (1977), 30-45; Gottlieb; Cushman and Pearce.

6. Ganz, pp. 83-96. Ganz also defines rules in terms of the absence of truth value and adoption. These characteristics are rejected by the present author. Their weakness is pointed out in the section entitled "Other Definitions," where Ganz's definition is discussed.

7. Fisher, p. 238.

8. Snyder, p. 162.

9. Ganz, p. 104.

10. Cushman and Pearce; Frentz and Farrell.

11. Peter Collett, *Social Rules and Social Behavior* (Totowa, N.J.: Rowman and Littlefield, 1977), p. 4; Ganz, p. 28.

12. Gumb, p. 38; Peter Winch, *The Idea of a Social Science and its Relation to Philosophy* (New York: Humanities Press, 1958).

13. Collett, p. 4; Ganz,

14. Ganz, pp. 31-32; in a note Ganz later admits that "certainly rules can be contradictory" (p. 52, n. 7).

15. Ganz, p. 72.

16. Gumb, p. 42.

17. Roger D. Abrahams and Rudolph C. Troike (eds.), *Language and Cultural Diversity in American Education* (Englewood Cliffs, N.J.: Prentice-Hall, 1972), pp. 14, 61, 327.

18. Leonard C. Hawes, "Lecture," Summer Symposium on Beyond the Ivory Tower, University of Southern California, 1977.

19. Although rules need not be followed to be rules, those which will probably be of the most interest to communication scholars will be those which are both followable and followed.

20. Toulmin, "Concepts," p. 87; Harré, p. 153; Snyder, p. 162; Cushman and Pearce, pp. 345, 348-52; Collett, pp. 4, 8; Gumb, p. 18; Ganz, pp. 48-65; W. Barnett Pearce and Donald P. Cushman, "Research About Communication Rules: A Critique and Appraisal," presented at Speech Communication Association Convention, Washington, D.C., December 1977; Ted Smith, "Practical Inference and its Implications for Communication Theory," unpublished manuscript, n.d.; Cushman, p. 35.

21. W. Barnett Pearce, "Naturalistic Study of Communication: Its Function and Form," *Communication Q.*, 25, 3 (1977), p. 54.

22. Toulmin, "Concepts," p. 87; Harré, p. 153; Snyder, p. 162.

23. Cushman and Pearce, pp. 345, 348-52; Pearce and Cushman; Smith; Cushman.

24. Toulmin, p. 87.

25. Cushman and Pearce, p. 345.

26. Penelope Brown and Stephen Levinson, "Universals in Language Usage: Politeness Phenomena," in *Questions and Politeness*, ed. Esther N. Goody (Cambridge: Cambridge Univ. Press, 1978), pp. 99-100.

27. Robin Lakoff, "What You Can Do With Words: Politeness, Pragmatics and Performatives," *Berkeley Studies in Syntax and Semantics*, 16 (1974), 14.

28. Susan B. Shimanoff, "Investigating Politeness," in *Discourse Across Time and Space*, eds. Elinor O. Keenan and Tina L. Bennett (Los Angeles: Univ. of Southern California Press, 1977), pp. 213-41.

29. Paula B. Johnson and Jacqueline W. Goodchilds, "How Women Get Their Way," *Psychology Today*, Oct. 1976, pp. 69-70.

30. Ganz, pp. 50, 84-85.

31. Ganz, p. 50.

32. G. H. von Wright, "The Logic of Practical Discourse," in *Contemporary Philosophy*, ed. Raymond Klikansky (Italy: La Nuava Italia Editrice, 1968), pp. 141-65; Cushman and Pearce, p. 349; Pearce and Cushman, p. 6; Smith, p. 17.

33. Gottlieb, p. 39; Smith, p. 34. Emphasis added.

34. von Wright, p. 143.

35. von Wright, p. 156.

36. Jack L. Ray, "Prescriptive Deontic Logic: A Study of Inference from Linguistic Forms Expressing Choice and Conditional Permission and Obligation," Ph.D. dissertation, University of Southern California, 1971, p. 83.

37. von Wright, p. 143.

38. Anita May Pomerantz, "Second Assessments: A Study of Some Features of Agreements/Disagreements," Ph.D. dissertation University of California, Irvine, 1975.

39. Robin Lakoff, *Language and Woman's Place* (New York: Harper & Row, 1975), p. 74.

40. William Labov, *Sociolinguistic Patterns* (Philadelphia: Univ. of Pennsylvania Press, 1972), pp. 218-32.

41. Labov, p. 231.

42. Labov, pp. 228-29.

43. Labov, pp. 230-32.

44. Ganz, pp. 37-47.

45. Gottlieb, p. 39; Cushman and Whiting, p. 228; Collett, p. 4; Ganz, p. 68; Frentz and Farrell, pp. 336-37. Some scholars use the term *conditional* rather than *contextual*, but one-time commands or agreements are also conditional, so *contextual* seems a better term to present the notion that a rule applies in all similar contexts.

46. This list of contextual features is similar to Kenneth Burke's pentad: act, scene, actor, agency, and purpose. See *A Grammar of Motives* (Berkeley: Univ. of California Press, 1945).

47. Ganz, p. 24.

48. Snyder, p. 163.

49. Pearce, p. 26.

50. Frentz and Farrell, pp. 336-37.

51. Kushner, "A Reconceptualization of Rules," presented at Western Speech Communication Association Convention, San Francisco, 1976, p. 32.

52. Kaufer, "Developing a Rule Theoretic Approach to Communication as Opposed to a Dictionary of Rules: Some Considerations and Criteria," Rules-Based Approaches to Communication Theory and Research: Their Form, Value, and Feasibility, Doctoral Honors Seminar, Amherst, Massachusetts, December 1976 (henceforth, this conference will be referred to as the Rules Honors Seminar), p. 7.

53. Philipsen, "Linearity of Research Design in Ethnographic Studies of Speaking," *Communication Q.*, 25, 3 (1977), 44.

54. Cushman and Whiting, p. 43.

55. Susan B. Shimanoff, "A Rule-Governed Model of Communication," Rules Honors Seminar, 1976, pp. 4-5.

56. Nofsinger, "The Demand Ticket: A Conversational Device for Getting the Floor," *Speech Monographs*, 42 (1975), 1-9.

57. *Speech Acts: An Essay in the Philosophy of Language* (Cambridge: Cambridge Univ. Press, 1969), p. 146.

58. Nofsinger, p. 4.

59. Ganz, p. 95.

60. Susan Ervin-Tripp, "On Sociolinguistic Rules: Alternation and Co-occurrence," in *Directions in Sociolinguistics: The Ethnography of Communication*, eds. John J. Gumperz and Dell Hymes (New York: Holt, Rinehart & Winston, 1972), pp. 213-50.

61. Robert E. Nofsinger, "On Answering Questions Indirectly: Some Rules in the Grammar of Doing Conversation," *Human Communication Research*, 2 (1976), 177.

62. Nofsinger, "Indirect Answers," p. 177.

63. Nofsinger, "Demand Ticket," p. 7.

64. Nofsinger, "Indirect Answers," p. 173.

65. Gumb, p. 35.
66. Gumb, p. 33.
67. Harold Garfinkel, *Studies in Ethnomethodology* (Englewood Cliffs, N.J.: Prentice-Hall, 1967), pp. 42-43.
68. Ganz, pp. 28-37.
69. Dan J. Slobin, *Psycholinguistics* (Glenview, Ill.: Scott, Foresman, 1971); Fisher; Snyder; Nofsinger, "Indirect Answers," p. 172.
70. Nofsinger, "Demand Ticket," pp. 2, 5.
71. Nofsinger, "Demand Ticket," p. 5.
72. Ganz, pp. 128-29; *Oxford English Dictionary*, pp. 881-83. References to the communication sources will be made as each synonym is discussed. The eleven synonyms were: *agreement, contract, critique, episode, expectation, explanation, logic, meta-rule, plan, presupposition*, and *self-concept*.
73. Delia, p. 54; Delia based his statement on a similar one by Daniel J. O'Keefe, "Constructivism and Communication Studies: Theoretical Essays," Ph.D. dissertation, University of Illinois, Urbana-Champaign, 1976, p. 115.
74. Ganz, pp. 80, 101, 103.
75. Ganz, p. 69.
76. Ganz admits this similarity; see p. 69, n. 22.
7. Philip Babcock Gore (ed.), *Webster's Third New International Dictionary of the English Language Unabridged* (Springfield, Mass.: G. & C. Merriam, 1976) p. 199.
78. Ganz, pp. 71-104. Ganz also compared *rule* with *model, methods, practices, mores, canons*, other religious terms, and other references for average behavior.
79. Ervin-Tripp, p. 213.
80. "Management of Meaning," p. 32.
81. Pearce makes much the same argument without using the same labels in "Management of Meaning," p. 32.
82. Ganz, p. 100.
83. Nofsinger, "Demand Ticket," p. 6.
84. p. 96.
85. p. 102.
86. H. Paul Grice, "The Logic of Conversation," in *Syntax and Semantics, Vol. 3: Speech Acts*, eds. Peter Cole and Jerry Morgan (New York: Academic Press, 1975), pp. 41-58.
87. Elinor O. Keenan, lecture, University of Southern California, 1976.
88. "A Conceptual and Measurement Model for Norms and Roles," *Pacific Soc. Rev.,* 9 (1966), 41.
89. W. Barnett Pearce, "Consensual Rules in Interpersonal Communication: A Reply to Cushman and Whiting," *Journal of Communication*, 23 (1973), 165; Aaron V. Cicourel, *Cognitive Sociology: Language and Meaning in Social Interaction* (New York: Free Press, 1974), p. 52; Mark L. Knapp, *Social Intercourse: From Greetings to Goodbye* (Boston: Allyn & Bacon, 1978), pp. 59-67; Snyder, p. 162.
90. pp. 35, 37.
91. William L. Kolb, "Norm," in *Dictionary of the Social Sciences*, eds. Julius Gould and William L. Kolb (New York: Free Press of Glencoe, 1964), p. 472.
92. "Phrases of Conflict in Small Group Development: A Markov Analysis," *Human Communication Research*, 1 (1975), 210.
93. p. 20.
94. Leonard C. Hawes, "Toward a Hermeneutic Phenomenology of Communication," *Communication Q.*, 25, 3 (1977), 38. In this article Hawes uses the term *logic* in a discussion about the logics of phenomenologists and positivists. However, in a lecture in

1977 he has used the term more broadly to include such logics as the logics of nursing home personnel and residents and half-way house occupants.

95. Harré, p. 153.

96. "Consensual Rules: A Reply," p. 166.

97. p. 153.

98. "The Coordinated Management of Meaning: A Rules-Based Theory of Interpersonal Communication," in *Explorations*, p. 21.

99. Unwanted episodes are discussed by Vernon E. Cronen, W. Barnett Pearce, and Lonna Snavely in "A Theory of Rule-Structure and Types of Episodes, and a Study of Perceived Enmeshment in Undesired Repetitive Patterns (URPs)," in *Communication Yearbook III*, ed. B. Ruben (New Brunswick, N.J.: Transaction Press, 1979).

100. "Communication Systems: Interpersonal Implication," in *Explorations*, p. 48.

101. Cushman and Craig, p. 49.

102. "Alternative Perspectives for the Study of Human Communication: Critique and Response," *Communication Q.*, 25, 1 (1977), 58.

103. p. 95.

104. Ganz, p. 93.

105. Ganz, p. 95.

106. Ganz, p. 94; Gumb, p. 21.

107. Ganz, pp. 71-79.

108. "A Foundation for the Study of Everyday Talk," *Communication Q.*, 25, 3 (1977), 4.

109. Ervin-Tripp.

110. Ganz, pp. 83-86.

111. Gottlieb, p. 157; Cushman and Whiting, p. 227; Pearce and Cushman; Ted Smith, "Practical Inference and its Implications for Communication Theory," unpublished manuscript, n.d., p. 2; Mary L. Hines, "Practical Force: Theoretical Implications of a Rules Based Approach to the Explanation of Human Communication," Rules Honors Seminar, p. 1.

112. p. 225.

113. "The Rhetoric of Nonverbal Communication in Interpersonal Encounters," Ph.D. dissertation, University of Southern California, 1976.

114. p. 6. Litton-Hawes also conceptualized rule as an explanation (p. 4). The weakness of this position has already been discussed.

115. *The Hidden Dimension* (Garden City, N.Y.: Anchor Books, 1969).

116. "The Current Status of Theory and Research in Interpersonal Communications," *Human Communication Research*, 4 (1978), 175.

117. Bochner, p. 188.

118. Gumb, p. 17.

119. 17-36.

120. Ganz, pp. 103-104.

121. Ganz, pp. 65-70.

122. p. 69.

123. A shorter version of the definition appears in the preface (pp. 5-6), but even it is a full paragraph.

124. Snyder, p. 163; Gottlieb, p. 156.

125. Gottlieb, p. 40.

126. Max Black, *Models and Metaphors* (Ithaca: Cornell Univ. Press, 1962), p. 106.

127. Gumb, p. 21.

128. Ganz, p. 13.

129. p. 39.

130. Collett, p. 6; Searle, p. 34.

131. Ray; Collett; D. Paul Snyder, *Modal Logic and Its Applications* (New York: Van Nostrand Reinhold, 1971).

132. Collett, p. 6.

133. Ray; von Wright; Cushman and Whiting; Cushman and Craig.

134. pp. 76-87.

135. Ray, p. 76.

136. Stephen E. Toulmin, *The Uses of Argument* (Cambridge: Cambridge Univ. Press, 1964), p. 28.

137. Ray, p. 179.

138. Emanuel A. Schegloff, "Sequencing in Conversational Openings," in *Directions in Sociolinguistics*, pp. 346-80. The numbers and brackets have been added.

139. Elaine Marie Litton-Hawes, "A Discourse Analysis of Topic Co-Selection in Medical Interviews," Ph.D. dissertation, Ohio State University, 1976, p. 69.

140. Nofsinger, "Indirect Answers," p. 176.

141. Litton-Hawes, p. 71.

142. p. 48.

143. p. 50.

144. pp. 50, 53.

145. Cushman and Craig, p. 53.

146. $*R_{(40)}$ was originally generated by Randy Sawyer, and $*R_{(41)}$ by Jacqueline E. Geiger. Both authors were students of mine. The revisions were done as part of a classroom exercise. Although there was limited supporting evidence for the revisions, they were not subjected to scientific verification.

147. Because a description of the data in terms of contextual variables may be misleading, Emanuel A. Schegloff and Harvey Sachs argue that such characterizations should not be given. "Opening Up Closings," *Semiotica*, 8 (1973), 291-92, n.#4. However, the position taken here is that if researchers do not specify the contextual limitations of their research the generalizability of proposed rules can never be assessed. Nor can investigations be compared.

148. Harré, p. 143.

149. Cushman and Whiting, p. 228.

150. Fisher, p. 238.

151. Searle, p. 34.

152. Collett, p. 5.

153. Black; Raymond D. Gumb, *Rule-Governed Linguistic Behavior* (Paris: Mouton, 1962).

154. Searle, p. 34.

155. Searle; Nofsinger; Sanders and Martin.

156. Searle, p. 35.

157. Searle, pp. 33-36; Collett, pp. 5-6; Robert E. Sanders and Larry W. Martin, "Grammatical Rules and Explanations of Behavior," *Inquiry*, 18 (1975), 68.

158. Sanders and Martin, p. 68; a similar point is made by John R. Searle, *Speech Acts*, pp. 33-36.

159. *Speech Acts.*

160. "Indirect Answers."

161. Slobin, p. 54.

162. Charles R. Berger et al., "Interpersonal Epistemology and Interpersonal Communication," in *Explorations*, pp. 168-69.

163. Harré, p. 94.

164. Snyder, p. 162.

165. Susan K. Blume, "Asking the Unanswerable: A Rule-Breaking Approach to Implicit Knowledge," Rules Honor Seminar, 1976, p. 1.

166. Slobin, p. 54.

167. Susan B. Shimanoff and Joanna C. Brunak, "Repairs in Planned and Unplanned Discourse," in *Discourse*, pp. 123-67.

168. Fisher, p. 246.

169. Cushman and Whiting, p. 219; Cushman and Pearce, p. 349; Cushman, p. 39.

Notes to Chapter 3

1. A rule need not be operative to be a rule, but it is of course more valuable to the communication scholar if it actually influences behavior. The material presented in this chapter will help researchers identify such rules.

2. This is similar to Chomsky's notion that the performances of actors may be used to determine the underlying systems of rules that inform those behaviors, known as competence. See Noam Chomsky *Aspects of the Theory of Syntax* (Cambridge, Mass.: MIT Press, 1965), p. 4.

3. Joan Safron Ganz, *Rules: A Systematic Study* (Paris: Mouton, 1971), p. 78. This notion was expressed in the negative by W. Barnett Pearce who argued that in rule-governed behavior there is not a logical relationship between antecedents and consequences; see "The Coordinate Management of Meaning: A Rules-Based Theory of Interpersonal Communication," in *Explorations in Interpersonal Communication*, ed. Gerald R. Miller (Beverly Hills: Sage, 1976), p. 26. The reader is also encouraged to see the section on the followability of rules in Chapter 2 for more details and references related to the notion of controllability.

4. W. Barnett Pearce, "Naturalistic Study of Communication: Its Function and Form," *Communication Q.*, 25, 3 (1977), 54.

5. Peter Collett, "The Rules of Conduct," in *Social Rules and Social Behavior*, ed. Peter Collett (Totowa, N.J.: Rowman and Littlefield, 1977), p. 21. A similar point is made by Jay Jackson for what he calls "norms," in "A Conceptual and Measurement Model for Norms and Rules," *Pacific Soc. Rev.*, 9 (1966), 35-47.

6. This rule is a paraphrase of a much longer one in Harvey Sacks, Emanuel A. Schegloff, and Gail Jefferson, "A Simplest Systematics for the Organization of Turn-Taking for Conversation," *Language*, 50 (1974), 704.

7. Anita Pomerantz, "Second Assessments: A Study of Some Features of Agreements Disagreements," Ph.D. dissertation, University of California, Irvine, 1975.

8. Jackson, pp. 36-41.

9. "A Rules-Based Approach to Communication Within a Formal Organization: Theory and Case Studies," unpublished paper, n.d., p. 49. (This paper was based on her dissertation done at the University of Massachusetts, Amherst, 1978.)

10. Collett, p. 146; Pearce, in "Management of Meaning" (p. 27), took a strong stand and argued that actors must be able to make these judgments. It is argued here, however, that other forms of evidence can be used to demonstrate the criticizability of rule-generated behavior.

11. *The Hidden Dimension* (Garden City, N.Y.: Anchor Books, 1969), p. 159.

12. Collett, pp. 25-26.

13. Roger Brown and Usula Bellugi, "Three Processes in the Child's Acquisition of Syntax," *Harvard Educ. Rev.*, 34 (1964), 133-51.

14. Janet Lynn Weathers, "The Effect of Assertive Communication and Presence of Audience on Students' and Teachers' Perceptions of the Rules Which Should Guide a Student in a Disagreement with a Teacher," Diss. Univ. of Southern California, 1979.

15. Pearce, "Naturalistic Study," p. 54.

16. Erving Goffman, *Behavior in Public Places* (New York: Free Press, 1963), p. 88.

17. Susan B. Shimanoff, "Male and Female Politeness," transcript, 1976, p. 5.

18. Gail Jefferson, "Sequential Aspects of Storytelling in Conversation," in *Studies in the Organization of Conversational Interaction*, ed. Jim Schenkein (New York: Academic Press, 1978), pp. 228-29. For an explanation of the special transcription symbols used in the dialogue, see pp. xi-xvi of the same book.

19. H. Paul Grice, "The Logic of Conversation," in *Syntax and Semantics, Volume 3: Speech Acts*, eds. Peter Cole and Jerry L. Morgan (New York: Academic Press, 1975), p. 46.

20. Jay Jackson, "Normative Power and Conflict Potential," *Soc. Methods and Research*, 4 (1975), 144-45.

21. Kathleen R. Boynton, "A Theory of Episode Deviation," presented at the Rules-Based Approaches to Communication Theory and Research: Their Form, Value and Feasibility Doctoral Honors Seminar, Amherst Massachusetts, December 1976. (Henceforth this conference will be referred to as the Rules Honors Seminar.)

22. "Speaking 'Like a Man' in Teamsterville: Culture and Patterns of Role Enactment in an Urban Neighborhood," *Q. J. of Speech*, 61 (1975), 13-22.

23. Ted Smith, "Practical Inference and Its Implications for Communication Theory," unpublished manuscript, pp. 39-40.

24. Mark L. Knapp, *Social Intercourse: From Greeting to Goodbye* (Boston: Allyn & Bacon, 1978), pp. 63-67.

25. "The Logic of Conversation," in *Syntax and Semantics Vol. 3: Speech Acts*, eds. Peter Cole and Jerry L. Morgan (New York: Academic Press, 1975), p. 49.

26. David Kaufer, "Developing a Rule Theoretic Approach to Communication as Opposed to a Dictionary of Rules: Some Considerations and Criteria," Rules Honors Seminar, p. 12.

27. Grice, p. 43.

28. Robert E. Nofsinger, "The Demand Ticket: A Conversational Device for Getting the Floor," *Speech Monographs*, 42 (1975), 7.

29. For a summary of the research on the incongruity thesis of humor, see Diana Marjorie Mechan, "A Factor Analysis of Humor," Ph.D. dissertation, San Diego State University 1975, pp. 12-17.

30. John Waite Bowers, Normal D. Elliot, and Roger J. Desmond, "Exploiting Pragmatic Rules: Devious Messages," *Human Communication Research*, 3 (1977), 235-42.

31. Bowers, Elliot, and Desmond, p. 239.

32. Janice Hocher Rushing, "Using Students as Participant Observers in Research on Conflict in Relationship Definitions," International Communication Association, 1976, p. 11.

33. "The Verbal Stare: Focus on Attention in Conversation," *Communication Monographs*, 43 (1976), 1-10.

34. "Language-Action: A Paradigm for Communication," *Q. J. of Speech*, 62 (1976), 345.

35. Wayne A. Beach and William Wilmot, "Self-Disclosure as Manipulation," presented at Western Speech Communication Association Convention, Seattle 1975; Susan B. Shimanoff, "The Tryanny of Politeness or How to Get the Fence White-Washed," presented at Western Speech Communication Association Convention, San Francisco 1976.

36. Susan B. Shimanoff and Joanne C. Brunak, "Repairs in Planned and Unplanned Discourse," in *Discourse Across Time and Space*, eds. Elinor O. Keenan and Tina L. Bennett (Los Angeles: Univ. of Southern California Press, 1977), p. 123.

37. Emanuel A. Schegloff, Gail Jefferson, and Harvey Sacks, "The Preference for Self-Correction in the Organization of Repair in Conversation," *Language*, 53 (1977), 361-82; Aaron Snyder, "Rules for Language," *Mind*, 80 (1971), 174; John Fisher, "Knowledge of Rules," *Review of Metaphysics*, 28 (1974), 239; Dan I. Slobin, *Psycholinguistics* (Glenview, Ill.: Scott, Foresman, 1971), p. 53; Shimanoff and Brunak.

38. Peck, "Palos Verdes," transcript, 1976, printed in Shimanoff and Brunak, p. 128.

39. Grice, p. 46.

40. Shimanoff and Brunak, pp. 128-42.

41. Livia Polanyi, "False Starts Can Be True," *Proceedings of the Fourth Annual Meeting of the Berkeley Linguistics Society*, 4 (1978), 628-39; Shimanoff and Brunak, pp. 133, 160.

42. Schegloff, Jefferson, and Sacks, p. 363.

43. Boynton; Stephen D. Krashen et al., "Two Studies in Language Acquisition and Language Learning," presented at Meeting of the Linguistic Society of America, 1976.

44. Schegloff, Jefferson, and Sacks, pp. 361-82.

45. "Remedial Interchanges," in *Relations in Public: Microstudies of the Public Order* (New York: Harper & Row, 1971), pp. 95-187.

46. Goffman, pp. 109-16.

47. "The Remedial Process: A Negotiation of Rules," presented at Speech Communication Association Convention, 1978.

48. Collett, p. 11; Pearce, p. 26; Slobin, p. 53.

49. Dorothy Lenk, "The Use of a Stochastic Model for Discerning Rule Guided Communication Behavior," Rules Honors Seminar, p. 14; W. Barnett Pearce does not specify that a 95 percent regularity is necessary; but he does emphasize that rules must result in statistical regularities, and "statistical regularity" is often associated with 95 percent certainty. See "Management of Meaning," p. 26.

50. Jean Berko, "The Child's Learning of English Morphology," *Word*, 14 (1958), 150-77.

51. Dell Hymes, *Foundations in Sociolinguistics: An Ethnographic Approach* (Philadelphia: Univ. of Pennsylvania Press, 1974), p. 62.

52. Jan-Petter Blom and John J. Gumperz, "Social Meaning in Linguistic Structures: Code Switching in Norway," in *Directions in Sociolinguistics: The Ethnography of Communication*, eds. John J. Gumperz and Dell Hymes (New York: Holt, Rinehart & Winston, 1972), pp. 407-34; John J. Gumperz, "Verbal Strategies in Multilingual Communication," in *Georgetown University Round Table on Language and Linguistics, No. 23*, ed. James E. Alatis (Washington, D.C.: Georgetown Univ. Press, 1970), 129-48; John J. Gumperz, "Dialect and Conversational Inference in Urban Communication," *Language in Society*, 7 (1978), 393-409.

53. David K. Lewis, *Convention: A Philosophical Study* (Cambridge, Mass.: Harvard Univ. Press, 1969), p. 42.

54. Lewis, pp. 100-107.

55. Lewis, pp. 102-03.

56. Ganz, p. 80.

57. Ganz, p. 80.

58. Percy H. Tannenbaum, Frederick Williams, and Carolyn S. Hiller, "Word Predictability in the Environments of Hesitations," *J. of Verbal Learning and Verbal Behavior*, 4 (1965), 134-40.

59. Peter Ball's research demonstrated that in conversation terminal-filled pauses ("er," "um," and so on.) delay the assumption of the floor, and he argued that filled pauses could be used to maintain the floor; see "Listener's Responses to Filled Pauses in Relation to Floor Apportionment," *British J. of Social and Clinical Psychology*, 14 (1975), 423-24.

60. Harry E. Collins and Harold Guetzkow, *A Social Psychology of Group Processes for Decision-Making* (New York: John Wiley, 1964), pp. 148-60.

61. David Mortensen, *Communication: The Study of Human Interaction* (New York: McGraw-Hill, 1972), p. 249; Arthur N. Wiens et al., "Interview Interaction Behavior of Supervisors, Head Nurses and Staff Nurses," *Nursing Research*, 13 (1965), 322-39.

62. Michael Argyle, Mansui Lalljee, and Mark Cook, "The Effects of Visibility of Interaction in a Dyad," *Human Relations*, 21 (1968), 3-17; Don H. Zimmerman and Candace West, "Sex Roles, Interruptions and Silence in Conversations," in *Language and Sex: Difference and Dominance*, eds. Barrie Thorne and Nancy Henley (Rowley, Mass.: Newbury House, 1975), pp. 105-29.

63. William T. Rogers and Stanley E. Jones, "Effects of Dominance Tendencies on Floor Holding and Interruption Behavior in Dyadic Interaction," *Human Communication Research*, 1 (1975), 113-22.

64. O'Brien, p. 52.

65. W. Barnett Pearce, "The Coordinated Management of Meaning: A Rules-Based Theory of Interpersonal Communication," in *Explorations in Interpersonal Communication*, ed. Gerald R. Miller (Beverly Hills: Sage, 1976), p. 26.

66. Aaron Snyder, "Rules of Language," *Mind*, 80 (1971), 172.

67. Keith Alder, "On the Falsification of Rules Theories," *Q. J. of Speech*, 64 (1978), 437.

Notes to Chapter 4

1. Donald P. Cushman and W. Barnett Pearce, "Generality and Necessity in Three Types of Theory about Human Communication, with Special Attention to Rules Theory," *Human Communication Research*, 3 (1977), 349; Donald P. Cushman, "The Rules Perspective as a Theoretical Basis for the Study of Human Communication," *Communication Q.*, 25, 1 (1977), 38-39; W. Barnett Pearce, "Naturalistic Study of Communication: Its Function and Form," *Communication Q.*, 25, 3 (1977), 53.

2. Donald P. Cushman and Gordon C. Whiting, "Approaches to Communication Theory: Toward Consensus on Rules," *J. of Communication*, 22 (1972), 217, 229; W. Barnett Pearce, "Consensual Rules in Interpersonal Communication: A Reply to Cushman and Whiting," *J. of Communication*, 23 (1973), 165.

3. Cushman and Whiting, p. 217.

4. p. 229.

5. Joan Safron Ganz makes a similar distinction in *Rules: A Systematic Study* (Paris: Mouton, 1971), p. 108.

6. Geneva Gay and Roger D. Abrahams, "Black Culture in the Classroom," in *Language and Cultural Diversity in American Education*, eds. Roger D. Abrahams and Rudolph C. Troike (Englewood Cliffs, N.J.: Prentice-Hall, 1972), p. 77.

7. Gay and Abrahams, p. 77.

8. For a good summary of language attitude research, see Frederick Williams et al., *Explorations of the Linguistic Attitudes of Teachers* (Rowley, Mass.: Newbury House, 1976).

9. Daniel J. O'Keefe, "Constructivism and Communication Studies: Theoretical Essays," Ph.D. dissertation, University of Illinois, Urbana-Champaign 1976, pp. 115-19; Jesse G. Delia, "Alternative Perspectives for the Study of Human Communication; Critique and Response," *Communcation Q.*, 25, 1 (1977), 54.

10. Stephen E. Toulmin, "Rules and Their Relevance for Understanding Human Behavior," in *Understanding Other People*, ed. Theodore Mischel (Oxford: Blackwell, 1974), pp. 185-215; Ganz; Peter Collett, "The Rules of Conduct," in *Social Rules and Social Behavior*, ed. Peter Collett (Totowa, N.J.: Rowman and Littlefield, 1977), pp. 8-27.

11. Toulmin, pp. 188-96.

12. Elaine N. Litton-Hawes, "A Foundation for the Study of Everyday Talk," *Communication Q.*, 25, 3 (1977), 5; Cushman, p. 37.

13. Ganz, pp. 26-37.

14. Ganz, p. 66.

15. Collett, p. 9.

16. Raymond D. Gumb, *Rule-Governed Linguistic Behavior* (Paris: Mouton, 1972), p. 70.

17. Ganz, p. 29; Collett (p. 9) maintains that it was one form of evidence.

18. John Fisher, "Knowledge of Rules," *Review of Metaphysics*, 28 (1974), p. 245; Dan I. Slobin, *Psycholinguistics* (Glenview, Ill.: Scott, Foresman, 1971), p. 53; Collett, p. 14; Snyder, p. 167.

19. Collett, p. 14; W. Barnett Pearce, "The Coordinated Management of Meaning: A Rules-Based Theory of Interpersonal Communication," in *Explorations in Interpersonal Communication*, ed. Gerald R. Miller (Beverly Hills: Sage, 1976), p. 27.

20. Suzette Haden Elgin, *A Primer of Transformational Grammar for Rank Beginners* (Urbana, Ill.: National Council of Teachers of English, 1975), p. 10.

21. Collett, p. 14; Slobin, p. 54; Pearce, "Management and Meaning," p. 27.

22. Slobin, p. 53; Collett, p. 11; Pearce, p. 26.

23. Stephen E. Toulmin, "Concepts and the Explanation of Behavior," in *Human Action*, ed. Theodore Mischel (New York: Academic Press, 1969), p. 87; Collett, p. 10; Pearce, "Management of Meaning," p. 27; Slobin, p. 54; Aaron Snyder, "Rules of Language," *Mind*, 80 (1971).

24. Harvey Sacks, Emanuel A. Schegloff, and Gail Jefferson, "The Preference for Self-Correction in the Organization of Repair in Conversation," *Language*, 53 (1977), 361-82; Susan B. Shimanoff and Joann C. Brunak, "Repairs in Planned and Unplanned Discourse," in *Discourse Across Time and Space*, eds. Elinor O. Keenan and Tina L. Bennett (Los Angeles: University of Southern California Press, 1977), pp. 123-67; Fisher, p. 239; Snyder, p. 174.

25. Frentz and Farrell, p. 339.

Notes to Chapter 5

1. John R. Searle, *Speech Acts: An Essay in the Philosophy of Language* (London: Cambridge Univ. Press, 1974).

2. David Kaufer, "Developing a Rule Theoretic Approach to Communication as Opposed to a Dictionary of Rules: Some Considerations and Criteria," Rules-Based Approaches to Communication Theory and Research: Their Form, Value and Feasibility, Doctoral Honors Seminar, Amherst, Massachusetts, December 1976 (henceforth, this conference will be referred to as Rules Honors Seminar), p. 7; William Labov, *Sociolinguistic Patterns* (Philadelphia: University of Pennsylvania, 1972), p. xiii.

Notes   279

3. Joseph N. Cappella, "Research Methodology in Communication: Review and Commentary," in *Communication Yearbook 1*, ed. Brent D. Ruben (New Brunswick, N.J.: Transaction, 1977), p. 49.

4. W. Barnett Pearce and Donald P. Cushman, "Research about Communication Rules: A Critique and Appraisal," presented at Speech Communication Association Convention, 1977, p. 11.

5. John Searle, "What Is a Speech Act?" in *Language and Social Context*, ed. Pier Paolo Giglioli (Middlesex, England: Penguin, 1976), pp. 136-54; H. Paul Grice, "Logic and Conversation," in *Syntax and Semantics, Vol. 3: Speech Acts*, eds. Peter Cole and Jerry L. Morgan (New York: Academic Press, 1975), pp. 41-58; Robert Nofsinger, "The Demand Ticket: A Conversational Device for Getting the Floor," *Speech Monographs*, 42 (1975), 1-9; Thomas S. Frentz and Thomas B. Farrell, "Language-Action: A Paradigm for Communication," *Q. J. of Speech*, 62 (1976), 333-49.

6. Searle, "What Is a Speech Act?" p. 153.

7. Kaufer, p. 12.

8. Grice, p. 46.

9. Nofsinger, "Demand Ticket," p. 4.

10. Frentz and Farrell, p. 341.

11. Frentz and Farrell, p. 341.

12. Robert Nofsinger, "On Answering Questions Indirectly: Some Rules in the Grammar of Doing Conversation," *Human Communication Research*, 2 (1976), 174.

13. Nofsinger, "Indirect Answers," p. 175.

14. Nofsinger, "Indirect Answers," pp. 177-78.

15. "Indirect Answers," pp. 176-78.

16. Cheris Kramer, "Folklinguistics: Wishy-Washy Mommy Talk," *Psychology Today*, June 1974, pp. 82-85; Cheris Kramer, "Women's Speech: Separate but Unequal?" *Q. J. of Speech*, 60 (1974), 14-24.

17. For a good summary of this research, see Nancy Henley and Barrie Thorne, *Language and Sex: Difference and Dominance* (Rowley, Mass.: Newbury House, 1975), pp. 257-63.

18. Labov, p. 198.

19. Labov, p. 199.

20. "Accent in Discourse: An Analysis of Function," Ph.D. dissertation, University of Southern California, 1978.

21. "Draft: Rules Article for Handbook of Communication, part #1," unpublished manuscript, State University New York, Albany, 1978, p. 58.

22. *The Politics of the Family and Other Essays* (New York: Vintage, 1971), p. 111.

23. Vernon E. Cronen and Leslie K. Davis, "Alternative Approaches for the Communication Theorist: Problems in the Laws-Rules-Systems Trichotomy," *Human Communication Research*, 4 (1978), 122, 127.

24. "Demand Ticket," p. 6; emphasis added.

25. Pearce and Cushman, p. 22; Cronen and Davis.

26. Robin Lakoff, "Language in Context," *Language*, 48 (1972), 907-27; Susan U. Philips, "The Role of the Listener in the Regulation of Talk: Some Sources of Cultural Variability ," presented at American Anthropological Association Convention, Mexico City, 1974.

27. Frentz and Farrell, p. 340; Pearce and Cushman, p. 20; Elinor Ochs Keenan, "The Universality of Conversational Postulates," *Languages in Society*, 5 (1975), 67-80; Jerry L. Morgan, "Some Remarks on the Nature of Sentences," in *Papers from the Parasession on Functionalism* (Chicago: Univ. of Chicago Press, 1975), p. 436.

28. Gail Jefferson, "A Case of Precision Timing in Ordinary Conversation: Overlap Tag-Positional Address Terms in Closing Sequences," *Semiotics*, 9 (1973), 49.

29. These rules are predicated in part on the research of Harvey Sacks, Emanuel A. Schegloff, and Gail Jefferson, "A Simplest Systematics for the Organization of Turn-Taking for Conversation," *Language*, 50 (1974), 696-735; Susan Ervin-Tripp, "On Sociolinguistic Rules: Alternation and Co-occurrence," in *Directions in Sociolinguistics: The Ethnography of Communication*, eds. John J. Gumperz and Dell Hymes (New York: Holt, Rinehart & Winston, 1972), pp. 213-50; Penelope Brown and Stephen Levinson, "Universals in Language Usage: Politeness Phenomena," in *Questions and Politeness: Strategies in Social Interaction*, ed. Ester N. Goody (Cambridge: Cambridge Univ. Press, 1976), pp. 56-289.

30. Kaufer, pp. 2, 7-12.

31. p. 7.

32. Nofsinger, "Indirect Answers," p. 177.

33. Nofsinger, "Indirect Answers," p. 177.

34. Kaufer, p. 11.

35. Kaufer, pp. 9-12.

36. Nofsinger, "Indirect Answers," p. 173.

37. David H. Smith, "Communication Research and the Idea of Process," *Speech Monographs*, 39 (1972), p. 179.

38. "Acquisition of an Aspect of Communication Competence: Learning What It Means to Talk Like a Lady," in *Child Discourse*, eds. Susan Ervin-Tripp and Claudia Mitchell-Kernan (New York: Academic Press, 1977), pp. 225-44. In an earlier, unpublished version of this paper, there were more references to rules. Some of these references are replaced with phrases like "sex stereotypes" and "sex-linkage of forms." This may reflect a tendency to view the perceived regularities less as rules, but there are, nonetheless, references to rules in this paper.

39. Robin Lakoff, *Language and Woman's Place* (New York: Harper & Row, 1975).

40. Cappella, p. 49.

41. Gerry Philipsen, "Linearity of Research Design in Ethnographic Studies of Speaking," *Communication Q.*, 25 (1977), 42-50; Pearce and Cushman.

42. Harold Garfinkel, *Studies in Ethnomethodology* (Englewood Cliffs, N.J.: Prentice-Hall, 1967).

43. Robert E. Nofsinger, "A Peek at Conversational Analysis," *Communication Q.*, 25, 3 (1977), p. 13.

44. Nofsinger, "Conversational Analysis," p. 13.

45. Pearce and Cushman, p. 11.

46. Nofsinger, "Conversational Analysis," p. 12; W. Barnett Pearce, "Naturalistic Study of Communication: Its Function and Form," *Communication Q.*, 25, 3 (1977), 52; Leonard C. Hawes, "The Naturalistic Perspective," presented at Speech Communication Association Convention, Houston 1975. (Hawes also uses the term *discourse analysis*.)

47. Cappella, p. 49.

48. *Webster's New Twentieth Century Dictionary of the English Language* (New York: Publishers Guild, 1943), p. 75.

49. *Webster's Dictionary*, p. 600.

50. *Oxford English Dictionary*, Compact Edition (New York: Oxford Univ. Press, 1971), I, 901.

51. Dell H. Hymes, "The Ethnography of Speaking," in *Anthropology and Human Behavior*, eds. Thomas Gladwin and William C. Sturtevant (Washington, D.C.: Anthropological Society of Washington, 1962), p. 16.

52. Garfinkel, p. 11.

53. *Introduction to Qualitative Research Methods* (New York: John Wiley, 1975), p. 16.

54. Nofsinger, "Conversational Analysis," p. 13.

55. Earl R. Babbie, *Survey Research Methods* (Belmont, Calif.: Wadsworth, 1973).

56. Pearce and Cushman, pp. 11, 13-16.

57. Philipsen, "Ethnographic Studies," p. 43.

58. Schegloff and Sacks, "Opening Up Closings," *Semiotics*, 8 (1973), 289-327; Schegloff, "Sequencing in Conversational Openings," in *Directions*, pp. 346-80; Sacks, Schegloff, and Jefferson, 696-735; Frentz and Farrell, pp. 342-46.

While these examples are representative, they are by no means exhaustive. For additional examples, see William Labov, "Rules for Ritual Insults," in *Studies in Social Interaction*, ed. Davis Sudnow (New York: Free Press, 1972), pp. 120-169, which is analyzed in the next chapter as an example of rules research; Elaine Marie Litton-Hawes, "A Discourse Analysis of Topic Co-Selection in Medical Interviews," Ph.D. dissertation Ohio State University, 1976; Jim Schenkein (ed.), *Studies in the Organization of Conversational Interaction* (New York: Academic Press, 1978); George Psathas (ed.), *Everyday Language: Studies in Ethnomethodology* (New York: Irvington, 1979).

59. Schegloff and Sacks, p. 296.

60. Schegloff, p. 362.

61. Sacks, Schegloff, and Jefferson, p. 704.

62. Frentz and Farrell, p. 345, taken from *The Presidential Transcripts* (New York: Delacorte Press, 1974), pp. 98-99.

63. Frentz and Farrell, p. 344.

64. Nofsinger, "Conversational Analysis," pp. 15-16.

65. *The Hidden Dimension* (Garden City, N.Y.: Doubleday, 1969).

66. Schegloff, p. 355; Starkey Duncan, Jr., "Some Signals and Rules for Taking Speaking Turns in Conversations," *J. of Personality and Social Psychology*, 23 (1972), 283-92; Sacks, Schegloff, and Jefferson, pp. 723-24; Frentz and Farrell, p. 345.

67. Schegloff, pp. 355-80.

68. Schegloff, p. 351.

69. Schegloff, p. 356.

70. Schegloff, p. 360.

71. Schegloff, p. 364.

72. Duncan, p. 285.

73. Schegloff and Sacks, p. 291.

74. This estimate was derived from personal experience and from comments made by other transcribers. Jefferson's system is published in Sacks, Schegloff, and Jefferson, pp. 731-33.

75. For two exceptions, see: Duncan, p. 284; Frentz and Farrell, pp. 342-43.

76. Sacks, Schegloff, and Jefferson, p. 700.

77. Sacks, Schegloff, and Jefferson, pp. 733-34.

78. Frederick Williams, "Communication and Sociolinguistics," *Journal of Communication*, 24, No. 2 (1974), 158-68.

79. Pearce, "Naturalistic Study," p. 56.

80. Sacks, Schegloff, and Jefferson.

81. Schegloff and Sacks, p. 291.

82. Duncan, p. 284.

83. Schegloff and Sacks, p. 291.

84. "The Role of the Listener."

85. "The Universality of Conversational Postulates."

282   COMMUNICATION RULES

86. This knowledge comes from discussing transcribing experiences with a number of trained transcribers and in comparing transcripts.

87. Hawes, "Naturalistic Study," p. 6.

88. Labov, p. 209.

89. Labov, *Sociolinguistics*, pp. 207-16; William Labov, "The Logic of Nonstandard English," in *Georgetown University Round Table on Languages and Linguistics, 1969,* ed. James E. Alatis (Washington, D.C.: Georgetown Univ. Press, 1970), pp. 1-44.

90. Labov, "Nonstandard English," p. 8.

91. Labov, "Nonstandard English," p. 7.

92. Labov, "Nonstandard English," pp. 9-10.

93. Labov, *Sociolinguistics,* pp. 209-11.

94. Susan B. Shimanoff, Katherine Yost, and Janet L. Weathers used an interesting method to hide the tape recorder. They cut a hole in a box and wrapped the box and lid separately in colorful paper. Then they punched pin holes through the paper where the hole was. They placed the microphone inside the box near this hole and put on the lid. Children thought it was a present or simply a colorful box. The only problem was that some children wanted to open it. "Communication Codes in Children's Dyads: As a Function of Social Class and Group Composition," unpublished manuscript, University of Southern California, 1976.

95. Stephen A. Taylor, "Conversational Practices for Children: An Investigation Using Two Methods," unpublished manuscript, State University of New York, Albany, n.d. This manuscript is based on his dissertation completed at the University of Illinois, Urbana-Champaign in 1976.

96. Nofsinger, "Conversational Analysis," p. 16.

97. Erving Goffman, *Relations in Public: Microstudies of the Public Order* (New York: Harper & Row, 1971), pp. 95-187; G.H. Morris, "The Remedial Process: A Negotiation of Rules," presented at Speech Communication Association Convention, 1978.

98. Garfinkel; Romano Harré and Paul Secord, *The Explanation of Social Behavior* (Totowa, N.J.: Littlefield, Adams, 1973), pp. 150, 172, 313.

99. Charles R. Berger, "The Covering Law Perspective as a Theoretical Basis for the Study of Human Communication," *Communication Q.*, 25, 1 (1977), 13.

100. Romano Harré, "Rules in the Explanation of Social Behavior," in *Social Rules and Social Behavior*, ed. Peter Collett (Totowa, N.J.: Rowman and Littlefield, 1977), pp. 28-41; Harré and Secord, pp. 39-41; Searle, pp. 50-53.

101. Harré, pp. 36-37.

102. Harré and Secord, p. 39.

103. Searle, pp. 50-53; Pearce, "Naturalistic Study," p. 53.

104. Hawes, "Naturalistic Study," p. 1.

105. Joan Safron Ganz, *Rules: A Systematic Study* (Paris: Mouton, 1971), pp. 130-33.

106. Nofsinger, "Conversational Analysis," p. 19.

107. Hawes, "Phenomenology."

108. Philipsen, "Ethnographic Studies," p. 49.

109. Pearce, "Naturalistic Study;" Hawes, "Naturalistic Study."

110. Jesse G. Delia and Lawrence Grossberg, "Interpretation and Evidence," *Western J. of Speech Communication*, 41 (1977), 32-42.

111. Jesse G. Delia, "Constructivism and the Study of Human Communication," *Q. J. of Speech*, 63 (1977), 77.
Interaction," Ph.D. dissertation, University of Illinois, Urbana-Champaign, 1975.

112. Herbert Blumer, *Symbolic Interactionism: Perspective and Method* (Englewood Cliffs, N.J.: Prentice-Hall, 1969), pp. 37, 41, 51.

113. W. Barnett Pearce, "The Coordinated Management of Meaning: A Rules-Based Theory of Interpersonal Communication," in *Exploration in Interpersonal Communica-*

tion, ed. Gerald R. Miller (Beverly Hills: Sage 1976), p. 27; Janet Horne, "Rules-Based Approaches to Communication Theory and Research: Investigating the Nature of Competence," Rules Honors Seminar, 1976, pp. 6-8; Donald Cushman and W. Barnett Pearce, "Generality and Necessity in Three Types of Theory about Human Communication with Special Attention to Rules Theory," *Human Communication Research,* 3 (1977), 351.

114. Mark L. Knapp et al., "The Rhetoric of Goodbye: Verbal and Nonverbal Correlates of Human Leave-Taking," *Speech Monographs,* 49 (1973), 182-98.

115. Hawes, "Phenomenology," pp. 31, 35-38.

116. Hawes, "Phenomenology," pp. 39-40.

117. Nofsinger, "Conversational Analysis," p. 19.

118. Pearce, "Naturalistic Study," p. 55.

119. Pearce, "Naturalistic Study," p. 55.

120. Harré and Secord, pp. 235-38.

121. Leonard Hawes, "Beyond the Ivory Palace," lecture in summer symposium, University of Southern California, 1977; Stanley Deetz, "An Understanding," *J. of Communication,* 23 (1973), 154.

122. Florence R. Kluckhohn, "The Participant Observer Technique in Small Communities," *Amer. J. of Sociology,* 46 (1940), 331.

123. Janice H. Rushing, "The Rhetoric of Nonverbal Communication in Interpersonal Encounters," Ph.D. dissertation, University of Southern California 1976, pp. 262-63; Philipsen, "Ethnographic Studies"; Harré and Secord, pp. 172, 313.

124. Garfinkel, pp. 116-85.

125. Harré and Secord, p. 112.

126. Rushing, p. 226.

127. Gerry Philipsen, "Speaking 'Like a Man' in Teamsterville: Culture Patterns of Role Enactment in an Urban Neighborhood," *Q. J. of Speech,* 61 (1975), 13-21; Donna M. Jurick, "The Enactment of Returning: A Naturalistic Study of Talk," *Communication Q.,* 25, 3 (1977), 21-29.

128. Philipsen, "Teamsterville," pp. 18, 20.

129. Philipsen, "Teamsterville," pp. 13-14, 22.

130. Jurdick, pp. 21-22; 28-29.

131. Philipsen, "Teamsterville," pp. 18, 21.

132. Jurdick, p. 28, 29.

133. Rushing, p. 263.

134. Janice Rushing, "Using Students As Participant Observers in Research on Conflict in Relationship Definitions," International Communication Association Convention, Portland, 1976, p. 5.

135. Philipsen, "Ethnographic Studies," p. 49.

136. Hall, pp. 154-57.

137. Frentz and Farrell, p. 339; Rushing, "Using Students," p. 3; Romano Harré, "Some Remarks on 'Rule' as a Scientific Concept," in *Understanding Other People,* ed. Theodore Mischel (Oxford: Blackwell, 1974), p. 152.

138. Janice Rushing, "Participant Observation: A Neglected Method for Small Group Communication Research," presented at Western Speech Communication Association Convention, Newport Beach, California, 1974, p. 16.

139. Rushing, "Participant Observation," p. 14.

140. Gerald R. Miller, "Research Setting: Laboratory Studies," in *Methods of Research in Communication,* ed. Philip Emmert and William D. Brooks (Boston: Houghton Mifflin, 1970), pp. 89-90.

141. Paul D. Krivonos and Mark L. Knapp, "Initiating Communication: What Do You Say When You Say Hello?" *Central States Speech J.*, 26 (1975), 115-25; Knapp et al., "Leave Taking."

142. Krivonos and Knapp, pp. 122, 124.

143. Knapp et al., p. 194.

144. Krivonos and Knapp; Knapp et al.

145. Rushing, "Using Students," p. 4.

146. Rushing, "Using Students," p. 3; Rushing, "Rhetoric of Nonverbal Communication," p. 270.

147. Rushing, "Rhetoric of Nonverbal Communication," p. 272.

148. Miller, pp. 86-87, 90.

149. O'Brien, "A Rules-Based Approach to Communication Within a Formal Organization: Theory and Case Studies," unpublished manuscript based on her Ph.D. dissertation, University of Massachusetts, Amherst, 1978; Weathers, "The Effects of Assertive Communication and Presence of Audience on Students' and Teachers' Perceptions of Rules Which Should Guide a Student in a Disagreement with a Teacher," Ph.D. dissertation, University of Southern California, 1979; Pearce and Conklin, "A Model of Hierarchical Meaning in Coherent Conversation and a Study of 'Indirect Responses,'" *Communication Monographs* 46 (1979), 75-87.

150. O'Brien, p. 25.

151. O'Brien, pp. 26, 37.

152. Weathers, pp. 68-69.

153. pp. 72-74.

154. Weathers, p. 90.

155. Pearce and Conklin, p. 85.

156. Taylor; Pearce, "Management of Meaning"; Pearce, "Naturalistic Study"; Pearce and Cushman.

157. Taylor, "Conversational Practices."

Notes to Chapter 6

1. Fred N. Kerlinger, *Foundations of Behavioral Research*, 2nd ed. (New York: Holt, Rinehart & Winston, 1973), p. 9.

2. Paul Davidson Reynolds, *A Primer in Theory Construction* (Indianapolis: Bobbs-Merrill, 1971), pp. 10-11.

3. Berger, "The Covering Law Perspective as a Theoretical Basis for the Study of Human Communication," *Communication Q.*, 25, 1 (1977), pp. 7-18; Gerald R. Miller and Charles R. Berger, "On Keeping the Faith in Matters Scientific," *Western J. of Speech Communication*, 42 (1978), 51-52.

4. Dray, *Laws and Explanation in History* (London: Oxford Univ. Press, 1957), p. 1.

5. Leonard C. Hawes, *Pragmatics of Analoguing: Theory and Model Construction in Communication* (Reading, Mass.: Addison-Wesley, 1975), p. 36; Peter Monge, "Theory Construction in the Study of Communication: The System Paradigm," *J. of Communication*, 23 (1973), 8; Donald P. Cushman and W. Barnett Pearce, "Generality and Necessity in Three Types of Human Communication Theory: Special Attention to Rules Theory," *Human Communication Research*, 3 (1977), 346.

6. Berger, pp. 8-9.

7. Carl G. Hempel, *Aspects of Scientific Explanation; And Other Essays in the Philosophy of Science* (New York: Free Press, 1965).

8. p. 9.

9. In a considerably shorter article, "Scientific Explanation," in *Philosophy of Science Today*, ed. Sidney Morgenbesser (New York: Basic Books, 1967), pp. 87-88, Hempel describes reason-giving explanations as laws on the grounds that they are generalizations. He further points out that Gilbert Tyle has called these generalizations law-like statements. Hempel does not present any reason-giving laws in this latter work, and such examples are absent from his *Aspects of Scientific Explanations*.

10. A similar position was expressed by Daniel M. Taylor in *Explanation and Meaning* (Cambridge: Cambridge Univ. Press, 1970), pp. 14-17.
Cambridge

11. p. 11.

12. p. 121.

13. p. 19.

14. Abraham Kaplan, *The Conduct of Inquiry: Methodology for Behavioral Science* (New York: Chandler, 1964), p. 103.

15. Reynolds, p. 93; Jack Gibbs, *Sociological Theory Construction* (Hinsdale, Ill.: Dryden Press, 1972); Virginia McDermott, "The Literature on Clasical Theory Construction," *Human Communication Research*, 2 (1975), 92-95.

16. Kenneth D. Bailer, "Evaluating Axiomatic Theories," in *Sociological Methodology*, ed. Edgar F. Borgatta (San Francisco: Jossey-Bass, 1970), pp. 48-71.

17. Hawes, pp. 33-38.

18. Harvey Sacks, Emanuel A. Schegloff, and Gail Jefferson, "A Simplest Systematics for the Organization of Turn-Taking in Conversation," *Language*, 50 (1974), 696-735.

19. Emanuel A. Schegloff, "Sequencing in Conversational Openings," in *Directions in Sociolinguistics: The Ethnography of Communication*, eds. John J. Sumperz and Dell Hymes (New York: Holt, Rinehart & Winston, 1972), pp. 346-80.

20. This relationship is commonly related to social movement. Negative-rule-reflective behavior may be thought of as the reaffirmation of rules. For example, the feminist movement has recommended new rules for male/female relationships; see *So You Want to Date a Feminist: A Complete Guide* (New York: Feminist Invention Group, 1974). For a discussion of subversion and reaffirmation rhetoric, see Walter R. Fisher, "A Motive View of Communication," *Q. J. of Speech*, 56 (1970), 131-39.

21. Many of the theoretical statements in this section have been inferred from: Kathleen R. Boynton, "A Theory of Episode Deviation," Rules-Based Approaches to Communication Theory and Research: Their Form, Value and Feasibility, Doctoral Honors Seminar, Amherst, Massachusetts, December 1976 (henceforth, this conference will be referred to as the Rules Honors Seminar); Susan B. Shimanoff, "A Rule Governed Model of Communication," Rules Honors Seminar, 1976.

22. Wayne A. Beach and William Wilmot, "Self-Disclosure as Manipulation," Western Speech Communication Association Convention, Seattle, 1975.

23. Susan B. Shimanoff, "The Tyranny of Politeness or How to Get the Fence White-Washed," Western Speech Communication Association Convention, San Francisco, 1976.

24. John Waite Bowers, Normal D. Elliot, and Roger J. Desmond, "Exploiting Pragmatic Rules: Devious Messages," *Human Communication Research*, 3 (1977), pp. 235-42.

25. Susan Ervin-Tripp, "On Sociolinguistic Rules: Alternation and Cooccurrence," in *Directions*, pp. 213-50; Roger Brown and Marguerite Ford, "Address in American English," in *Language in Culture and Society: A Reader in Linguistics and Anthropology* (New York: Harper and Row, 1964), pp. 234-44.

26. Ervin-Tripp; Brown and Ford.

27. The author is grateful to Barbara Ryon Howard for first pointing out to her that rules and psychological variables may be interrelated; see "Interpersonal Attraction as a Function of Communicative Rules Consensuality," unpublished manuscript, University of Southern California, 1978.

28. Kerlinger, p. 7.

29. McDermott, pp. 83-103.

30. Cushman and Pearce; Vernon E. Cronen, and Leslie K. Davis, "Alternative Approaches for the Communication Theorist: Problems in the Laws-Rules-Systems Trichotomy," *Human Communication Research*, 4 (1978), 120-28; the entire issue of *Communication Q.*, 25, 1 (1977), 3-73.

31. Georg Henrik von Wright, *Explanation and Understanding* (Ithaca, N.Y.: Cornell University Press, 1971), p. 1.

32. Taylor; Leonard C. Hawes, *Pragmatics of Analoguing: Theory and Model Construction in Communication* (Reading, Mass.: Addison-Wesley, 1975), pp. 100-102.

33. Robert E. Nofsinger, "On Answering Questions Indirectly: Some Rules in the Grammar of Doing Conversation," *Human Communication Research*, 2 (1976), 23.

34. John R. Searle, "What Is a Speech Act?" in *Language and Social Context*, ed. Pier Paolo Giglioli (Middlesex, England: Penguin Books, 1976), p. 153.

35. Monge, p. 7.

36. p. 7.

37. Cushman and Pearce; W. Barnett Pearce, "The Coordinated Management of Meaning: A Rules-Based Theory of Interpersonal Communication," in *Explorations in Interpersonal Communication*, ed. Gerald R. Miller (Beverly Hills: Sage, 1976); Donald P. Cushman, "The Rules Perspective as a Theoretical Basis for the Study of Human Communication," *Communication Q.*, 25 (1977), 30-45; W. Barnett Pearce and Donald P. Cushman, "Research about Communication Rules: A Critique and Appraisal," Speech Communication Association Convention, Washington, D.C. 1977.

38. Cushman and Pearce; Pearce; Pearce and Cushman.

39. von Wright, p. 96; von Wright used the generic "he" instead of "she" in his original statement.

40. Gerald R. Miller and Charles R. Berger, "On Keeping the Faith in Matters Scientific," *Western J. of Speech Communication*, 42 (1978), Persistent Problems and Promising Directions in Interpersonal Research," *Human Communication Research*, 4 (1978), 188-90.

41. "Coordinated Meaning," p. 29.

42. Stephen Edelston Toulmin, *The Uses of Argument* (London: Cambridge Univ. Press, 1958); Walter R. Fisher and Susan B. Shimanoff, "The Logic Rules Theory," unpublished manuscript, 1979.

43. Berger, p. 12.

44. Romano Harré and Paul F. Secord, *The Explanation of Social Behavior* (London: Blackwell, 1972), pp. 181-82.

45. Ervin-Tripp; Brown and Ford.

46. Ervin-Tripp; Brown and Ford.

47. Susan U. Philips, "Participant Structures and Communicative Competence: Warm Springs Children in Community and Classroom," in *Functions of Language in the Classroom*, eds. Courtney B. Cazden, Vera P. John, and Dell Hymes (New York: Teachers College Press, 1972), pp. 370-94.

48. Berger, p. 13.

49. Jessie Delia makes a point similar to this one. He argues that covering laws have "nothing to say about communication qua communication" (p. 46), in "Alternative

Perspectives for the Study of Human Communication: Critique and Response," *Communication Q.*, 25 (1977), 46-62.

50. Anatol Rapoport, "Foreward," in *Modern Systems Research for the Behavioral Scientist*, ed. Walter Buckley (Chicago: Aldine, 1968), p. xvii.

51. Miller and Berger, p. 48.

52. For examples of scholars who exclude mental-concepts, see: F. Kenneth Boulding, *General and Social Systems* (New Brunswick, N.J.: Rutgers Univ. Press, 1968), pp. 192-94; B. Aubrey Fisher, "Communication Study in System Perspective," in *General Systems Theory and Human Communication*, eds. Brent D. Ruben and John Y. Kim (Rochelle Park, N.J.: Hayden, 1975), p. 30. For examples of scholars who include mental-concepts in their research, see: Harold M. Schroder, Michael J. Driver, and Siegfried Streufest, "Intrapersonal Organization," in *General Systems Theory and Human Communication*, pp. 96-113; Janet L. Weathers, "A Model of the Classroom as a Communication System," unpublished paper, University of Southern California, 1977.

53. Peter R. Monge, "The Systems Perspective as a Theoretical Basis for the Study of Human Communication," *Communication Q.*, 25, 1 (1977), 25-28.

54. Cushman and Pearce, pp. 346-48.

55. Cronen and Davis, pp. 121-22.

56. Cronen and Davis argue that a good example of a combined systems and rules approach was Donald P. Cushman and Robert T. Craig, "Communication Systems: Interpersonal Implications." in *Explorations*, pp. 37-58. However, it has already been argued that Cushman and Craig's "rules" are not rules, but self-concept beliefs. Peter Monge also argues that systems theory could embrace rules. He offers the following as an example of systems research: Paul Watzlawick, Janet Helmich Beavin, and Don D. Jackson, *Pragmatics of Human Communication* (New York: W. W. Norton, 1967). This work also refers to rules. It is possible then, to combine rule and system analysis, but this has not been typical of systems research in communication.

57. Croven and Davis; Monge; Watzlavick, Beavin, and Jackson. See also notes 56 and 80 for this chapter.

58. Gerald R. Miller, "The Current Status of Theory and Research in Interpersonal Communication," *Human Communication Research*, 4 (1978), p. 176; Pearce, pp. 30-32.

59. Emanuel Schegloff and Harvey Sacks, "Opening Up Closings," *Semiotica*, 8 (1973), 289-327.

60. Schegloff and Sacks; James Heringer, "Pre-Sequences and Indirect Speech Acts," in *Discourse Across Time and Space*, eds. Elinor O. Keenan and Tina L. Bennett (Los Angeles: Univ. of Southern California Press 1977), pp. 169-80; A. Terasaki, "Pre-Announcement Sequences in Conversation," unpublished manuscript, University of California, Irvine, 1976.

61. Toulmin, Fisher, and Shimanoff.

62. For example, see McDermott, p. 83.

63. Kerlinger, p. 9.

64. Watzlawick, Beavin, and Jackson; Dell Hymes, "Introduction," in *Functions in the Classroom*, eds. Courtney B. Cazden, Vera P. John, and Dell Hymes (New York: Teachers College Press, 1972), p. xxxix; Charlene Edna O'Brien, "A Rules-Based Approach to Communication Within a Formal Organization: Theory and Case Studies," unpublished manuscript based on her Ph.D. dissertation at the University of Massachusetts, Amherst, 1968.

65. Stephen Krashen, "An Adult Second Language Acquisition and Learning: A Review of Theory and Applications," unpublished manuscript, University of Southern California, 1978.

288 COMMUNICATION RULES

66. Stephen D. Krashen, "Formal and Informal Linguistic Environments in Language Acquisition and Language Learning," *TESOL Q.*, 10 (1976), 157-68.

67. Krashen, "Theory and Applications."

68. Virginia McDermott discussed these ideas at the Rules Honors Seminar. Gail Theus Fairhurst, "A Rules-Based Approach to the Divorce Transition," Rules Honors Seminar, 1976.

69. Berger and Richard J. Calabrese, "Some Explorations in Initial Interaction and Beyond: Toward a Development Theory of Interpersonal Communication," *Human Communication Research*, 1 (1975), 99-112.

70. Berger and Calabrese, p. 103.

71. Berger, pp. 7-12.

72. For examples of recent research which may be viewed as law-like, see: Michael Burgoon and Lyle B. King, "The Mediation of Resistance to Persuasion Strategies by Language Variables and Active-Passive Participation," *Human Communication Research*, 1 (1974), 30-41; Richard D. Halley, "Distractibility of Males and Females in Competing Aural Message Situations: A Research Note," *Human Communication Research*, 2 (1975), 79-82; Thomas J. Saine, "Cognitive Complexity, Affective Stimulus Valence, and Information Transmission," *Human Communication Research*, 2 (1976), 281-88; Vicki S. Freimuth, "The Effects of Communication Apprehension on Communication Effectiveness," *Human Communication Research*, 2 (1976), 289-98; Charles L. Montgomery and Michael Burgoon, "An Experimental Study of the Interactive Effects of Sex and Androgyny on Attitude Change," *Communication Monographs*, 44 (1977), 130-35; Mary John Smith, "The Effects of Threats to Attitudinal Freedom as a Function of Message Quality and Initial Receiver Attitude," *Communication Monographs*, 44 (1977), 196-206; Virginia Richmond, "The Relationship Between Opinion Leadership and Information Acquisition," *Human Communication Research*, 4 (1977), 38-43; Timothy G. Plax, Edward M. Bodaken, and Kenneth K. Sereno, "Anxiety Arousing Messages and Ego-Involvement as Determinants of Communicative Predisposition," *Human Communication Research*, 3 (1977), 335-43.

Two other examples of law-like studies warrant mentioning because they deviate from the general pattern. In one study the researchers use only self-report data—they did not manipulate anything—but they claim to be concerned with developing laws; see John Saltiel and Joseph Woelfel, "Inertia in Cognitive Processes: The Role of Accumulated Information in Attitude Change," *Human Communication Research*, 1 (1975), 333-44. In another study where authors express a concern for causal relationships, communication serves as the dependent rather than independent variable; see William T. Rogers and Stanley E. Jones, "Effects of Dominance Tendencies on Floor Holding and Interruption Behavior in Dyadic Interaction," *Human Communication Research*, 1 (1975), 113-22.

Studies which claim to use a systems or rules perspective, those which explain the results in terms of "violation or expectancies" or social norms, or those which investigate the effectiveness of treatments without appealing to general laws or causal relationships have been purposely excluded from the above list. Other law-like research has been excluded because of limited space.

73. Charles R. Berger, "Proactive and Retroactive Attribution Processes in Interpersonal Communications," *Human Communication Research*, 2 (1975), 33-50.

74. Charles R. Berger has offered a similar description of his own research from the actors' perspective: "The types of information generally exchanged during the course of initial interactions often lead to predictions about attitudes and beliefs that have not yet been revealed. . . . Such predictive attempts are often aimed at moving from the sociological level to the psychological level without directly sampling the latter level." See Berger et al., "Interpersonal Epistemology and Interpersonal Communication," in *Explorations*, p. 152.

75. Fisher, p. 202.

76. H Paul Grice, "The Logic of Conversation," in *Syntax and Semantics, Vol. 3: Speech Acts*, eds. Peter Cole and Jerry L. Morgan (New York: Academic Press, 1975), pp. 41-58.

77. Anita May Pomerantz, "Second Assessments: A Study of Some Features of Agreements/Disagreements," Ph.D. dissertation, University of California, Irvine, 1975.

78. "The Systems Perspective as a Theoretical Basis for the study of Human Communication," *Communication Q.*, 25, 1 (1977), 21.

79. Fisher, pp. 201-203.

80. For examples of communication research from a systems perspective see: B. Aubrey Fisher, "Decision Emergence: Phases in Group Decision Making," *Speech Monographs*, 37 (1970), 53-66; Leonard C. Hawes, "The Effects of Interviewer Style on Patterns of Dyadic Communication," *Speech Monographs*, 39 (1972), 114-23; Leonard C. Hawes and Joseph M. Foley, "A Markov Analysis of Interview Communication," *Speech Monographs*, 40 (1973), 208-19; Ernest L. Stech, "Sequential Structure in Human Social Communication," *Human Communication Research*, 1 (1975), 168-79; Edward A. Mabry, "An Instrument for Assessing Content Themes in Group Interaction," *Speech Monographs*, 42 (1975), 291-97.

81. Donald G. Ellis and B. Aubrey Fisher, "Phases of Conflict in Small Group Development: A Markov Analysis," *Human Communication Research*, 1 (1975), 195-212.

82. William Labov, "Rules for Ritual Insults," in *Studies in Social Interaction*, ed. David Sudnow (New York: Free Press, 1972), pp. 120-69.

83. Whereas Labov wrote one interpretive rule, the present author has argued that there can be no such thing as an interpretive rule. Rather, production rules are used to explain (interpret) behavior whether one is an actor, researcher, or both. Labov's interpretive rule can easily be rewritten as a production rule, and it is rewritten later in the present paper.

84. Labov, p. 14.

85. p. 156.

86. p. 159.

87. pp.148-53.

88. p. 151.

89. p. 161.

90. pp. 148-53.

91. p. 162.

92. p. 149.

93. p. 143.

Notes To Chapter 7

1. Examples of rules research along these lines have been presented throughout this document. For a quick but partial list of such research, the reader may refer to footnotes 11 thru 17 in Chapter 1.

2. Charlene Edna O'Brien, "A Rules-Based Approach to Communication Within A Formal Organization: Theory and Case Studies," unpublished manuscript, n.d.; based on her Ph.D. dissertation at the University of Massachusetts, Amherst, 1978.

3. Barry E. Collins and Harold Guetzkow, *A Social Psychology of Group Processes for Decision-Making* (New York: John Wiley, 1964), pp. 170-72.

4. Miller, p. 176; Frank E. Miller and L. Edna Rogers, "A Relational Approach to Interpersonal Communication," in *Explorations in Interpersonal Communication* (Beverly Hills: Sage, 1976), p. 87.

5. Miller, p. 176.

6. Murray S. Davis, *Intimate Relations* (New York: Free Press, 1973).

7. Shirley J. Gilbert, "Empirical and Theoretical Extensions of Self-Disclosure," in *Explorations*, pp. 197-216.

8. Emanuel Schegloff and Harvey Sacks, "Opening up Closings," *Semiotica*, 8 (1973), 289-327; James Heringer, "Pre-Sequences and Indirect Speech Acts," in *Discourse Across Time and Space*, eds. Elinor O. Kernan and Tina L. Bennett (Los Angeles: Univ. of Southern California, 1977), pp. 169-80; A. Terasaki, "Pre-Announcement Sequences in Conversation," unpublished manuscript, Univ. of California, Irvine, 1976.

9. Don D. Jackson, "The Study of the Family," *Family Process*, 4 (1965), 1-20; Don D. Jackson, "Family Rules: Marital Quid Pro Quo," *Archives of General Psychiatry*, 12 (1965), 589-94; Paul Watzlawick and John Weakland (eds.), *The Interactional View: Studies at the Mental Research Institute, Palo Alto, 1965-1974* (New York: W. W. Norton, 1977); Virginia McDermott, "Progress Report on Research on Changes in Communicative Rules in Retirement," presented at the Rules-Based Approaches to Communication Theory and Research: Their Form, Value and Feasibility; Doctoral Honors Seminar, Amherst, Massachusetts, December 1976 (henceforth known as the Rules Honors Seminar); Gail Theus Fairhurst, "A Rules Approach to the Divorce Transaction," Rules Honors Seminar; Kathleen Boynton and W. Barnett Pearce, "Personal Transitions and Interpersonal Communication Among Submariners' Navy Wives," in *Military Families: Adaption to Change*, ed. Edna J. Hunter and Stephen D. Nice (New York: Praeger, 1978), pp. 130-41; Vernon E. Cronen, W. Barnett Pearce, and Lonna Snavely, "A Theory of Rule-Structure and Types of Episodes, and a Study of Perceived Enmeshment in Undesired Repetitive Patterns (URPs)," in *Communication Yearbook III*, ed. B. Ruben (New Brunswick, N.J.: Transaction Press, 1979); Arno A. Bellack, et al., *The Language of the Classroom* (New York: Teachers College Press, 1972); Janet Lynn Weathers, "The Effect of Assertive Communication and Presence of Audience on Students' and Teachers' Perceptions of the Rules Which Should Guide a Student in a Disagreement with a Teacher," Ph.D. dissertation, University of Southern California, 1979; Elaine Marie Litton-Hawes, "A Discourse Analysis of Topic Co-Selection in Medical Interviews," Ph.D. dissertation, Ohio State University, 1976.

10. Kathleen R. Boynton, "A Theory of Episode Deviation," Rules Honors Seminar; Susan B. Shimanoff, "A Rule-Governed Model of Communication," Rules Honors Seminar.

11. Wayne A. Beach and William Wilmot, "Self-Disclosure as Manipulation," presented at Western Speech Communication Association Convention, Seattle 1975; Susan B. Shimanoff, "The Tyranny of Politeness or How to Get the Fence White-Washed," presented at Western Speech Communication Association Convention, San Francisco 1976; John Waite Powers, Normal D. Elliot, and Roger J. Desmond, "Exploiting Pragmatic Rules: Devious Messages," *Human Communication Research*, 3 (1977), 235-42.

12. Barbara Ryan Howard, "Interpersonal Attraction as a Function of Communicative Rules Consensuality," unpublished manuscript, University of Southern California, 1978.

13. Here I am referring to variables like ego-involvement, dogmatism, cognitive dissonance, memory, attitude, and so forth. I am not including rules research that has focused on a rules approach to meaning. For examples of such research, see: W. Barnett Pearce, "The Coordinate Management of Meaning: A Rules Based Theory of Interpersonal Communication," in *Explorations in Interpersonal Communication* (Beverly Hills: Sage, 1976), pp. 17-36; W. Barnett Pearce and Forrest Conklin, "A Model of Hier-

archical Meanings in Coherent Conversation and a Study of 'Indirect Responses,'" *Communication Monographs*, 46 (1979), 75-87; Thomas B. Farrell and Thomas S. Frentz, "Communication and Meaning: A Language-Action Synthesis," *Philosophy and Rhetoric*, in press.

14. Paul Watzlawick, Janet H. Beavin, and Don J. Jackson, *Pragmatics of Human Communication: A Study of Interactional Patterns, Pathologies and Paradoxes* (New York: W. W. Norton, 1967); Dell Hymes, "Introduction," in *Functions of Language*, p. xxxix; O'Brien.

15. Stephen D. Krashen, "Formal and Informal Linguistic Environments in Language Acquisition and Language Learning, *TESOL Quarterly*, 10 (1976), 157-68.

16. Advocates of the rules perspective are footnoted extensively throughout the present study; for three particularly strong pieces, see: Donald P. Cushman and Gordon C. Whiting, "An Approach to Communication Theory: Towards Consensus on Rules," *J. of Communication*, 22 (1972) 217-38; Thomas S. Frentz and Thomas B. Farrell, "Language-Action: A Paradigm for Communication," *Q. J. of Speech*, 62 (1976), 333-49; Donald P. Cushman and W. Barnett Pearce, "Generality and Necessity in Three Types of Human Communication Theory: Special Attention to Rules Theory," *Human Communication Research*, 3 (1977), 344-53. For critiques of the rules perspective, see: Charles R. Berger, "The Covering Law Perspective as a Theoretical Basis for the Study of Human Communication," *Communication Q.*, 25, 1 (1977), 7-13; Gerald R. Miller, "The Current Status of Theory and Research in Interpersonal Communication," *Human Communication Research*, 4 (1978), 174-77; Gerald R. Miller and Charles R. Berger, "On Keeping the Faith in Matters Scientific," *Western J. of Speech Communication*, 42 (1978), 44-57; Art Bochner, "On Taking Ourselves Seriously: An Analysis of Some Persistent Problems and Promising Directions in Interpersonal Research," *Human Communication Research*, 4 (1978), 187-90; Dean E. Hewes, "A Critique of An Elaboration of the Concept of "Rule": A Case Study with the Military' by Kathleen Boynton and Gail Fairhurst," presented at the International Communication Association Convention, Chicago, 1978, pp. 1-7.

A SELECT BIBLIOGRAPHY

Abdul-Ghani, Christina. "Accent in Discourse: An Analysis of Function." Ph.D. dissertation, University of Southern California, 1978.

Abrahams, Roger D. and Rudolph C. Troike, eds. *Language and Cultural Diversity in American Education.* Englewood Cliffs, N.J.: Prentice-Hall, 1972.

Alder, Keith. "On the Falsification of Rules Theories." *Q. J. of Speech*, 64 (1978), 427-38.

Argyle, Michael, Mansui Lalljee, and Mark Cook. "The Effects of Visibility of Interaction in a Dyad." *Human Relations*, 21 (1968), 3-17.

Austin, J. L. *How To Do Things With Words.* Oxford: Oxford Univ. Press, 1962.

Babbie, Earl R. *Survey Research Methods.* Belmont, Calif.: Wadsworth, 1973.

Bailey, Kenneth D. "Evaluating Axiomatic Theories." In *Sociological Methodology.* Edited by Edgar F. Borgatta. San Francisco: Jossey-Bass, 1970, pp. 48-71.

Ball, Peter. "Listener's Responses to Filled Pauses in Relation to Floor Apportionment." *Brit. J. of Social and Clinical Psychology*, 14 (1975), 423-24.

Bauman, Richard and Joel Sherzer, eds. *Explorations in the Ehtnography of Speaking.* London: Cambridge Univ. Press, 1974.

Beach, Wayne A. and William Wilmot. "Self-Disclosure as Manipulation." Western Speech Communication Association Convention, Seattle, 1975.

Bellack, Arno A. et al. *The Language of the Classroom.* New York: Teachers College Press, 1972.

Berger, Charles R. "The Covering Law Perspective as a Theoretical Basis for the Study of Human Communication." *Communication Q.* 25, 1 (1975), 7-18.

Berger, Charles R. "Proactive and Retroactive Attribution Processes in Interpersonal Communications." *Human Communication Research*, 2 (1975), 33-50.

Berger, Charles R. and Richard J. Calabrese. "Some Explorations in Initial Interaction and Beyond: Toward a Developmental Theory of Interpersonal Communication." *Human Communication Research*, 1 (1975), 99-112.

Berger, Charles R. et al. "Interpersonal Epistemology and Interpersonal Communication." In *Explorations in Interpersonal Communication.* Edited by Gerald R. Miller. Beverly Hills: Sage, 1976, pp. 149-72.

Berko, Jean. "The Child's Learning of English Morphology," *Word*, 14 (1958), 150-77.

Black, Max. *Models and Metaphors.* Ithaca, N.Y.: Cornell Univ. Press, 1962.

Blom, Jan-Petter and John J. Gumperz, "Social Meaning in Linguistic Structure. Code Switching in Norway." In *Direction in Sociolinguistics: The Ethnography Communication.* Edited by John J. Gumperz and Dell Hymes. New York: Holt, Rinehart & Winston, 1972, pp. 407-34.

Blume, Susan K. "Asking the Unanswerable: A Rule-Breaking Approach to Implicit Knowledge." Rules-Based Approaches to Communication Theory and Research: Their Form, Value and Feasibility. Doctoral Honors Seminar, Amherst, Massachusetts, December 1976.

Blumer, Herbert. *Symbolic Interactionism: Perspective and Method.* Englewood Cliffs, N.J.: Prentice-Hall, 1969.

Bochner, Art. "On Taking Ourselves Seriously: An Analysis of Some Persistent Problems and Promising Directions in Interpersonal Research." *Human Communication Research*, 4 (1978), 179-91.

Brogdan, Robert and Steven J. Taylor. *Introduction to Qualitative Research Methods*. New York: John Wiley, 1975.

Boulding, F. Kenneth. *General and Social Systems*. New Brunswick, N.J.: Rutgers Univ. Press, 1963.

Bowers, John Waite, Normal D. Elliot, and Roger J. Desmond. "Exploiting Pragmatic Rules: Devious Messages." *Human Communication Research*, 3 (1977), 235-42.

Boynton, Kathleen R. "A Theory of Episode Deviation." Rules-Based Approaches to Communication Theory and Research: Their Form, Value and Feasibility. Doctoral Honors Seminar, Amherst, Massachusetts, December 1976.

Boynton, Kathleen Reardon and Gail Theus Fairhurst. "An Elaboration of the Concept 'Rule': A Case Study with the Military." International Communication Association Convention, Chicago, 1976.

Boynton, Kathleen and W. Barnett Pearce. "Personal Transitions and Interpersonal Communication Among Submariners' Navy Wives. In *Military Families: Adaption to Change*, edited by Edna J. Hunter and Stephen D. Nice. New York: Praeger, 1978, pp. 130-41.

Brown, Penelope and Stephen Levinson. "Universals in Language Usage: Politeness Phenomena." In *Questions and Politeness: Strategies in Social Interaction*, Edited by Ester N. Goody. Cambridge: Cambridge Univ. Press, 1978, pp. 56-289.

Brown, Roger and Marguerite Ford. "Address in American English." In *Language in Culture and Society: A Reader in Linguistics and Anthropology*. Edited by Dell Hymes. New York: Harper & Row, 1964, pp. 234-44.

Brown, Roger and Usula Bellugi. "Three Processes in the Child's Acquisition of Syntax." *Harvard Educ. Rev.*, 34 (1964), 133-51.

Burke, Kenneth. *A Grammar of Motives*. Berkeley: Univ. of Calif. Press, 1945.

Burke, Kenneth. *Language As Symbolic Action: Essays on Life, Literature, and Method*. Berkeley: Univ. of California Press, 1968.

Burke, Kenneth. "(Nonsymbolic) Motion/(Symbolic) Action." *Critical Inquiry*, 4 (1978), 809-38.

Burke, Kenneth. *The Rhetoric of Religion*. Boston: Beacon, 1961.

Cappella, Joseph N. "Research Methodology in Communication: Review and Commentary." In *Communication Yearbook I*. Edited by Brent D. Ruben. New Brunswick, N.J.: Transaction, 1977, pp. 37-55.

Carroll, Lewis. *Alice's Adventures in Wonderland* and *Through the Looking-Glass*. Edited by Roger Lancelyn Green. New York: Oxford Univ. Press, 1971.

Chomsky, Noam. *Aspects of the Theory of Syntax*. Cambridge, Mass.: Massachusetts Institute of Technology, 1965.

Chomsky, Noam. *Language and Mind*. New York: Harcourt, Brace & Jovanovitch, 1968.

Chomsky, Noam. "Problem in Linguistics." In *Explanation in the Behavioral Sciences*. Edited by Robert Borger and Frank Cioffi. Cambridge: Cambridge Univ. Press, 1970, pp. 425-51.

Cline, Rebecca J. and Bonnie M. Johnson. "The Verbal Stare: Focus on Attention in Conversation." *Communication Monographs*, 43 (1976), 1-10.

Collett, Peter. "The Rules of Conduct." In *Social Rules and Social Behavior*. Edited by Peter Collett. Totowa, N.J.: Rowman and Littlefield, 1977, pp. 1-27.

Collett, Peter. *Social Rules and Social Behavior*. Totowa, N.J.: Rowman and Littlefield, 1977.

Collins, Harry E. and Harold Guetzkow. *A Social Psychology of Group Processes for Decision-Making.* New York: John Wiley, 1964.

Cronen, Vernon E. and Leslie K. Davis. "Alternative Approaches for the Communication Theorist: Problems in the Laws-Rules-System Trichotomy." *Human Communication Research*, 4(1978), 120-28.

Cronen, Vernon E., W. Barnett Pearce, and Lonna Snavely. "A Theory of Rule-Structure and Types of Episodes, and a Study of Perceived Enmeshment in Undesired Repetitive Patterns (URPs)." In *Communication Yearbook III.* Edited by B. Ruben. New Brunswick, N.J.: Transaction Press, in press.

Cushman, Donald P. "Draft: Rules Article for Handbook of Communication, Part #1." Unpublished manuscript, State University of New York, Albany, 1978.

Cushman, Donald P. "The Rules Perspective as a Theoretical Basis for the Study of Human Communication." *Communication Q.*, 25, 1 (1977), 30-45.

Cushman, Donald P. and Robert T. Craig. "Communication Systems: Interpersonal Implications." In *Explorations in Interpersonal Communication.* Edited by Gerald R. Miller. Beverly Hills: Sage, 1976, pp. 37-58.

Cushman, Donald P. and W. Barnett Pearce. "Generality and Necessity in Three Types of Human Communication Theory with Special Attention to Rules Theory." *Human Communication Research*, 3 (1977), 344-53.

Cushman, Donald P. and Gordon C. Whiting. "An Approach to Communication Theory: Towards Consensus on Rules." *J. of Communication,* 22(1972), 217-38.

Davis, Murray S. *Intimate Relations.* New York: Free Press, 1973.

Deetz, Stanley. "An Understanding." *J. of Communication*, 23 (1973), 139-59.

Delia, Jesse G. "Alternative Perspectives for the Study of Human Communication: Critique and Response." *Communication Q.*, 25, No. 1 (1977), 46-62.

Delia, Jesse G. "Constructivism and the Study of Human Communication." *Q. J. of Speech*, 63 (1977), 66-83.

Delia, Jesse G. and Lawrence Grossberg. "Interpretation and Evidence." *Western J. of Speech Communication*, 41 (1977), 32-42.

de Saussure, Ferdinand. *Cours de Linguistique Generale.* 5th ed. Translated by Wade Baskin. *Course in General Linguistics.* New York: Philosophical Library, 1959.

Dray, William. *Laws and Explanation in History.* London: Oxford Univ. Press, 1957.

Duncan, Starkey, Jr. "Some Signals and Rules for Taking Speaking Turns in Conversation." *J. of Personality and Social Psychology*, 23 (1972), 283-92.

Duncan, Starkey, Jr. "Toward a Grammar for Dyadic Conversation." *Semiotica*, 9 (1973), 29-46.

Edelsky, Carole. "Acquisition of an Aspect of Communication Competence: Learning What It Means to Talk Like a Lady." In *Child Discourse.* Edited by Susan Ervin-Tripp and Claudia Mitchell-Kernan (New York: Academic Press, 1977), pp. 225-44.

Elgin, Suzette Haden. *A Primer of Transformational Grammar for Rank Beginners.* Urbana, Ill.: National Council of Teachers of English, 1975.

Ellis, Donald G. and B. Audrey Fisher. "Phrases of Conflict in Small Group Development: A Markov Analysis." *Human Communication Research*, 1 (1975), 195-212.

Ervin-Tripp, Susan. "On Sociolinguistic Rules: Alternation and Co-occurrence." In *Directions in Sociolinguistics: The Ethnography of Communication.* Edited by John J. Gumperz and Dell Hymes. New York: Holt, Rinehart & Winston, 1972, pp. 213-50.

Ervin-Tripp, Susan. "Sociolingusitics." In *Advances in Experimental Social Psychology.* Edited by R. Berkowitz. New York: Academic Press, 1969.

Fairhurst, Gail Theus. "A Rules Based Approach to the Divorce Transition." Rules-Based Approaches to Communication Theory and Research: Their Form, Value and Feasibility. Doctoral Honor Seminar, Amherst, Massachusetts, December 1976.

Farb, Peter. *Word Play: What Happens When People Talk.* New York: Bantam, 1973.

Farrell, Thomas B. and Thomas S. Frentz. "Communication and Meaning: A Language-Action Synthesis." *Philosophy and Rhetoric.* In press.

Feminist Invention Group. *So You Want to Date a Feminist: A Complete Guide.* New York: Feminist Invention Group, 1974.

Fisher, B. Aubrey. "Communication Study in System Perspective." In *General Systems, Theory and Human Communication.* Edited by Brent D. Ruben and John Y. Kim. Rochelle Park, N.J.: Hayden, 1975, pp. 191-206.

Fisher, John. "Knowledge of Rules." *Review of Metaphysics,* 28 (1974), 237-60.

Fisher, Walter R. "A Motive View of Communication." *Q. J. of Speech,* 56 (1970), 131-39.

Fisher, Walter R. and Susan B. Shimanoff. "The Logic of Rules Theory." Unpublished manuscript, 1979.

Frentz, Thomas S. "A Generative Approach to Episodic Structure." Western Speech Association Convention, San Francisco, 1976.

Frentz, Thomas S. and Thomas B. Farrell. "Language-Action: A Paradigm for Communication." *Q. J. of Speech,* 62 (1976), 333-49.

Frentz, Thomas S. and Robert E. Nofsinger. "Some Preliminaries to Language-Action." Western Speech Communication Association Convention, Phoenix 1977.

Ganz, Joan Safron. *Rules: A Systematic Study.* Paris: Mouton, 1971.

Garfinkel, Harold. *Studies in Ethnomethodology.* Englewood Cliffs, N.J.: Prentice-Hall, 1967.

Gay, Geneva and Roger D. Abrahams. "Black Culture in the Classroom." In *Language and Cultural Diversity in American Education.* Edited by Roger D. Abrahams and Rudolph D. Troike. Englewood Cliffs, N.J.: Prentice-Hall, 1972, pp. 67-84.

Gibbs, Jack. *Sociological Theory Construction.* Hinsdale, Ill.: Dryden, 1972.

Gilbert, Shirley J. "Empirical and Theoretical Extensions of Self-Disclosure." In *Explorations in Interpersonal Communication.* Edited by Gerald R. Miller. Beverly Hills: Sage, 1976, pp. 197-216.

Goffman, Erving. *Behavior in Public Places: Notes on the Social Organization of Gatherings.* New York: Free Press, 1963.

Goffman, Erving. *Encounters.* Indianapolis: Bobbs-Merrill, 1961.

Goffman, Erving. *Relations in Public: Microstudies of the Public Order.* New York: Harper and Row, 1971.

Goffman, Erving. "Remedial Interchanges." In *Relations in Public: Microstudies of the Public Order.* New York: Harper & Row, 1971, pp. 95-187.

Goodwin, Charles. "The Interactive Construction of the Sentence Within the Turn at Talk in Natural Conversation." Annual Meeting of the American Anthropological Association, San Francisco, 1975.

Gottlieb, Gidon. *Logic of Choice: An Investigation of the Concepts of Rule and Rationality.* New York: Macmillan, 1968.

Grice, H. Paul. "The Logic of Conversation." In *Syntax and Semantics Volume 3: Speech Acts.* Edited by Peter Cole and Jerry L. Morgan. New York: Academic Press, 1975, pp. 41-58.

Gumb, Raymond D. *Rule-Governed Linguistic Behavior.* Paris: Mouton, 1972.

Gumperz, John J. "Dialect and Conversational Inference in Urban Communication." *Language in Society,* 7 (1978), 393-409.

Gumperz, John J. "Verbal Strategies in Multilingual Communication." In *Georgetown University Round Table on Language and Linguistics, No. 23.* Edited by James E. Alatis. Washington, D.C.: Georgetown Univ. Press, 1970, pp. 129-48.

Gumperz, John J. and Dell Hymes. *Directions in Sociolinguistics: The Ethnography of Communications.* New York: Holt, Rinehart & Winston, 1972.

Gumperz, John J. and Dell Hymes. *The Ethnography of Communication.* Washington, D.C.: American Anthropologist Association, 1964; Special issue of the *American Anthropologist,* Part 2, Vol. 66, No. 6, December 1964.

Hage, Dorothy. "There's Glory for You." *Aphra,* 3 (1972), 2-14.

Hall, Edward T. *The Hidden Dimension.* Garden City, N.Y.: Anchor Books, 1969.

Harré, Romano. "Rules in the Explanation of Social Behavior." In *Social Rules and Social Behavior.* Edited by Peter Collett. Totowa, N.J.: Rowman and Littlefield, 1977, pp. 28-41.

Harré, Romano. "Some Remarks on 'Rule' as a Scientific Concept." In *Understanding Other People.* Edited by Theodore Mischel. Oxford: Blackwell, 1974, pp. 143-84.

Harré, Romano and Paul Secord. *The Explanation of Social Behavior.* Totowa, N.J.: Littlefield, Adams, 1973.

Hawes, Leonard C. "How Writing is Used in Talk: A Study of Communicative Logic-In-Use." *Q. J. of Speech,* 62 (1976), 350-60.

Hawes, Leonard C. "The Naturalistic Study of Human Communication: A Naturalistic Perspective." Speech Communication Association Convention, Houston, 1975.

Hawes, Leonard C. *Pragmatics of Analoguing: Theory and Model Construction in Communication.* Reading, Mass.: Addison-Wesley, 1975.

Hawes, Leonard C. "Toward a Hermeneutic Phenomenology of Communication." *Communication Q.,* 25, 3 (1977), 63-68.

Hempel, Carl G. *Aspects of Scientific Explanation: And Other Essays in the Philosophy of Science.* New York: Free Press, 1965.

Hempel, Carl G. "Scientific Explanation." In *Philosophy of Science Today.* Edited by Sidney Morgenbesser. New York: Basic Books, 1967, pp. 79-88.

Henley, Nancy and Barrie Thorne. *Language and Sex: Difference and Dominance.* Rowley, Mass.: Newbury, 1975, pp. 257-63.

Heringer, James. "Pre-Sequences and Indirect Speech Acts." In *Discourse Across Time and Space.* Edited by Elinor O. Keenan and Tina L. Bennett. Los Angeles: Univ. of Southern California Press, 1977, pp. 169-80.

Hewes, Dean. "A Critique of 'An Elaboration of the Concept of "Rule": A Case Study with the Military' by Kathleen Boynton and Gail Fairhurst." International Communication Association Convention, Chicago 1978.

Horne, Janet. "Rules-Based Approaches to Communication Theory and Research: Investigating the Nature of Competence." Rules-Based Approaches to Communication Theory and Research: Their Form, Value and Feasibility. Doctoral Honors Seminar, Amherst, Massachusetts, December 1976.

Howard, Barbara Ryon. "Interpersonal Attraction as a Function of Communicative Rules Consensuality." Unpublished manuscript, University of Southern California, 1978.

Hymes, Dell H. "The Ethnography of Speaking." In *Anthropology and Human Behavior.* Eds. Thomas Gladwin and William C. Sturtevant. Washington, D.C.: Anthropological Society of Washington, 1962, pp. 13-53.

Hymes, Dell. *Foundations in Sociolinguistics.* Philadelphia: Univ. of Pennsylvania Press, 1974.

Hymes, Dell. "Introduction." In *Functions of Language in the Classroom.* Edited by Courtney B. Cazden, Vera P. John, and Dell Hymes. New York: Teachers College Press, 1972.

Hymes, Dell. "On Communicative Competence." In *Sociolinguistics: Selected Readings.* Edited by J. B. Pride and Janet Holmes. Harmondsworth, England; Penguin, 1972, pp. 269-93.

Jackson, Don D. "The Study of the Family." *Family Process,* 4 (1965), 1-20.

Jackson, Jay. "A Conceptual and Measurement Model for Norms and Roles." *Pacific Soc. Rev.*, 9 (1966), 35-47.

Jackson, Jay. "Normative Power and Conflict Potential." *Soc. Methods and Research*, 4 (1975), 237-63.

Jefferson, Gail. "A Case of Precision Timing in Ordinary Conversation: Overlapped Tag-Positioned Address Terms in Closing Sequences." *Semiotica*, 9 (1973), 49-96.

Jefferson, Gail. "Sequential Aspects of Storytelling in Conversation." In *Studies in the Organization of Conversational Interaction.* Edited by Jim Schenkein. New York: Academic Press, 1978, pp. 219-48.

Johnson, Paula B. and Jacqueline W. Goodchilds. "How Women Get Their Way." *Psychology Today*, Oct. 1976, pp. 69-70.

Jurick, Donna M. "The Enactment of Returning: A Naturalistic Study of Talk." *Communication Q.* 25 (1977), 21-29.

Kallen, Horaces M. "Behaviorism." *Encyclopedia of the Social Sciences.* Vol. 1. New York: Macmillan, 1937, pp. 495-98.

Kaplan, Abraham. *The Conduct of Inquiry: Methodology for Behavioral Science.* New York: Chandler, 1964.

Kaufer, David. "Developing a Rule Theoretic Approach to Communication as Opposed to a Dictionary of Rules: Some Considerations and Criteria." Rules-Based Approaches to Communication Theory and Research: Their Form, Value and Feasibility. Doctoral Honors Seminar, Amherst, Massachusetts, December 1976.

Keenan, Elinor Ochs. "The Universality of Conversational Postulates." *Language in Society*, 5 (1976), 67-80.

Kerlinger, Fred N. *Foundations of Behavioral Research.* 2nd ed. New York: Holt, Rinehart & Winston, 1973.

Knapp, Mark L. *Social Intercourse: From Greeting to Goodbye.* Boston: Allyn & Bacon, 1978.

Knapp, Mark L. et al. "The Rhetoric of Goodbye: Verbal and Nonverbal Correlates of Human Leave-Taking." *Speech Monographs*, 40 (1973), 182-98.

Kluckhohn, Florence R. "The Participant Observer Technique in Small Communities." *Amer. J. of Sociology*, 46 (1940), 331-43.

Kolb, William L. "Norm." *Dictionary of the Social Sciences.* Edited by Julius Gould and William L. Kolb. New York: Free Press of Glencoe, 1964, pp. 472-73.

Kramer, Cheris. "Folklinguistics: Wishy-Washy Mommy Talk." *Psychology Today*, June 1974, pp. 82-85.

Kramer, Cheris. "Women's Speech: Separate but Unequal?" *Q. J. of Speech*, 60 (1974), 14-24.

Krashen, Stephen. "An Adult Second Language Acquisition and Learning: A Review of Theory and Applications." Unpublished manuscript, University of Southern California, 1978.

Krashen, Stephen D. "Formal and Informal Linguistic Environments in Language Acquisition and Language Learning." *TESOL Q.*, 10 (1976), 157-68.

Krashen, Stephen D. "Some Issues Relating to the Monitor Model." In *On TESOL '77.* Edited by H. Brown, C. Yorio, and R. Crymes. In press.

Krashen, Stephen D. et. al. "Two Studies in Language Association and Language Learning," Meeting of the Linguistic Society of America, 1976.

Krivonos, Paul D. and Mark L. Knapp. "Initiating Communication: What Do You Say When You Say Hello?" *Central States Speech J.* 26 (1975), 115-25.

Kushner, Malcom. "A Reconceptualization of Rules." Western Speech Communication Association Convention, San Francisco, 1976.

Labov, William. "The Logic of Nonstandard English." In *Georgetown University Round Table on Languages and Linguistics 1969*. Edited by James E. Alatis. Washington, D.C.: Georgetown Univ. Press, 1970, pp. 1-44.

Labov, William. "Rules for Ritual Insults." In *Studies in Social Interaction*. Edited by David Sudnow. New York: Free Press, 1972, pp. 120-69.

Labov, William. *Sociolinguistic Patterns*. Philadelphia: Univ. of Pennsylvania Press, 1972.

Laign, Ronald D. *The Politics of the Family and Other Essays*. New York: Vintage, 1971, p. 111.

Lakoff, Robin. *Language and Woman's Place*. New York: Harper & Row, 1975.

Lakoff, Robin. "Language in Context." *Language*, 48 (1972), 907-27.

Lakoff, Robin. "What You Can Do With Words: Politeness, Pragmatics and Performatives." *Berkeley Studies in Syntax and Semantics*, 16 (1974), 1-55.

Lenk, Dorothy. "The Use of a Stochastic Model for Discerning Rule Guided Communicative Behavior." Rules-Based Approaches to Communication Theory and Research: Their Form, Value and Feasibility. Doctoral Honors Seminar, Amherst, Massachusetts, December 1976.

Lewis, David K. *Convention: A Philosophical Study*. Cambridge, Mass.: Harvard Univ. Press, 1969.

Litton-Hawes, Elaine Marie. "A Discourse Analysis of Topic Co-Selection in Medical Interviews," Ph.D. dissertation, Ohio State University, 1976.

Litton-Hawes, Elaine M. "A Foundation for the Study of Everyday Talk." *Communication Q.*, 25, 3 (1977), 2-11.

McDermott, Virginia. "The Literature on Classical Theory Construction." *Human Communication Research*, 2 (1975), 83-102.

Meehan, Diana Marjorie. "A Factor Analysis of Humor." M.A. Thesis, San Diego State University, 1975.

Mischel, Theodore. "Scientific and Philosophical Psychology: A Historical Introduction." In *Human Action*. Edited by Theodore Mischel. New York: Academic Press, 1969, pp. 1-40.

Millar, Frank E. and L. Edna Rogers. "A Relational Approach to Interpersonal Communication." In *Explorations in Interpersonal Communication*. Edited by Gerald R. Miller. Beverly Hills: Sage, 1976, pp. 87-104.

Miller, Gerald R. "The Current Status of Theory and Research in Interpersonal Communication." *Human Communication Research*, 4 (1978), 164-78.

Miller, Gerald R. "Research Setting: Laboratory Studies." In *Methods of Research in Communication*. Edited by Philip Emmert and William D. Brooks. Boston: Houghton Mifflin, 1970, pp. 77-104.

Miller, Gerald R. and Charles R. Berger. "On Keeping the Faith in Matters Scientific." *Western J. of Speech Communication*, 42 (1978), 44-57.

Monge, Peter R. "The Systems Perspective as a Theoretical Basis for the Study of Human Communication." *Communication Q.*, 25, 1 (1977), 19-29.

Monge, Peter R. "Theory Construction in the Study of Communication: The System Paradigm." *J. of Communication*, 23 (1973), 5-16.

Morgan, Jerry L. "Some Remarks on the Nature of Sentences." In *Papers from the Parasession on Functionalism*. Chicago: Univ. of Chicago Press, 1975, pp. 433-47.

Morris, G. H. "The Remedial Process: A Negotiation of Rules." Speech Communication Association Convention, 1978.

Mortensen, C. David. *Communication: The Study of Human Interaction*. New York: McGraw-Hill, 1972.

Nofsinger, Robert E. "Answering Questions Indirectly." *Human Communication Research*, 2 (1976), 172-81.

Nofsinger, Robert E. "The Demand Ticket: A Conversational Device for Getting the Floor." *Speech Monographs*, 42 (1975), 1-9.

Nofsinger, Robert E. "A Peek at Conversational Analysis." *Communication Q.*, 25 (1977), 12-20.

O'Brien, Charlene Edna. "A Rules-Based Approach to Communication Within a Formal Organization: Theory and Case Studies." Unpublished manuscript based on her Ph.D. dissertation at the University of Massachusetts, Amherst, 1978.

O'Keefe, Daniel J. "Constructivism and Communication Studies: Theoretical Essays." Ph.D. dissertation, University of Illinois, Urbana-Champaign, 1976.

Oxford English Dictionary. Vol. VIII. Oxford: Clarendon House, 1961.

Pearce, W. Barnett. "Consensual Rules in Interpersonal Communication: A Reply to Cushman and Whiting." *J. of Communication*, 23 (1973), 160-68.

Pearce, W. Barnett. "The Coordinate Management of Meaning: A Rules-Based Theory of Interpersonal Communication." In *Explorations in Interpersonal Communication*. Edited by Gerald R. Miller. Beverly Hills: Sage, 1976, pp. 17-36.

Pearce, W. Barnett. "Naturalistic Study of Communication: Its Function and Form." *Communication Q.* 25, 3 (1977), 51-56.

Pearce, W. Barnett and Forrest Conklin. "A Model of Hierarchical Meaning in Coherent Conversation and a Study of 'Indirect Responses.'" *Communication Monographs*, 46 (1979), 75-87.

Pearce, W. Barnett and Donald P. Cushman. "Research About Communication Rules: A Critique and Appraisal." Speech Communication Association Convention, Washington, D.C., 1977.

Philips, Susan U. "Participant Structures and Communicative Competence: Warm Springs Children in Community and Classroom." In *Functions of Language in the Classroom*. Edited by Courtney B. Cazden, Vera P. John, and Dell Hymes. New York: Teachers College Press, 1972, pp. 370-94.

Philips, Susan U. "The Role of the Listener in the Regulation of Talk: Some Sources of Cultural Variability." American Anthropological Association Convention, Mexico City, 1974.

Philipsen, Gerry. "Linearity of Research Design in Ethnographic Studies of Speaking." *Communication Q.*, 25, 3 (1977), 42-50.

Philipsen, Gerry. "Speaking 'Like a Man' in Teamsterville: Culture and Patterns of Role Enactment in an Urban Neighborhood." *Q. J. of Speech*, 61 (1975), 13-22.

Pomerantz, Anita May. "Second Assessments: A Study of Some Features of Agreements/ Disagreements." Ph.D. dissertation, University of California, Irvine, 1975.

Psathas, George, ed. *Everyday Language: Studies in Ethnomethodology*. New York: John Wiley, 1979.

Rapoport, Anatol. "Foreword." In *Modern Systems Research for the Behavioral Scientist*. Edited by Walter Buckley. Chicago: Aldine, 1968, pp. xiii-xxii.

Ray, Jack L. "Prescriptive Deontic Logic: A Study of Inference from Linguistic Forms Expressing Choice and Conditional Permission and Obligation." Ph.D. dissertation, University of Southern California, 1971.

Reynolds, Paul Davidson, *A Primer in Theory Construction*. Indianapolis: Bobbs-Merrill, 1971.

Rogers, William T. and Stanley E. Jones. "Effects of Dominance Tendencies on Floor Holding and Interruption Behavior in Dyadic Interaction." *Human Communication Research*, 1 (1975), 113-22.

Rosenfield, Lawrence W. "A Game Model of Human Communication." Minnesota Symposium in Speech Communication, 1968.

Rushing, Janice Hocker. "Participant Observation: A Neglected Method for Small Group Communication Research." Western Speech Communication Association Convention, Newport Beach, California, 1974.

Rushing, Janice Hocker. "The Rhetoic of Nonverbal Communication in Interpersonal Encounters." Ph.D. dissertation, University of Southern California, 1976.

Rushing, Janice Hocker. "Using Students as Participant Observers in Research on Conflict in Relationship Definitions." International Communication Association Convention, Portland 1976.

Sacks, Harvey. "An Analysis of the Course of a Joke's Telling in Conversation." In *Explorations in the Ethnography of Speaking.* Edited by Richard Bauman and Joel Sherzer. London: Cambridge Univ. Press, 1974, pp. 337-43.

Sacks, Harvey, Emanuel A. Schegloff, and Gail Johnson. "A Simplest Systematics for the Organization of Turn-Taking in Conversation." *Language*, 50 (1974), 696-735.

Sander, Robert E. and Larry W. Martin. "Grammatical Rules and the Explanation of Behavior." *Inquiry*, 18 (1975), 65-82.

Schachter, Stephen. "Deviation, Rejection and Communication." *J. of Abnormal and Social Psychology*, 46 (1951), 190-207.

Schegloff, Emanuel A. "Sequencing in Conversational Openings." In *Direction in Sociolinguistics: The Ethnography of Communication.* Edited by John J. Gumperz and Dell Hymes. New York: Holt, Rinehart & Winston, 1972, pp. 346-80.

Schegloff, Emanuel A. and Harvey Sacks. "Opening Up Closings." *Semiotica*, 8 (1973), 289-327.

Schegloff, Emanuel A., Gail Jefferson, and Harvey Sacks. "The Preference for Self-Correction in the Organization of Repair in Conversation." *Language*, 53 (1977), 361-82.

Schenkein, Jim, ed. *Studies in the Organization of Conversational Interaction.* New York: Academic Press, 1978.

Schroder, Harold N., Michael J. Driver, and Siegried Streufest. "Intrapersonal Organization." In *General Systems Theory and Human Communication.* Edited by Brent D. Ruben and John Y. Kim. Rochelle Park, N.J.: Hayden, 1975, pp. 96-113.

Searle, John R. "Indirect Speech Acts." In *Syntax and Semantics, Volume 3: Speech Acts.* Edited by Peter Cole and Jerry L. Morgan. New York: Academic Press, 1975, pp. 59-82.

Searle, John R. *Speech Acts: An Essay in the Philosophy of Language.* Cambridge: Cambridge Univ. Press, 1969.

Searle, John R. "What is a Speech Act?" In *Language and Social Context.* Edited by Pier Paolo Giglioli. Middlesex, England: Penguin, 1972, pp. 136-54.

Shimanoff, Susan B. "Investigating Politeness." In *Discourse Across Time and Space.* Edited by Elinor O. Keenan and Tina L. Bennett. Los Angeles: Univ. of Southern California, 1977, pp. 213-41.

Shimanoff, Susan B. "Male and Female Politeness." Transcript, 1976.

Shimanoff, Susan B. "A Rule Governed Model of Communication." Rules-Based Approaches to Communication Theory and Research: Their Form, Value and Feasibility. Doctoral Honors Seminar, Amherst, Massachusetts, December 1976.

Shimanoff, Susan B. "The Tyranny of Politeness or How to Get the Fence White-Washed." Western Speech Communication Association Convention, San Francisco 1976.

Shimanoff, Susan B. and Joanna C. Brunak. "Repairs in Planned and Unplanned Discourse." In *Discourse Across Time and Space.* Edited by Elinor O. Keenan and Tina L. Bennett. Los Angeles: Univ. of Southern California, 1977, pp. 123-67.

Shimanoff, Susan B., Katherine Yost, and Janet L. Weathers. "Communication Codes in Children's Dyads: As a Function of Social Class and Group Composition." Unpublished manuscript. University of Southern California, 1976.

Slobin, Dan J. *Psycholinguistics.* Glenview, Ill.: Scott, Foresman, 1971.

Smith, David H. "Communication Research and the Idea of Process." *Speech Monographs*, 39 (1972), 174-82.

Smith, Ted. "Practical Inference and Its Implications for Communication Theory." Unpublished manuscript, n.d.

Snyder, Aaron. "Rules of Language." *Mind*, 80 (1971), 161-78.

Snyder, D. Paul. *Modal Logic and Its Applications.* New York: Van Nostrand Reinhold, 1971.

Sudnow, David, ed. *Studies in Social Interaction.* New York: Free Press, 1972.

Tannenbaum, Percy K., Frederick Williams, and Carolyn S. Hiller. "Word Predictability in the Environments of Hesitations." *J. of Verbal Learning and Verbal Behavior*, 4 (1965), 134-40.

Taylor, Daniel M. *Explanation and Meaning.* Cambridge: Cambridge Univ. Press, 1970.

Taylor, Stephen A. "Conversational Practices for Children: An Investigation Using Two Methods." Unpublished manuscript. State University of New York, n.d.

Teraski, A. "Pre-Announcement Sequences in Conversation." Unpublished paper. University of California, Irvine, 1976.

Toulmin, Stephen E. "Concepts and the Explanation of Behavior." In *Human Action.* Edited by Theodore Mischel. New York: Academic Press, 1969, pp. 71-104.

Toulmin, Stephen E. "Rules and Their Relevance for Understanding Human Behavior." In *Understanding Other People.* Edited by Theodore Mischel. Oxford: Blackwell, 1974, pp. 185-215.

Toulmin, Stephen Edelston. *The Uses of Argument.* London: Cambridge Univ. Press, 1958.

von Wright, Georg Henrik. *Explanation and Understanding.* Ithaca, N.Y.: Cornell Univ. Press, 1971.

von Wright, Georg Henrik. "The Logic of Practical Discourse." In *Contemporary Philosophy.* Edited by Raymond Klikansky. Italy: La Nuava Italia Editrice, 1968, pp. 141-67.

Walum, Laurel Richardson. "The Changing Door Ceremony: Notes on the Operation of Sex Roles in Everyday Life." *Urban Life and Culture*, 2 (1974), 506-15.

Watzlawick, Paul and John Weakland, eds. *The Interactional View: Studies at the Mental Research Institute, Palo Alto 1965-74.* New York: W. W. Norton, 1977.

Watzlawick, Paul, Janet H. Beavin, and Don J. Jackson. *Pragmatics of Human Communication: A Study of Interactional Patterns, Pathologies and Paradoxes.* New York: W. W. Norton, 1967.

Weathers, Janet Lynn. "The Effects of Assertive Communication and Presence of Audience on Students' and Teachers' Perceptions of the Rules Which Should Guide a Student in a Disagreement with a Teacher." Ph. D. dissertation, University of Southern California, 1979.

Weathers, Janet L. "A Model of the Classroom as a Communication System." Unpublished paper. Univ. of Southern California, 1977.

Webster's New Twentieth Century Dictionary of the English Language. New York: Publishers Guild, 1943.

Wiemann, John W. and Mark L. Knapp. "Turn-Taking in Conversations." *J. of Communication*, 25 (1975), 75-92.

Wiens, Arthur N. et. al. "Interview Interaction Behavior of Supervisors, Head Nurses and Staff Nurses." *Nursing Research*, 13 (1965), 422-39.

Williams, Frederick. "Communication and Sociolinguistics." *J. of Communication*, 24, No. 2 (1974), 158-68.

Williams, Frederick et al. *Explorations of the Linguistic Attitudes of Teachers*. Rowley, Mass.: Newbury House, 1976.

Winch, Peter. *The Idea of a Social Science and its Relation to Philosophy*. New York: Humanities Press, 1958.

Wittgenstein, Ludwig. *Philosophical Investigations*. Oxford: Blackwell, 1953.

Zimmerman, Don H. and Candace West. "Sex Roles, Interruptions and Silence in Conversations." In *Language and Sex: Difference and Dominance*. Edited by Barrie Thorne and Nancy Henley. Rowley, Mass.: Newbury, 1975, pp. 105-29.

INDEX

Action vs. motion, 33, 39, 172, 174. See also social data vs. physical data; brute facts vs. institutional facts

Agreement, 59, 62-63

Antecedent conditions, 170-171, 187, 193-194. See also presuppositions; context

Anthropological case study, 155

Appropriateness, 93-94, 129

Acquisition vs. learning, 235-236, 262-263

As a rule, 120, 121. See also law-related behavior; mechanistic behavior

Axiomatic theory, 199, 205-216

Brute facts vs. institutional facts, 172-173. See also social data vs. physical data; action vs. motion

Can, cannot, 77

Categorical rules, 45. See also obligatory rules

Causation, 193-194, 199, 223-229

Choice, 32-33, 39, 90, 201

Classroom, 260

Code-switching, 104-105

Command, 59, 67-68

Compliant. See rule-compliant

Conditional. See context

Constitutive vs. regulative rules, 84-85, 117-118

Constructivism, 174

Context, 77, 78, 82-83, 103-105, 108, 115. See also antecedent conditions; contex-

tual; culture; presupposition; scope conditions; universality

Contextual, 46-50, 75, 78, 82, 89, 103-105, 106, 109. See also context

Contract, 59, 66

Control, 234-239. See also practical utility

Controllable, 89, 90, 105, 106, 109, 115

Convention, 58, 109-110, 115

Conversational analysis, 155, 156, 174

Correction. See repair

Criterion, 59, 62

Criticizable, 89, 91-103, 105, 106-107, 108, 109, 115

Crystalization, 97, 212, 232, 236

Culture, 226-227. See also context; universality

Custom, 58, 110, 115

Description vs. prescription, 39, 45, 49, 68, 72, 76, 80, 88, 268-269

Direction, 59, 69-70

Discourse analysis, 155, 156

Doctor/patient, 260

Domain of rules, 50-54, 82

Episode, 59, 66, 258

Ethnography, 155-156, 174

Ethnomethodology, 155-156

Evaluating behavior, 83, 86, 87. See also criticizable

Expectation, 59, 65

Experimentation, 188-194, 195, 196, 198; research examples, 189-191; advantages

305

ABOUT THE AUTHOR

SUSAN B. SHIMANOFF is Assistant Professor in the Department of Rhetoric at the University of California, Davis. She received her doctorate in speech communication with a minor in linguistics from the University of Southern California. Her research interests include conversational rules, politeness strategies, repair behavior, and the communication of males and females.